D1322273

THE
HIGHLANDS

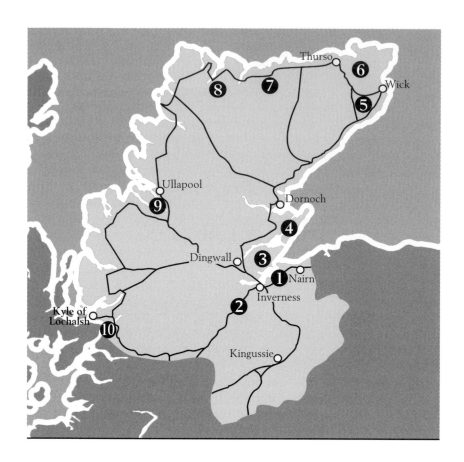

EXCURSIONS

EXPLORING SCOTLAND'S HERITAGE

RCAHMS

THE

HIGHLANDS

• •

Joanna Close-Brooks

Series Editor: Anna Ritchie

EDINBURGH: HMSO

Crown copyright 1995
First published 1986
This edition 1995

Applications for reproduction should be made to HMSO.

Cover photography: Historic Scotland (Urquhart Castle) and Audrey Henshall (Wester Balblair symbol stone)

End papers by Elisa Trimby

British Library Cataloguing in Publication Data

A catalogue record for this book is available from the British Library Royal Commission on the Ancient and Historical Monuments of Scotland John Sinclair House, 16 Bernard Terrace, Edinburgh EH8 9NX 0131-662 1456

The Royal Commission, which was established in 1908, is responsible for compiling a national record of archaeological sites and historic buildings of all types and periods. The Royal Commission makes this record available both through its publications (details of which can be obtained from the above address) and through the maintenance of a central archive of information, known as the National Monuments Record of Scotland. This contains the national collection of pictorial and documentary material relating to Scotland's ancient mounuments and historic buildings and is open Monday to Friday for public reference at the above address.

HMSO Bookshops
71 Lothian Road, Edinburgh EH3 9AZ
0131-228 4181 Fax 0131-229 2734
49 High Holborn, London WC1V 6HB
(counter service only)
0171-873 0011 Fax 0171-831 1326
68-69 Bull Street, Birmingham B4 6AD
0121-236 9696 Fax 0121-236 9699
33 Wine Street, Bristol BS1 2BQ
0117 9264306 Fax 0117 9294515
9-21 Princess Street, Manchester M60 8AS
0161-834 7201 Fax 0161-833 0634
16 Arthur Street, Belfast BT1 4GD
01232 238451 Fax 01232 235401
The HMSO Oriel Bookshop
The Friary, Cardiff CF1 4AA
01222 395548 Fax 01222 384347
Published by HMSO and available from:

HMSO Publications Centre
(Mail, fax and telephone orders only)
PO Box 276, London SW8 5DT
Telephone orders 0171-873 9090
General enquiries 0171-873 0011
(queuing system in operation for both numbers)
Fax orders 0171-873 8200

HMSO's Accredited Agents
(see Yellow Pages)
and through good booksellers

ISBN 0 11 495293 0

CONTENTS

FOREWORD

Twentieth-century Scotland has a heritage of human endeavour stretching back some ten thousand years, and a wide range of man-made monuments survives as proof of that endeavour. The rugged character of much of the Scottish landscape has helped to preserve many antiquities which elsewhere have vanished beneath modern development or intensive deep ploughing, though with some 10,200 km of coastline there has also been an immeasurable loss of archaeological sites as a result of marine erosion. Above all, perhaps, the preservation of such a wide range of monuments should be credited to Scotland's abundant reserves of good building stone, allowing not only the creation of extraordinarily enduring prehistoric houses and tombs but also the development of such remarkable Scottish specialities as the medieval tower-house and the iron-age broch. This volume is one of a series of nine handbooks which have been designed to provide up-to-date and authoritative introductions to the rich archaeological heritage of the various regions of Scotland, highlighting the most interesting and best preserved of the surviving monuments and setting them in their original social context. The time-scale is the widest possible, from relics of World War II or the legacy of 19th century industrial booms back through history and prehistory to the earliest pioneer days of human settlement, but the emphasis varies from region to region, matching the particular directions in which each has developed. Some monuments are still functioning (lighthouses for instance), others are still occupied as homes, and many have been taken into the care of the State or the National Trust for Scotland, but each has been chosen as specially deserving a visit.

Thanks to the recent growth of popular interest in these topics, there is an increasing demand for knowledge to be presented in a readily digestible form and at a moderate price. In sponsoring this series, therefore, the Royal Commission on the Ancient and Historical Monuments of Scotland broadens the range of its publications with the aim of making authentic information about the man-made heritage available to as wide an audience as possible.

This is the second edition of the series, in which more monuments, museums and visitor centres have been added in order to reflect the way in which the management and presentation of Scotland's past have expanded over the last decade. The excursions section proved very popular and has been both enlarged and illustrated in colour.

The author, Joanna Close-Brooks, is now a freelance archaeologist, but her earlier career began in the field of Italian iron-age studies, based in the British School at Rome, until she returned to British archaeology, working first in the Ashmolean Museum, Oxford, and then as Assistant Keeper in the National Museum of Antiquities of Scotland in Edinburgh (now the National Museums of Scotland). Her interest in the Highlands of Scotland has led both to fieldwork and to excavations in the area, with a special emphasis upon the burials, forts and stone-carving of the Picts.

Monuments have been grouped according to their character and date and, although only the finest, most interesting or best preserved have been described in detail, attention has also been drawn to other sites worth visiting in the vicinity. Each section has its own explanatory introduction, beginning with the most recent monuments and gradually retreating in time back to the earliest traces of prehistoric man. Each major monument is numbered and identified by its district so that it may easily be located on the end- map, but it is recommended that the visitor should also use the relevant 1:50,000 maps published by the Ordnance Survey as its Landranger Series, particularly for the more remote sites. Sheet nos. 7, 9, 10, 11, 12, 15, 16, 17, 19, 20, 21, 24, 25, 26, 27, 33, 34, 35, and 36 cover the area of this volume, which is the modern administrative area of Highland, with the exceptions of the island of Skye and the Lochaber area, which are included in the volume on Argyll and the Western Isles. Within the Highland area, sites are listed for convenience according to the old counties of Caithness, Sutherland, Ross and Cromarty, Nairn and Inverness-shire. The National Grid Reference for each site is provided (eg ND 351609) as well as local directions at the head of each entry.

An asterisk (*) indicates that the site is subject to restricted hours of opening; unless attributed to Historic Scotland or the National Trust for Scotland (NTS), the visitor should assume the monument to be in private ownership **and should seek permission locally to view it**. It is of course vital that visitors to any monument should observe the country code and take special care to fasten gates. Where a church is locked, it is often possible to obtain the key from the local manse, post office or general store.

We have made an attempt to estimate how accessible each monument may be for disabled visitors, indicated at the head of each entry by a wheelchair logo and a number: 1=easy access for all visitors, including those in wheelchairs; 2=reasonable access for pedestrians but restricted access for wheelchairs; 3=restricted access for all disabled but a good view from the road or parking area; 4=access for the able-bodied only.

Many of the sites mentioned in this handbook are held in trust for the nation by the Secretary of State for Scotland and cared for on his behalf by Historic Scotland. Further information about these monuments, including details of guidebooks to individual properties, can be obtained from Historic Scotland, Longmore House, Salisbury Place, Edinburgh EH9 1SH. Information about properties in the care of the National Trust for Scotland can be obtained from the National Trust for Scotland, 5 Charlotte Square, Edinburgh EH2 4DU. The abbreviation NMS refers to the National Museums of Scotland, Edinburgh, whose collections include important material from the Highlands.

ANNA RITCHIE
Series Editor

ACKNOWLEDGEMENTS

Numerous friends and colleagues have helped with this volume. Particular thanks are due to Miss M Harman, Mrs E Gibb, Miss K Butler, the Hon Fiona Campbell and Dr Ellen Macnamara who gave of their time, energy and expertise in helping with fieldwork: Mrs J Durham who contributed her wide knowledge of the north; Miss M Bennett and Miss J Bower who helped with fieldwork in 1993-94.

The records and archives of the Royal Commission on the Ancient and Historical Monuments of Scotland and the National Monuments Record of Scotland contain invaluable information, much of it the work of their own staff. The descriptive lists of buildings, arranged in Districts and Parishes, and prepared by Historic Scotland are equally invaluable. I would like to thank the staff of these and other bodies for their courteous assistance: RCAHMS and NMRS, particularly Dr Graham Ritchie, Mrs L Ferguson, Mr G Stell, Mr R Mowat, Mr I Gow, Miss C H Cruft, Dr M Oglethorpe; the photographic staff under Mr G B Quick, especially Mr J Keggie for his new photographs; Mr I Fleming who checked all the grid references, and Mr I Parker and Mr J Borland who prepared some of the line illustrations. I am particularly grateful to Mr J G Dunbar and Mr I Fisher for reading and advising on the text. Among the staff of Historic Scotland thanks are due to Dr D Breeze, Dr J Hume, Dr R Fawcett, Mr P J Ashmore, Mr C J Tabraham, and in particular to Miss A Riches and Mrs E Beaton formerly of the Historic Buildings Division.

Mr G Watson supplied invaluable information on Caithness sites. Many other people responded to questions, among them Dr D Omand, Mr R G Curtis, Mr and Mrs S Maxwell, Mrs Munro of Foulis, Miss M Morrison, Lord Strathnaver, Dr R G Cant, Mr L Masters, Mr D Lockhart, Mr J Blair and the Rev A G MacAlpine (re Croick). Many museums gave information, among them Inverness (Mrs C Niven), Tain (Mrs R Mackenzie), Groam House Museum, Rosemarkie (Mrs J D Marshall) and the Royal Museum of Scotland, Queen Street, Edinburgh (Mr T G Cowie, Mrs R Wilson, Mr J Wilson and the Country Life Section); as did the staff of the National Trust for Scotland, the Forestry Commission, the India Office Library, the Scottish National Portrait Gallery, the Scottish United Services Museum and the North of Scotland Hydro-Electric Board. I am indebted to the council of the Scottish History Society for permission to reproduce material from the Sutherland Estate Papers. I am particularly grateful to Mr R G Gourlay, for much helpful advice and for air photographs. The editor, Dr Anna Ritchie, has provided help and encouragement throughout the work; and I must thank my mother for her support while I was writing the text.

INTRODUCTION

**Eilean Donan
Castle**

The Highlands of Scotland, that most evocative of names, may conjure up romantic visions in the modern imagination: stern castles looming over dark lochs, thatched huts in the glens below great mountains, clan warfare and cattle-reiving, and the battlefield of Culloden. An over-romantic view of the Highlands (popular among the Victorians) belies the tough struggle for life in the harsh mountainous interior or on the treacherous northern seas, but there is an extra dimension to life in the far north, where people are scattered thinly across the landscape, and nature often seems more important than the works of man. 'My heart's in the Highlands' wrote Burns, and the region has captured the imagination of both native and stranger, who are drawn not only by the beauty of the scenery but by some sense that their roots are there. Man-made structures in the Highlands, often erected in direct response to some natural phenomenon, bridging ravines, sited in naturally defensive positions, or built of stone won from the hills, convey to us an unusual understanding of and identity with the past.

Everywhere there is magnificent scenery, round the coast high cliffs and long sandy beaches, and inland mountains rising above the eastern fringe of cultivated land. Much of the centre and west consists of a series of mountain ranges where man has never lived. The most extensive area of high mountains is the granite massif of the Cairngorms, skirted by the main road north, but of all the many mountains, the most distinctive are those in western Sutherland, Suilven, Stac Polly and Canisp among them, curiously shaped sandstone outcrops standing high above the ancient gneiss plateau. The region is cut up by sea, rivers and mountains, while the mountainous parts are themselves divided in two by the Great Glen, a geological fault-line which provided a natural southwest-northeast route. In the west is a network of long sea inlets and inland lochs running between mountain ranges. Even the east coast is cut by the three great estuaries of the Dornoch, Cromarty and Moray Firths. While both coasts were linked to the south by sea, and the east coast also by a circuitous land route, inland areas even far south remained isolated until the great period of road building in the early 19th century.

Occupation by man, now and in the past, has been restricted to lowland areas. The thin soil of much of the Highlands, derived from ancient, underlying gneiss and schist rocks, is extremely poor, but in Caithness, down the east coast and round the Moray Firth are more fertile soils overlying sedimentary rocks, and the river valleys have sand and gravel deposits. These lower areas also have a better climate with less cold and rain than higher ground, and occupation has always been concentrated there. Originally the population was spread more or less evenly over the inhabited areas, but over the last five hundred years or so there has been a gradual but inexorable concentration in the relatively few towns and villages.

Prehistory

People first came into Scotland after the last ice age around 8000 to 7000 BC, when a tundra landscape had been succeeded first by grassland and then by trees up to around 750 m above sea level. Small bands of stone- age hunters and fishers, known as mesolithic peoples, roamed over the north, often visiting the coast or lochs where they could catch fish and seals as well as animals, such as deer, and collect plant food and shellfish. Their tiny chipped flints, used to arm arrowheads and knives, have been found in several places including Red Point on Loch Torridon, Wester Ross. These people may have affected their environment, for instance by burning woods to create more grassland, but they have left no visible monuments.

Neolithic farmers settled in the British Isles before 4000 BC and spread over all the areas then suitable for habitation. These folk have left an array of stone monuments built over a period of some 2000 years, mostly huge stone cairns covering burial chambers built of great stone slabs. They were farmers, keeping cattle, sheep and pigs, growing barley and wheat in small fields, and cutting down trees with stone axes. While neolithic forts or other defensive earthworks have not been identified in the Highlands, as they have elsewhere, it would be a mistake to think these people lived an idyllic, peaceful existence. An adult killed by a stone arrowhead, who was buried in a cairn at Loch Calder, Caithness, is one of several such instances in Britain.

Changes took place towards the end of the 2nd millennium BC. New arrivals introduced a style of decorated pottery known as beakers, and bronze largely replaced stone for the manufacture of tools and weapons. Much of the copper ore required for making bronze was obtained in the Highlands, and stone moulds have been found for casting bronze axes and spearheads. Sheet bronze buckets and cauldrons were used for feasting and drinking, and wealth and power were also displayed in gold bracelets and other gold ornaments. Burial was at first by inhumation in individual graves under round cairns, often accompanied by pots and by jet necklaces for women, and then by cremation in large pottery urns. Later on cairns were no longer piled over graves, and few burials from later bronze age and iron age times are known. Stone circles were erected early in the bronze age, and other stone settings of equally mysterious purpose were laid out, such as the stone rows in Caithness. Houses were now round, with low timber or stone walls and thatched roofs; some of the hut circles to be seen in the area belong to the bronze age.

An increased population, changing social and political conditions, and perhaps the rise of petty kingdoms, led to the construction of strong stone-walled forts on hilltops in the first millennium BC, though there are fewer forts in the north than elsewhere in Scotland. The relationship between the large forts, the smaller stone-walled duns and the numerous scattered groups of undefended huts is unknown, as are their exact dates. However the small duns and the extraordinary broch towers, a unique development from a widespread tradition of circular stone buildings, seem to belong to a society organised on a local, almost family basis. The growing power of tribal kingdoms may have been disorganised, perhaps by repercussions from the Roman occupation of southern Scotland in the first century AD. In any case the terrain made central control difficult to maintain.

The people who constructed the fortifications and the huts were essentially farmers, now using iron which had begun to replace bronze as the standard utilitarian metal somewhere around the 6th century BC. We know from Greek and Roman historians that people living in Scotland in the early centuries AD spoke Celtic languages and had Celtic tribal names, but the date at which the Celts first arrived in the British Isles, in the first millennium BC or even earlier, is presently uncertain. The Romans themselves barely penetrated the fringes of the Highlands, and there are no Roman monuments within the area covered by this volume, although some coastal communities acquired Roman goods by way of barter or loot.

Picts, Scots and Norse

The people living in the north of Scotland from the 4th to the 9th century AD are known to history as Picts. They spoke a Celtic language, closely related to old Welsh but differing considerably from Irish and Scots Gaelic. Pictish may have incorporated traces of an earlier, non-Indo-European language, but any elements of this are difficult to recognise, and we have no idea how significant the pre-Celtic element in the population was. We know little about the Picts from historical sources save the names of their kings, their constant battles with their neighbours, and their links with the Christian church in Ireland, Dalriada and Northumbria. The Pictish kingdom was divided into two by the Grampian mountains; at first the power centre seems to have been around the Moray Firth, where St Columba met a sub-king of Orkney who had given hostages to the Pictish King Bridei, but later southern Pictland, between the Forth and the Mounth, was more important.

Scots from Ireland had settled in former Pictish territory in Argyll before AD 500 to form the kingdom of Dalriada. Eventually, by a mixture of force and skilful marriage alliances, they won control of the whole Pictish kingdom: the Scottish king Kenneth MacAlpin was the first ruler of the combined kingdoms around AD 843. How the Scots imposed their Gaelic language and institutions on the Picts is something of a mystery, but Norse raids on Pictish coastlands from around AD 800 may have been an important factor. Later the Scots took over Lothian and the Borders from the Angles of Northumbria, and finally the kingdom of Strathclyde from the Britons.

A few ruined structures survive from Pictish times, and archaeology may one day reveal more. There are buildings of Pictish date constructed from the stone of fallen brochs at Yarrows (no. 105), Carn Liath (no. 90) and Forse (no. 94). More numerous are Pictish carved stones, both the unique and mysterious symbol stones, which may have originated around the Moray Firth, and the intricately carved cross-slabs, of which some outstanding examples have been found in northern Scotland. Both types of carving occur mainly along the east coast.

Following the Viking raids on the north and west from around AD 800, and subsequent Norse settlement in the area, the famous Norse chieftains Thorstein the Red and Sigurd the Mighty, first Earl of Orkney, conquered northern Scotland as far as the River Oykell. Thereafter the Earls of Orkney held Orkney from the King of Norway and the area now called Caithness and Sutherland from the King of Scotland. As the power of the Scottish kings grew in the north, the earls were deprived of much of this huge area, with Sutherland erected into a separate earldom for the De Moravia (Moray) family in the 1220s. The Sinclair family resigned the Orkney earldom to the King of Scotland in 1470, but kept their remaining mainland estates and the title of Earl of Caithness.

Few signs remain of the extensive Norse settlement in the north. There will have been many Norse farmsteads, the farmhouse typically a long building with a byre in one end, as in the Northern Isles, but only one has yet been excavated, at Freswick in Caithness, and that is now covered over again. One visible relic is the cross with a Norse inscription in Thurso Museum (no. 8), while objects from pagan Norse graves found at Castletown, Caithness, and Durness, Sutherland, are in the National Museums of Scotland. There are only four standing but ruinous structures in the north which may date to the time of the Norse Earls in the twelfth or thirteenth centuries AD; one is the tiny St Mary's Chapel at Crosskirk (no. 63); the others are the tower of Old Wick (no. 53), the chapel at Skinnet (ND 130620) and the tower at Forse (ND 224338).

Placenames

While standing monuments of the first millennium AD are few, placenames show something of the extent of the areas once inhabited by Pictish, Norse or Gaelic-speaking peoples. The modern district names have this diverse background. Cait and Moray were Pictish names for provinces (Caithness has had the Norse *nes,* 'promontory' added); Sutherland comes from the Norse sudrland, 'the south land' as it appeared to those in Caithness and Orkney. Inverness District takes its Gaelic name from the town, and means 'mouth of the river Ness'.

Many Pictish names gave way to Gaelic in the west and even more to Norse in the north, but some Pictish names for rivers and straths have survived; in Ross and Cromarty, for example, there are the two Carrons, the Conon, the Orrin, the Calvie of Glencalvie and the Peffer of Strathpeffer. The common Pictish/British word *aber,* 'the mouth of a river', is rare in the north, but the few surviving instances include Aberchalder by Loch Oich and less obviously Applecross (no. 64), once aber-crossan 'the mouth of the river Crossan'. In some cases, *aber* may have been translated into the Gaelic equivalent *inbhir,* an element found in Inverness, Invermoriston, Invershin and the like.

There are many Norse placenames in Caithness, thinning out southwards towards the Moray Firth and down the west coast. These include topographical elements such as *nes,* 'promontory', as in Tarbat Ness; *gjá,* 'sea inlet or geo', as in Whaligoe (no. 14); *vik,* 'bay', as in Wick (no. 7). Ullapool may mean 'the bay of (the river) Ulla'. Other names are indicative of settlement, as are those incorporating the elements *bólstathr* and *ból,* 'farm or farmstead', such as Lybster, Scrabster, Embo, Skelbo and Cadboll. Others incorporate *setr,* 'dwelling', as in Wester, Caithness, or dalr, 'dale or valley', as in Berriedale and Helmsdale. Another Norse survival in Caithness was the system of land division by pennylands, in use until the early 19th century and still to be found in placenames such as Pennyland, west of Thurso.

Gaelic placenames are widespread in the Highlands outside Caithness, and cover most topographical features. Besides *inbhir,* they incorporate elements like *sròn,* 'nose', often used of promontories, and *ceann,* 'head', which appears in placenames as 'kin', as in Kinlochbervie and Kincardine. *Cill,* 'church or burial-ground', usually occurs with the names of Celtic saints, thus Kildonan in Sutherland is 'the church of Donnan', who was a younger contemporary of St Columba. *Sìthean,* 'a fairy mound', is often applied to burial cairns (no. 104) and *achadh,* 'cultivated field', is a common element. English was first used on the east coast and in towns in the 12th century. An early record of an English placename is that of Wardlaw near Beauly in 1210.

Medieval

During the 12th and 13th centuries the Kings of Scotland made determined, and ultimately successful, efforts to extend their authority to the northern mainland. Moray, long a source of dangerous dynastic rivals to the Canmore kings, was annexed and reorganised by David I (1124-53) and his successors, with burghs and castles established at Elgin, Forres, Inverness, Auldearn and Nairn, while William the Lion (1165-1214) built castles at Redcastle and Dunskeath in Ross. By the time of Alexander III (1249-86) Caithness too, although still linked with the Norse earldom of Orkney, could be considered an integral part of the Scottish kingdom. During the first half of the 13th century cathedrals were established at Dornoch and Fortrose and monasteries at Beauly and Fearn; no doubt a number of stone parish churches had also been built by this time, though few now survive.

A serious threat arose in the 15th century when the Lords of the Isles added the earldom of Ross to their possessions and extended their power-base to the east coast, issuing charters from Tain, Dingwall, Inverness and Urquhart. However, by the end of the century the Lords of the Isles had lost all their territories, though attempts to restore the dynasty continued in the West Highlands for some fifty years.

During the later Middle Ages there came to be a marked difference between the Gaelic-speaking Highlander and the English-speaking Lowlander in Scotland as a whole, with a similar division occurring within the present Highland region between the coastlands fringing the Moray Firth and the rest of the area. Each side knew little of the other, and distrusted what they knew. John Major wrote in 1521 'one half of Scotland speaks Irish (Gaelic) and all these we reckon to belong to the wild Scots'. When abrupt changes finally came to the Highlands in the 19th century, linguistic and cultural differences accentuated the problems of the transition.

18th-20th Centuries

This period has been one of mixed fortunes for the Highlands. It began with the Jacobite risings of 1715, 1719 and 1745, which led to a determined effort by the Government to integrate the Highlands with the rest of Scotland. The hereditary jurisdictions of local chiefs were abolished and communications opened up, firstly by the military roads in the 18th century, and then the parliamentary roads of the 19th century. Money was spent by the government and others on projects intended to improve economic conditions and provide employment. Down the east coast, a string of settlements resulted whose population has, despite setbacks, shown overall growth. Both in towns and in the countryside, almost all the houses and other structures that we see have been built in the last two or three hundred years, partly because new developments have destroyed earlier structures, but mostly because so many early buildings were of perishable materials such as timber, turf and mud. Only castles and churches as standing buildings provide visible witness to the medieval occupation of the region.

The 18th century saw a growth of population, but the traditional farming methods then practised over wide areas could not cope with the increased need for food, and there were recurrent famines and widespread emigration. Despite this, the population continued to grow. The reaction of landlords varied; some went bankrupt trying to feed their tenants, others took in those cleared from other areas, but many evicted the tenants from the poorer farms on their estates to create new and more profitable sheep farms. The large-scale and well-documented clearances on the Sutherland estates had more complex roots, for they were optimistically intended to improve the lot of the tenants as well as yield higher rents from the land. The population was rehoused in coastal villages where employment, generally in fishing, would provide a livelihood instead of the subsistence agriculture practised inland. Large sums of money from the Marquess of Stafford's English estates were spent on measures such as roads, harbours and setting up local industries, but in practice too little attention was paid to the practical difficulties of the enforced moves, and none to the wishes of the tenants, and much human misery resulted. Clearances continued spasmodically until halted by the Crofters Holdings Act of 1886, but this did not alleviate the conditions that led to depopulation of rural areas. From around the mid-19th century the population of the Highlands decreased, and only in the last few years has it started to rise again, with oil-related industries, so long as they last, providing a new source of employment.

From the 18th century onwards, many buildings illustrate the development of the region; graceful 18th-century houses built by the larger landowners, massive Victorian baronial edifices, some built by successful businessmen, parliamentary roads with fine stone bridges, railways with long viaducts, aluminium factories, gasworks, distilleries, dams for hydro-electricity, and everywhere examples of simple vernacular architecture, the stone-built houses that most people lived in. Inevitable economic development has meant some destruction: Helmsdale Castle was recently demolished so that a new bridge could be built to carry the A 9 over the Helmsdale river. Yet there is space in the Highlands for old and new to survive side by side. The great variety of buildings and monuments in the region provides a three-dimensional, illustrated history of life in the Highlands: how people have lived and what they have built from prehistory to the present day.

PHOTOGRAPH
ACKNOWLEDGEMENTS

Most of the photographs come from the archives of the National Monuments Record of Scotland, and some are the work of the RCAHMS photographic staff. Others are by the author (pp. 17, 20, 22, 23, 24, 26, 28, 32, 33, 34, 36, 38, 40, 45, 48, 49, 50, 52, 53, 57, 59, 63, 65, 67, 69, 70, 73, 75, 77, 79, 80, 82, 83, 86, 87, 89, 91, 92, 98, 102, 104, 106, 112, 113, 115, 126, 127, 129, 130, 133, 134, 135, 137, 139, 140, 141, 144, 145, 146, 150, 151, 159, 161, 162, 164). The T Sandby illustration on p. 93 is reproduced by gracious permission of Her Majesty The Queen (copyright reserved; RL 14724). For the rest, author and publisher are indebted to the following institutions and individuals: Historic Scotland (Crown copyright, pp. 18 Fort George, 26 Camster, 39, 95, 96, 97, 107, 108, 109, 112 Fort George, 113 Fort George, 117, 119, 120, 121, 129 Strathpeffer, 132, 142, 143, 144 Dun Troddan, 155, 159-60 Camster); National Trust for Scotland (pp. 44 Abertarff House, 79 Culloden); Inverness Museum and Art Gallery (p. 44 Inverness Town Steeple); Cawdor Castle (Tourism) Ltd (p. 105); J R Hume (pp. 50 Wick, 51, 55, 56, 57 Foyers, 61 Castlehill, 62, 68 Dunnet Head); M Sharp (pp. 153, 154, 157 Achavanich); R Gourlay (pp. 29, 31 Coille na Borgie, 84, 140 Dun Lagaidh); R Lamb (p. 110); A Grandjean (p. 152); Mrs J Scott (p. 148); T E Gray (p. 126 Creich); D Walker (p. 109); G Ritchie (p. 31); The Still Moving Picture Company (p. 9 Eilean Donan Castle).

EXCURSIONS

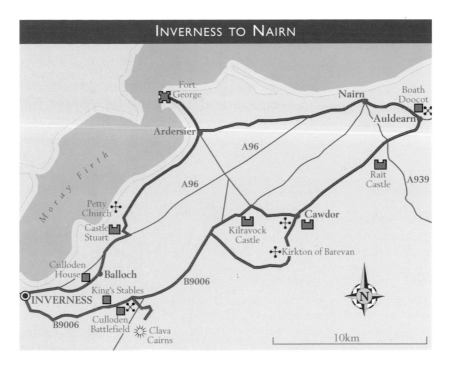

INVERNESS TO NAIRN

Clava cairn

Culloden Visitor Centre (NTS) on the B9006 is signposted from the A9 south of Inverness. Shortly before the centre, King's Stables cottage (no. 27) may be seen on the left of the road. Through the visitor centre is the 18th-century thatched cottage of Old Leanach (no. 27). Much of Culloden battlefield is laid out with paths. Turn right at next crossroads, then cross the B851 and follow signposts to the Clava cairns (no. 99), three most impressive round cairns surrounded by stone circles. Close by are the 28 stone arches of the Culloden Moor Viaduct built for the Highland Railway in 1898. Return to B9006, and fork right on B9091 to Kilravock Castle (no. 44; check opening day) and right again on B9090 to splendid Cawdor Castle (no. 48) with its 15th-century tower. Cawdor church in the village has an unusual tower built in 1619, with a later belfry at the top. From here a minor road passes the ruined medieval church at Kirkton of Barevan (NH 836472). Return to Cawdor, and follow B9090 and 9101 to turning to Raitcastle Farm. Down the track past the farm is the ruined 14th-century hall-house of Rait Castle (no. 51).

Fort George

From Rait take the B 9109 northeast to Auldearn to see Boath Doocot (no. 32), signposted north from the main street, which stands within a medieval earthwork. On to Nairn for three museums (check opening days) and attractive cast-iron bandstand of late 19th-century date on the east links. A 96 and B 9092 to Ardersier and out to Fort George (no. 41), a magnificent Georgian artillery fortress deserving a half-day visit to itself. Return west on B 9039 along coast, passing Castle Stuart, an early 17th-century tower-house bristling with turrets: sometimes open. Behind it is Petty church, where there is an 1824 watchhouse in the kirkyard and a splendid pair of black cats guarding the door of the Mackintosh burial aisle. In the garden west of the kirkyard is an overgrown medieval motte mound.

Rejoin A 96, and take loop road south through Smithton and Balloch to see an octagonal dovecote (no. 31), beside the road. Behind it is the elegant 18th-century Culloden House (no. 37).

Culloden House

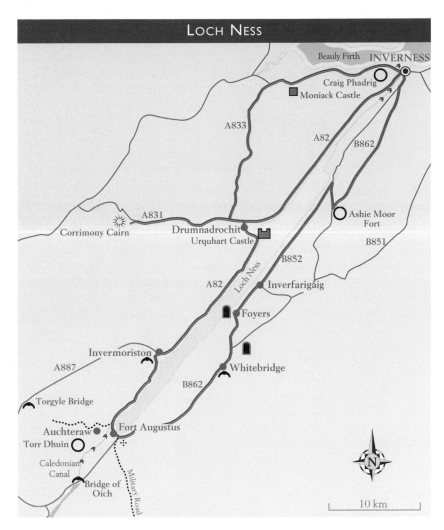

Leave Inverness on the minor road to Essich Moor, between B 861 and B 862. Continue on this road to its junction with B 862 in moorland at Ashie Moor. Here there is a small iron-age fort on a hillock not far east of the road (NH 600316). Both the road just driven over, continuing south as the B 862, and the B 852 beside Loch Ness are military roads. Those interested in iron-age hut circles may wish to explore examples shown on the OS map in many places, for instance close to the B 861 centred on NH 675381 (marked 'Settlement & Field System', the tiny circles on the map are individual huts).

At Ashie Moor turn back north on B 862 down to Loch Ness, and then south again on B 852 to Inverfarigaig. Here there is a small Forestry Commission exhibition about the Loch Ness area, toilets and the start of forest trails. Continue south to just past Foyers Hotel where a road leads down to the lochside at Lower Foyers. On the right part way down is an old aluminium factory of 1896 (no. 10) with contemporary housing nearby. Continue towards Whitebridge, but turn north briefly on B 862 to see old dam on Loch Mhor (NH 513181; see no. 10). At Whitebridge, bypassed by the new road, is a particularly fine Wade bridge with ashlar masonry.

Whitebridge

In Fort Augustus is the Victorian *St Benedict's Abbey, on the site of the fort built, at the suggestion of General Wade, after the 1715 rising. It now houses an exciting exhibition on the fort (parts of which are incorporated in the abbey), monasticism, the Scottish Highlander and so on. Open all year, but check times. The 20th-century Abbey Church is always open. Also in Fort Augustus there is an impressive flight of five locks on the Caledonian Canal (no. 20) as it drops down to join Loch Ness. Military roads which may be tackled by the hardy walker led west from here to Bernera barracks and south over the Corrieyairack Pass to Garva Bridge (no. 23), Dalwhinnie and Perth.

Continue south on the A 82 to just past Aberchalder to see the Bridge of Oich, probably by James Dredge of Bath, and now bypassed by a concrete bridge of 1932. Bridge of Oich is a suspension bridge with iron chains and pylons. It is effectively a cable-stayed bridge, but differs from modern bridges of this type in having the inclined stays supported by the suspension chains rather than the pylons. Several of Dredge's bridges have lasted nearly a century and a half, but this is the only one in original condition in Scotland.

Back in Fort Augustus take minor road southwest to Forest Office at Auchteraw for leaflet, then to carpark for Torr Dhuin Forest Walk. A marked path leads to Torr Dhuin on a knoll overlooking the river, the Caledonian Canal and Kyltra Lock. The small vitrified dun on top has a defended platform below and an outer stone rampart. There is an old excavation trench inside, and the vitrification is hard to see. Return up the west side of Loch Ness, through Invermoriston with its old bridge (see no. 22).

Corrimony cairn

Detour west on the A 887, if time, to see Torgyle Bridge (no. 22). Further along Loch Ness are the extensive ruins of the great medieval fortress of Urquhart Castle (no. 52). Here another deviation west may be made on the A 831 to see the impressive cairn at Corrimony (no. 100). Return to Inverness by the A 82, or turn off at Drumnadrochit, and take the A 833 over the moors and return to Inverness by the coast, passing Moniack Castle (no. 36), and Craig Phadrig vitrified fort (no. 76).

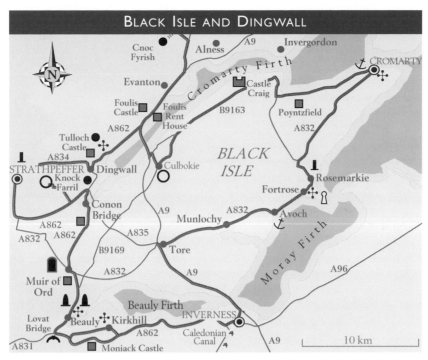

BLACK ISLE AND DINGWALL

From Inverness take the A 9 and the Kessock Bridge across the Beauly Firth to the Black Isle. At Tore roundabout, turn right on A 832 to Fortrose. Note the cloutie well (rag well) on the right side of the road shortly before Munlochy (NH 640536). Avoch is a fishing village with a harbour of 1813-15 designed by Telford and a warehouse. In Fortrose the Cathedral ruins (no. 61) are surrounded by 18th-century and later houses on the sites of the manses of the cathedral clergy. Past Fortrose turn right to Chanonry Point, where the ferry crossed to Ardersier. Here is a pier and a lighthouse built in 1846 by Alan Stevenson, and there are two large icehouses in a private garden nearby. A short distance on is Rosemarkie, with a fine Pictish cross-slab (no. 70) and other fragments in Groam House Museum, near the church.

The A 832 leads on to the 18th-century burgh of Cromarty (no. 3), with its East Kirk, Hugh Miller's Cottage and much else to explore. Return along the north coast on B 9163, looking in on 18th-century Poyntzfield House (no. 35), a smaller country mansion. On the north coast a minor turning to Craigton, and a walk over a field, crop permitting, leads to Castle Craig, a ruined 16th-century tower-house of the Bishops of Ross (interior unsafe). Then keep straight on to Culbokie, where turn left on minor road, unsigned, to Crasky: in about 0.6 km there is a carpark in the wood on the right, and a short path from it to a dun with multiple defences on a low hill, now cleared of trees (NH 613587). The small space inside, with room for perhaps one house, is defended by a stone rampart, two outer banks and a ditch.

Rejoining the A 9, cross the Cromarty Firth to see Foulis Rent House (no. 30) with a picnic spot overlooking the Firth: the mansion house of Foulis Castle (no. 34), not visible from the road, can be seen by appointment. Go north on A 9, B 9176 and turn west on minor road to Boath for path to top of Cnoc Fyrish and unusual monument (no. 39). Back down the A 862 to

Rosemarkie

Dingwall: there is a small museum in the old Tolbooth, the parish church of 1801 in Church Street, and a worn Pictish symbol stone with symbols on both sides (it has been re-used) near the kirkyard gate. On the south side of Dingwall take turning off the A 826 signed 'Tower' for the memorial to General Sir Hector Macdonald 'Fighting Mac', built in 1907, a tall stone tower in a cemetery on a hill. Tower is sometimes open, and there are fine views from the top.

Take the A 834 west and before Strathpeffer note turning to Castle Leod (NH 485593), a Mackenzie Castle, home of the Earl of Cromartie. This splendid early 16th-century tower is occasionally open (tel. Cromartie Estate Office, Strathpeffer 421264). Strathpeffer spa (no. 2) has unusual 19th-century spa architecture and a good Pictish symbol stone (no. 71). In the old Railway Station is a Museum of Childhood. Continue to Contin, and turn back east on the A 835 to approach Knock Farril vitrified fort (no. 77) from the south, on a minor road to Lochussie and Knockfarril. The fort has easy access at the west end and fine views.

Return south through Conon Bridge: named from Telford's bridge of 1807 (since demolished), the village was laid out in 1829. An octagonal tollhouse with verandah still stands by the new bridge. On the south edge of the town a green plot interrupts the houses on the right of the road. The bumps in the grass are a small henge monument, a circular area defined by a ditch with a bank outside, believed to be a bronze-age ceremonial site some 4,000 years old. South again to the west of the road notice the fine 1822 steading of Conan Mains as you pass; it has an octagonal dovecot, and another dovecot in the tower over the entrance. At Muir of Ord turn west on A 832 for Glen Ord distillery (tours) and Ord House Hotel, a house of the Mackenzies of Ord, the present harled house perhaps earlier 18th century, refronted in 1810 with some later alterations.

South of Muir of Ord note standing stones either side of the road. In Beauly are the ruins of the 13th-century and later Priory (no. 62). Immediately after junction with A 831, the road crosses Telford's fine Lovat Bridge of 1814 over the Beauly River. Take B 9164 north through Kirkhill and side road to Wardlaw Cemetery for burial aisle of the Frasers of Lovat with a splendid turreted stone belfry, added to the old church (now gone) in 1634 by John Ross, master mason (see no. 4); or take A 862 and turn south to Moniack Castle (no. 36) to see another traditional laird's house of many periods, winery and worn Pictish stone. Back to Inverness past turning to Craig Phadrig vitrified fort (no. 76) and over Caledonian Canal (no. 20) at Muirtown Basin.

Foulis rent house

Kirkhill belfry

Foulis mansion-house (Right)

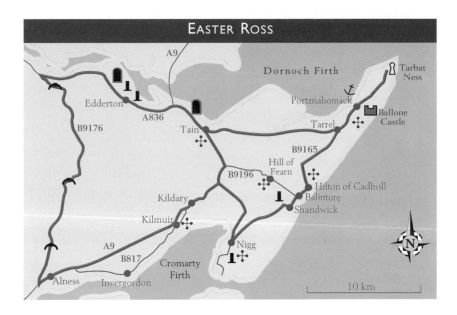

EASTER ROSS

In Tain are the fine Tolbooth (no. 4) and the medieval church of St Duthac (no. 59); leave Tain on minor road east to Tarrel, perhaps turning off to see the fishing village of Inver with its single-storey cottages. On to Portmahomack; the harbour has a pier built for Lord Tarbat in 1697 and later improved by Telford, and two estate warehouses, now converted to houses, by the harbour; the smaller one may date to around 1700. Fixed in the harbour shore are rows of old anchors. Tarbat old church, on the edge of Portmahomack, has a curious stone dome, perhaps once used as a sea-light, and a medieval vault (torch needed); key and booklet from the manse. Fragments of Pictish cross-slabs have been found in the church and church-yard (most in NMS) and it may be another Pictish monastic site. The road leads on to a carpark and the tall tower of Tarbat Ness lighthouse, built by Robert Stevenson in 1830 and rebuilt in 1892.

Tarbat Ness, lighthouse

Turning south, a minor road leads down to Rockfield fishing vil-lage on the shore, whence follow shore path to impressive ruin of Ballone Castle (no. 45). Continue south on B 9165, and take loop road along coast through three characteristic fishing villages. In Hilton of Cadboll is the grassed-over site of a medieval or later chapel (Historic Scotland) where a Pictish cross-slab was found, now in NMS. Go on through Balintore and Shandwick and follow the road uphill to see a splendid Pictish cross-slab (no. 68) in its original position, but under a glass roof. Left at T-junction to Nigg, where inside old church at west end is another great cross-slab (no. 69). From here either return to Tain, or take minor road east to Hill of Fearn, where just south on the B 9165 is the 14th-century church of Fearn Abbey with its plain lancet windows, now reroofed and used as the parish church.

Shandwick Stone

For a longer trip, continue west on A 9. In Kildary take B 817 to Kilmuir, where the parish church of Kilmuir Easter was built in 1798 but has an ear-lier belfry tower with a conical stone roof built in 1616 and related to that

Edderton parish church, 1842

Parish church, 1743

Easter Kilmuir, belfry

on Tain Tolbooth (no. 4). Rejoin A 9, and at junction with B 9176 turn right on the parliamentary road, earlier a drove road, over Struie Hill. On this road are three bridges; high single-span arches over the gorges of the Alness river at the south end, and the Easter Fearn burn at the north end, and in the moorland between a two-arched stone bridge over the Strathrory burn beside a carpark. There was a drove stance on the bleak moor by the Aultnamain Inn (NH 665813), and a drover's inn here, though the present building is more recent. Near the north end of this road is a viewpoint looking over the Dornoch Firth into Sutherland.

Return east along A 836, and turn north at crossroads in Edderton to see Pictish symbols carved on a bronze-age standing stone (no. 72) and Balblair Distillery just beyond. Back on A 836 in Edderton, see first the current rather handsome parish church of 1842, the galleries inside supported on cast iron columns, and then, about 1 km further east, the charming former parish church of 1743, a low building originally thatched, with outside stairs to the galleries and a fine Pictish cross-slab in the churchyard (no. 67). Pass the ferry point and pier for the old Meikle Ferry and the new A 9 road bridge over the Firth to Dornoch, and visit Glenmorangie distillery on the outskirts of Tain.

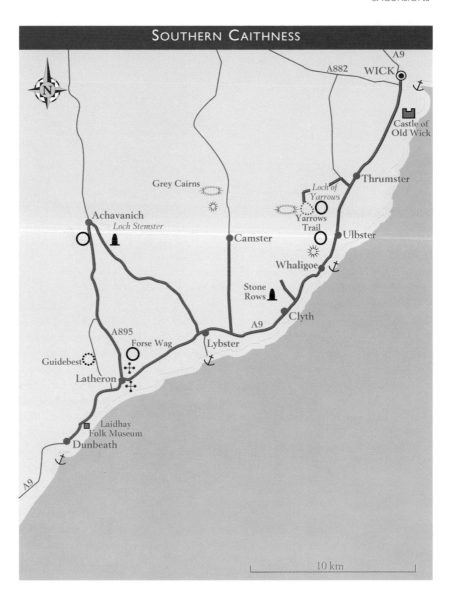

In Wick (no. 7) get Yarrows Archaeology Trail leaflet from Tourist Information Centre. Then out to coast south of harbour for the ruined tower of Old Wick (no. 53). Go south on A 9 past Loch Hempriggs and turn off in Thrumster for South Yarrows for trail (no. 105), to see broch with later outbuildings and two long cairns, and then on up Warehouse Hill for more chambered cairns, standing stone and a fort if time. Return to A 9 and on to Ulbster, and a crossroads with a telephone box. Here the minor road south goes to Whaligoe (no. 14), a tiny fishing harbour reached by steps down a cliff. The road north leads to the signposted path to Cairn of Get chambered cairn (no. 103), some ten to fifteen minutes walk, and Garrywhin hillfort just beyond. Further down the A 9 at Mid Clyth are the curious multiple stone rows (no. 98), a short distance down a signposted side road. Before Lybster another minor road goes north to Watten. Some 8 km along this road are the impressive Grey Cairns of Camster (no. 101) with accessible, roofed chambers.

Mid Clyth stone rows

Return to A 9, past Lybster with an attractive fishing harbour and old warehouses, and continue down A 9. On the cliff at Latheron is the white-harled early 18th-century church with 1822 north aisle and dumpy belfry-tower, now the Clan Gunn centre; look for a big graveslab of 1642 behind the church. An earlier detached stone bell-tower, perhaps 17th century, some 0.5 km north can be seen from the A 895. Beside the road between Latheron and Dunbeath is the restored crofthouse of Laidhay Folk Museum (no. 25). Turn off at Latheron onto A 895 noting detached bell tower of Latheron church on right to see Forse Wag (no. 94), a ruined broch with unusual outbuildings. On another minor road running west of and parallel to the A 895 is Guidebest stone circle, in the bottom of a valley by the Burn of Latheronwheel, but rather overgrown (ND 180351). Continue up the A 895 past Loch Rangag and the grassed-over mound of a broch with outworks

Camster round cairn (Below)

Forse Wag (Bottom Left)

Latheron 18th-century church (Right)

between the loch and the road, and turn right on a minor road back to Lybster to see the remarkable stone setting at Achavanich, south of Loch Stemster (no. 97).

For those continuing south on the A 9, there is another fishing harbour at Dunbeath, and a charming harbour in a tiny creek at Berriedale, with an icehouse and the last remnants of a castle on the cliff at the mouth of the burn. Otherwise return to Wick (no. 7) by the A 9. In Wick see the herring curing-yard and fishing displays at the Wick Heritage Centre, and glass blown the traditional way in the Caithness Glass factory.

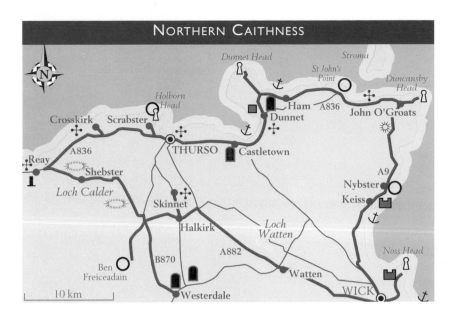

NORTHERN CAITHNESS

From Wick (no. 7) take minor road on north side of Wick Bay out to Staxigoe, with a tiny harbour and three store houses, then on to Noss Head. From carpark take signposted path to dramatic ruins of Castle Girnigoe (no. 47) on rock stack. Beyond is Noss Head lighthouse, built in 1849 by Alan Stevenson (usually open to visitors in the afternoon, as are the other lighthouses on this route). Back to the A 9, and north to Keiss (no. 13) for fishing harbour, Telford church and manse, and coastal path past two ruined brochs to the fine ruined tower of Keiss Castle (no. 44). Back on the A 9 there is a third broch beside the road near the war memorial. Past Keiss a turning is marked to Nybster broch (no. 92) on a headland. The Northlands Viking Centre, Auckengill, in an old Schoolhouse beside the A 9, near the turning to Nybster broch, has displays on Caithness archaeology (open in summer). Continuing north, the road swings round Warth Hill, on top of which is a bronze-age round cairn (ND 371698; park in quarry) with good views on a fine day. Beyond is John O'Groats and Duncansby Head lighthouse (built by D A Stevenson, 1924).

Turn back on A 836 to Kirkstyle for the white-harled parish church of Canisbay with its saddle-back west tower (no. 57). Beyond Canisbay a minor road north and a walk lead to St John's Point, with an iron-age fort on the headland defended by a rampart and ditch. Later it was perhaps an Early Christian site, for behind the modern wall at the east end of the rampart are the foundations of a tiny chapel where a dark-age cross-slab with incised outline cross was found. Continue west on minor road with a distant view of the Castle of Mey, a 16th-century towerhouse restored by the Queen Mother and now her Scottish home. At Ham is a fine ruined mill and a harbour built for the flagstone trade with wide quay and breakwater faced with vertical flags. Then out to Dunnet Head for another lighthouse

Castle Girnigoe

(no. 19). Minor road to West Dunnet and the traditional croft complex at Mary Ann's Cottage (no. 26). Return through Dunnet, where the church has a medieval west tower. Next comes Castletown, with a trail round the flagstone works, Castlehill harbour and a flagstone centre (no. 15).

Dunnet Head lighthouse

North from Thurso (no. 8), where the local museum displays include dark-age carved stones, the flagstone industry and coastal transport and shipping, is the busy harbour of Scrabster, and beyond it Holborn Head lighthouse (David and Thomas Stevenson, 1862), with the lighthouse tower set over one wing of the keepers' houses. Past the lighthouse, walk on to an iron-age promontory fort (ND 108715) near the point of Holborn Head, with a single, overgrown rampart.

Continuing west on A 836, take signposted side road north to Crosskirk and walk out to the small 12th-century chapel of St Mary (no. 63) on the cliff. Shortly after rejoining the A 836 there is an attractive early 19th-century mill and miller's house at Bridge of Forss. On to Reay, with a white-harled 18th-century kirk with belfry tower; south of the road is the old kirk-yard, where in an aisle of the old church is a worn dark-age cross-slab (key from Post Office close by). From Reay return east on minor road, and at Shebster crossroads turn north on road to Achreamie for signposted path to two impressive though grassgrown long cairns on top of Cnoc Freiceadain (no. 104; easy walk up hill). Return to Shebster, and continue east and then south past Loch Calder if not too wet, to see three more ruined chambered cairns at the north end of the loch, not far from the road (ND 067618, 069618, 070619). Their chambers, excavated in the 1960s, have been left open and are fairly intact but unroofed. One cairn is long, one short and horned with a chamber at each end, and one round; the loch is now washing them away.

**Camster long
cairn, aerial view**

Rejoin B 870, and turn south on minor road to Dorrery to see Ben Freiceadain hillfort (no. 82). Return to Wick on B 870, passing an attractive mill at Westerdale, with water still flowing down the mill lade and splashing into the river, and make a short detour to Spittal, where the working flagstone quarry can sometimes be seen, the huge flags detached the traditional way with wedges and hammers; there is also a fossil centre here, open in summer. Alternatively return via A 882 to Halkirk, an agricultural village with a grid of streets laid out by Sir John Sinclair in the early 19th century. Here detour north to Skinnet and walk out to the ruins of a medieval chapel in a graveyard where two Pictish cross-slabs have been found; one with symbols is now in Thurso Museum, the other stands south of the chapel and has worn interlace decoration on a cross in a circle. At Watten the road crosses the Wick River on a Telford bridge, and just south of Watten is another disused meal mill at Achingale (ND 240534).

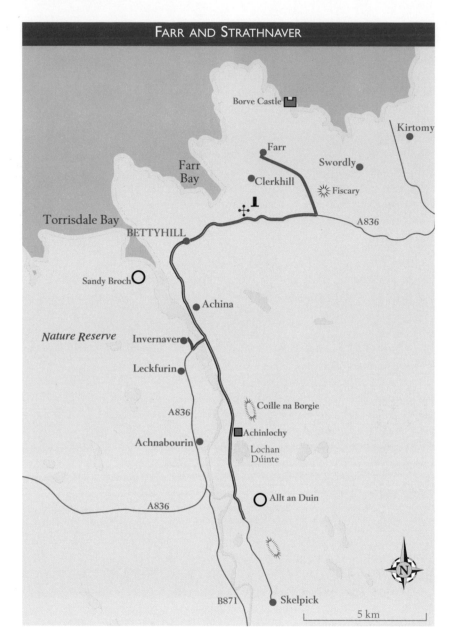

Take the Ordnance Survey Landranger map on this trip to locate the archaeological sites. East of Bettyhill on the A 836 is a Tourist Information Centre with useful local leaflets and toilets. Park there to visit white-harled Farr Church, now the Strathnaver Museum, with a fine Pictish cross-slab outside the church at the west end (no. 66). Ask at Tourist Information Centre for keyholder if museum is shut.

There is a surprising number of neolithic cairns in the area, attesting considerable early settlement. Many have survived as they are in places not suitable for medieval or modern cultivation. Three great round mounds of stones can be seen in moorland east of the minor road to Farr. Two stand close together on a ridge (NC 732625) with fine views all round. The northern cairn has a typical entrance passage and a chamber divided into three compartments; some of this can be seen as the cairn was dug into in the last century. The large southern cairn, probably also chambered, seems to be intact. An unusual feature is a low platform of stones round the south cairn with a spread of stones linking it to the north cairn, perhaps an addition but still neolithic. To the southeast is another large round cairn, which may be neolithic, and to the west a smaller, partly overgrown cairn, probably bronze age. Strike north from Farr over rough moorland to the cliffs, to reach the last remains of Borve Castle (NC 725640), once belonging to the McKays. This was built on a dramatic headland with a natural arch beneath, defended by a bank on the saddle joining it to the mainland and a bank and ditch at the far end. The foundations of a square tower and other buildings can be discerned in the grass.

Fiscary cairns

Return to Bettyhill and the A 836 west. At Invernaver, if time, stop and walk out along the coast and up the hillside by a burn to the Sandy Broch (NC 697609). All the land to the west is nature reserve with an interesting fauna, mountain plants being found here near sea level. Otherwise leave A 836 at the bridge over the Naver and follow minor road to Skelpick. About 1.2 km along are the two fine neolithic cairns at Coille na Borgie (no. 106) one with vertical slabs in its facade. Shortly after is the small township of Achinlochy, from which 7 families were moved to new lots on the north coast in 1819. Park in quarry east of road by site, which has an information board and numbered structures, including one corn-drying kiln with a well preserved bowl. Just before the road crosses the Skelpick burn, a rough walk east and up the hillside is needed to visit the broch Allt an Duin (NC

Coille na Borgie chambered cairn

723575), on a high knoll by a burn overlooking what must then have been farmland. It has not been excavated, but some features are visible, and the large triangular stone by it was once the lintel over the door, as at Caisteal Grugaig (no. 85). Continue down the road, and before the next house strike across country and ford the Skelpick burn (wellingtons needed) to see another well preserved long horned cairn, Skelpick Long, with a chamber at the north end (NC 722567). There are yet more neolithic cairns nearby. If you prefer not to go across country but to follow marked paths, omit brochs and Skelpick Long cairn, return to Naver bridge, and take the B 871 south to Syre, passing Skail cairn by the road and then visiting Rosal pre-clearance township (no. 29; see northern Sutherland excursion).

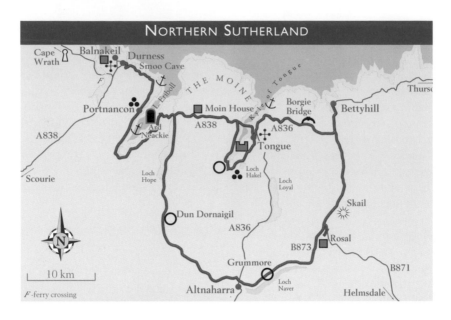

This route includes dramatic coastal scenery and beautiful white sandy beaches. The Ordnance Survey Landranger maps will help to locate archaeological sites.

Castle Varrich

From Bettyhill take A 836 west to Tongue. Stop to see the earthwork just south of the road before Borgie Bridge, a flat-topped circular mound some 18 m in diameter, set on the edge of a natural scarp, and defended by a large ditch with an entrance causeway. Its date is unknown but probably medieval. The slight ruined structure in it may be later. At Borgie is an early 19th-century two-arched rubble bridge, now bypassed. Before Tongue take the road to Skullomie, where massive stone revetments between rocks form a tiny harbour. In Tongue is the old parish church, a low T-shaped building, white-harled with crow-step gables, rebuilt in 1680 and again in 1728. Inside at the west end is the Reay loft with 18th-century panelling, though the older columned canopy to this loft has been taken down and is in store. Tongue House, partly 17th century, is hidden by trees and walls but can be seen when the garden is open. Down by the shore, overlooking the new causeway and bridge, is a small early 19th-century octagonal tower with slated roof, the former ferry-house and lookout.

Leave Tongue by minor road south: on the edge of the village a sign points to Castle Varrich on a ridge overlooking the Kyle, a tiny roofless towerhouse with a storeroom on ground level and one room and an attic above, entry having been by ladder to the first-floor door. Its date is perhaps

16th century. Further on the road passes Lochan Hakel on the east. There is a large boulder with many cupmarks and some worn rings at the south end of the lochan, but it is quite a trudge round to reach it (best viewed in a low light). Tradition says the marks were made by the high heels of a fairy dancing on the stone. Another cup-marked stone lies just west of the road at NC 561527 but can be hard to spot: the 'Symbol Stone' marked by it on some maps is only a stone scratched by a plough. Continue round the head of the estuary, where Dun na Maigh broch (no.88) on a high rocky bluff looking north up the Kyle is well worth the trouble of climbing up to it. Return up west side of Kyle, cross A 836 and go on to Talmine for a ruined corn mill with part of its wheel.

Rejoin the A 836 west, and about halfway across the desolate area known as The Moine notice Moin House, just south of the new road at NC 518600. Just three rooms and a loft, it was built in 1830 by the Duke of Sutherland as a refuge for travellers crossing this 'deep and dangerous morass', as it was before the Sutherlands built the road. As the road descends to Loch Eriboll, a T-shaped promontory can be seen in the loch. This is Ard Neackie (no. 12) with an interesting group of inn, ferry pier, lime-kilns and limestone quarry, and easy access. On the opposite shore at Portnancon is a corresponding pier for the ferry and a former storehouse. Some 600 m north again, past the Port Camul turning and beside the road is Laid souterrain (no. 96: see entry for directions; take torch). Follow the road on to the mouth of the loch, where at Rispond is a salmon fishing station built in 1788, with a harbour and quay, fish house with outside stair, icehouse and dwelling houses, one of which had salmon boiling houses in its wings. The harbour is in a creek sheltered from the north by a crag. Sir Walter Scott had 'an ample Highland breakfast' here in 1814 during his voyage on the Lighthouse Yacht, before going on to explore Smoo Cave and to see the site for a new light at Cape Wrath. Rispond is private, but could be viewed across the creek from the

Dun na Maigh broch

south. The road to Durness passes the huge natural Smoo Cave, not to be missed. Quartz flakes (prehistoric) and shell middens (here iron age or later) have been found, left by people using the cave in the past, the shells either food debris or the result of baiting lines for fishing.

Go through Durness, where there is a Tourist Information Centre with local leaflets, and out to Balnakeil. On the way is a ruined early 19th-century mill on the right of the road. Balnakeil House was built in about 1720-40 on the foundations of a castle of the Bishops of Caithness and later the Lords of Reay. It incorporates old vaulted basement storerooms and kitchen in the east wing. The white-harled house stands alone, save for its steading and garden, in a vast sweep of green grass leading to white sandy beaches and

Ard Neackie

blue sea with Faraidh Head behind. Balnakeil Church is a roofless ruin in the graveyard by the beach, a T-shaped structure with crow-stepped gables built in 1619 perhaps on an earlier site, with a north aisle added in 1692. In the east gable is an upper door for an outside stair leading to a former laird's loft. Inside the church is an arched tomb recess with carved 17th-century graveslabs, one dated 1623 to the notorious local villain, Donald MacMurdoch, who '... hier lies low, was ill to his friend, waur (worse) to his foe ...'. In the churchyard is an attractive monument erected in 1827 to Rob Don, the 18th-century Gaelic poet; it is a short obelisk on a square plinth with inscriptions in four languages. From here there is a pleasant walk out over the dunes to the cliffs of Faraidh Head with colonies of puffins and other seabirds.

At Keoldale a small ferry takes people (not cars) across the Kyle of Durness to the vast wild headland at the north west tip of Scotland. There is one mini-bus on the far side which runs trips out to Cape Wrath lighthouse, on a promontory above sheer cliffs. The nearest boat-landing place is over a mile east. The lighthouse and keepers' cottages were built by Robert Stevenson, grandfather of Robert Louis Stevenson, in 1827-28 (ask if you may see over in the afternoons). The cliffs are famous for their seabirds.

On the return journey, a deviation south on slower, single-track roads may be made down the east side of Loch Hope to Altnaharra, to pass Dun Dornaigil (no. 89) an impressive broch beside the road. Then return up Strathnaver, passing Grummore broch between the road and Loch Naver, a large stoney mound with some wall-faces showing. At Syre, turn west on the B 871 for carpark for Rosal (no. 29), the best place to see a pre-clearance township, carefully laid out by the Forestry Commission. Heading for Bettyhill, note the chambered cairn by the road at Skail (NC 712468). The stones have mostly been robbed away, and the upright slabs of the chamber, formerly linked by drystone walling, stand exposed.

Balnakeil House

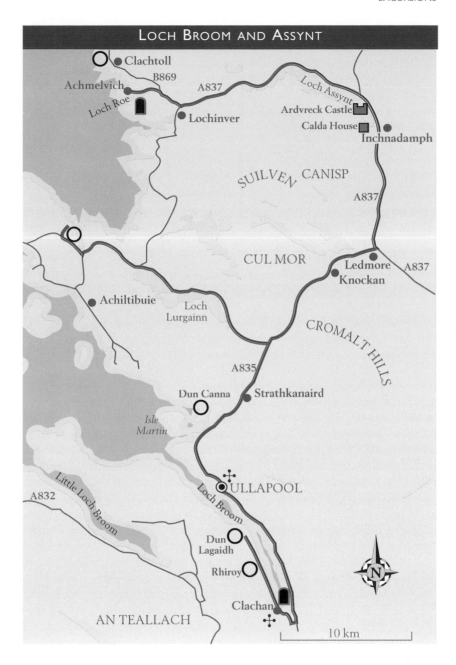

LOCH BROOM AND ASSYNT

From Ullapool (no. 6), a planned fishing village with a museum in a Telford church, drive south to the head of Loch Broom. Note the remains of low, angular drystone walls in the shallows near the head of the loch: these are yairs or tidal fish-traps. Take minor road west over river and north up the side of Loch Broom to Rhiroy broch (no. 86); go on to end of road then follow path to the fort and dun of Dun Lagaidh (no. 79) with the ruins of the township of Newton Loggie south and west of the fort. Return round the loch, visiting Loch Broom church in Clachan at the head of the loch (keyholder Mr Duncan Mackenzie, Cherry Bank, Ardindrean, near Rhiroy; tel Loch Broom 248). This plain but attractive harled church built in 1817 has its original galleries and interior fittings including two long central

Dun Lagaidh

communion tables, a rare survival. Back on the A 835 and some 5 km east is the spectacular Corrieshalloch Gorge and the 45 m high Falls of Measach (NTS).

The trail continues back through Ullapool and on north. At Ardmair look west to Isle Martin, where a fishing station for curing red herrings (kippers) was set up in 1775 before the foundation of Ullapool. In Strathkanaird stop in layby on main road for long walk out through Blughasary (where the former carpark is now shut) to the fort of Dun Canna (no. 80) on a headland with a sandy beach to the south. Then continue on A 835 towards Ledmore junction. A deviation may be made west on a single track road out towards Achiltibuie. Take the turning to Brae of Achnahaird, and then east to the carpark on the cliff. Here walk south a short distance down a path which crosses good examples of recent spade-cultivation ridges to reach a small dun (NC 017138). This has a thick, irregular but more or less oval wall and

Rhiroy broch

is set on the neck of a small headland with traces of other foundations beyond it, perhaps later buildings. The yellow sands of Achnahaird are visible in the distance. Where the road to Achiltibuie passes Loch Raa there are good hut circles either side of the road, the best near the south end of the loch by the burn.

Back on the A 835, before Ledmore the road passes Knockan Cliff where there are Geology and Nature Trails open all year and a Nature Conservancy Visitor Centre (open summer). The first part of the trail is easy, with yellow saxifrage by the path; the upper part needs a good head for heights but has a marvellous view over Inverpolly nature reserve and the mountains of Cul Mor and Canisp. Around Ledmore are many chambered cairns marked on the OS maps, and often near the road: clearly neolithic farmers some 5,000 years ago appreciated the good soils in this limestone area. At Ledmore take A 837 to Assynt.

Near Inchnadamph there are caves in the valley of the Allt na Uamh where bones of late ice-age animals such as reindeer, bear and Arctic fox have been found, dating from between 25,000 and 8,000 BC, but as yet no certain traces of human activities have been found with them.

A little further on the romantic ruin of Ardvreck Castle (no. 46) stands on an almost islet in Loch Assynt, with the later ruin of Calda House by the road; look out for the chambered cairn between castle and road. East of the road, near the layby south of the castle, is a huge round millstone. This was used in a panmill, perhaps early this century, set vertically with the edge used to crush limestone for spreading on acid ground or for road metal. On the hillside above the millstone and a waterfall are the ruins of 18th-century Achmore (NC 243238) not the usual township but the ruins of a tacksman's house, farmsteading and a few cottages. (Tacksmen held land from the laird and rented it out to subtenants.)

Ullapool

Follow the A 837 round Loch Assynt and towards Lochinver, and turn north on B 869 to Clachtoll to see a broch (no. 87) sited on the rocky foreshore. On the way is the remains of a quern quarry on the shore of Loch Roe (NC 069242), best visited in spring, by late summer seaweed has grown over it. Turn off to Achmelvich, and halfway there take track south to Loch Dubh, then a path along its north shore; where a burn runs out to Loch Roe are the remains of two mills, the smaller one a horizontal mill. Leave the path and scramble west over slippery boulders at the foot of the cliff to the quarry on the shore. Circular marks can be seen where quern rough-outs have been detached. These were for small handquerns, not millstones. (At the end of the quarry is a wall.)

Ardvreck Castle

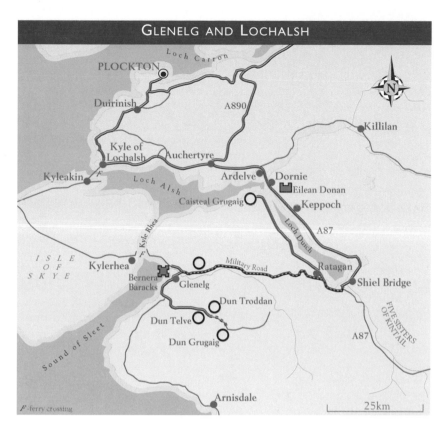

GLENELG AND LOCHALSH

This excursion offers a selection of fortifications, from iron-age brochs and forts to 18th-century barracks. At Shiel Bridge on the A 87 take the minor road west over Mam Ratagan to Glenelg, a military road built by Major Caulfield in the 1750s to link Bernera with Fort Augustus and later rebuilt by Telford. Most of the hairpin bends on the steep eastern slopes have now been replaced by a new road. At the top is a carpark with fine views back over Loch Duich and the Five Sisters of Kintail. Continue through Glenelg, and turn south at the coast and then east into Glen Beag to see the spectacular brochs of Dun Telve and Dun Troddan (nos 83, 84). Dun Telve is better preserved than any other broch except Mousa in Shetland. Continue to the end of the road, and walk on up the track to Dun Grugaig (NG 851159), a galleried dun perched on a knoll high above the burn. It has been partly dug out, and the entrance, chambers and galleries can be seen among the tumbled stones. The track continuing up the strath was once a drove route for cattle being driven from Skye to Falkirk.

Glenelg view

Return to Glenelg, and take the road to the Kylerhea ferry. Some 700 m along the road is a footbridge across the river on the left, with a path leading over the plain to the ruins of Bernera Barracks (no. 43) in the distance. From here there is a choice of routes. Perhaps take the ferry across to

Kylerhea, visit the otter watch hide on the far shore, explore part of Skye and return by the new bridge to Kyle of Lochalsh. Otherwise take the road back towards Shiel Bridge. Before crossing Ratagan, note the iron-age fort of Am Baghan Burblach (NG 831200), at the top of a steep and slippery hill. It has a collapsed stone rampart round the top of the hill, an entrance at the east end, and remains of recent structures inside. Back at Loch Duich, take the road west along the south side of the loch up to Totaig, and park by cottage and slipway. A track continues west, becoming a path through the wood, to a broch, Caisteal Grugaig (no. 85). On the way back, look for the baitholes near the slipway (see no. 85).

Dun Telve broch

Return to Shiel Bridge, and take A87 round the head of Loch Duich and on to Eilean Donan Castle (no. 50) just before Dornie. Though restored, it gives a good impression of a medieval castle, inside and out and has a spectacular setting at the junction of three lochs. This can be seen from the minor road above the A87. Go on to Kyle of Lochalsh, and then, as a change from fortifications, visit Plockton (no. 5), an attractive planned village laid out in 1794 (NTS) looking over Loch Carron. Continue east to Stromeferry and the A 890 back to Dornie.

Eilean Donan castle

TOWNS AND BURGHS

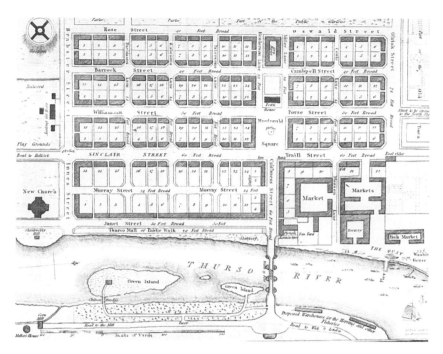

Sir John Sinclair's plan for the New Town of Thurso (published in 1812)

The pattern of settlement in the Highlands was for long one of a widely dispersed population living in small clusters of farms scattered over the areas of cultivable land, with very few larger villages or towns amongst them. This pattern has changed in recent centuries both by the natural growth of some of the few larger towns, and by the great number of deliberately planned new villages, or extensions to existing settlements. The result is that today the greater part of the population of the Highlands lives in settlements, mostly round the coasts, and a far smaller proportion lives in the hinterland.

The early royal burghs near the Moray Firth were established as part of the attempts of the Scottish kings to control the province of Moray. Most of these early burghs seem to have been existing settlements, which had grown up at places favourable for trade, usually with harbours. A royal castle was often built in the same place. Inverness (no. 1), Auldearn (no. 32) and Nairn were all burghs before 1214. In the north, Wick and Thurso (nos 7 and 8) were both small medieval towns with their origins in the Norse period, and only became royal burghs later, as did Tain. The population of Wick in 1660 is thought to have been around 500 people. Dingwall was another Norse settlement, its name meaning 'Field of the Thing', 'thing' being a Norse general court of justice which met in the open air. Dingwall and Cromarty (no. 3) were royal burghs by 1314.

The official establishment of a town as a 'burgh' gave it legal rights favourable to trade. The matters dealt with in the charters granted by William the Lion (1165-1214) to Inverness show something of a burgh's activities. The charters mention tolls and burgh lands, and stipulate that a weekly market could be held, that no cloth could be cut and dyed outside the burgh, and that there were to be no taverns outside Inverness, save where the lord of the village was of knight's rank. Besides the royal burghs, sizable communities grew up round the cathedrals of Dornoch (no. 60) and Fortrose (no. 61).

There has been a long history of landowners and others trying to establish or extend settlements in the Highlands, often in an attempt to provide employment for the population other than subsistence farming. One of the early developers was Lord Tarbat who built the first pier at Portmahomack, Easter Ross (NH 915846) in the early 18th century, creating a port out of what had been 'a handful of cottages on an empty heath'. He also attempted to open a fishing station at Ullapool some 100 years before the British Fisheries Society did the same, sending round a cargo of supplies, including two wheelbarrows, by ship from Leith. Grantown-on-Spey was founded by Sir James Grant of Castle Grant in 1776, Ullapool and Pulteneytown (nos 6 and 7) by the British Fisheries Society at the turn of the 18th and 19th centuries, and Plockton was founded by the Earl of Seaforth around 1794. In Caithness, Louisburgh, a northern suburb of Wick, was founded by Sir Benjamin Dunbar who also began villages at Broadhaven (ND 379513) and Staxigoe (ND 384524), and a village was laid out at Lybster (ND 2435) by General Patrick Sinclair. Sir John Sinclair laid out the inland grid-pattern settlement at Halkirk (ND 1359) as well as the large extensions to Thurso (no. 8). A string of villages along the Sutherland coast was established or enlarged by the Sutherland estate to house the people moved from small settlements in inland areas which were to become sheep-farms. At Helmsdale (ND 0215), Portgower (ND 0013) and Brora (ND 9003) curing- yards, warehouses and piers were constructed, while at Brora a coalmine, saltpans, brewery and brick- and tile-works were also established (no. 11).

Other towns and villages grew in response to particular industries, thus Castletown, Caithness (no. 15) expanded with the flagstone industry at the end of the 18th century, and Foyers (no. 10), with the aluminium works established in 1896. Cromarty (no. 3) grew in response to the light industries established by Sir George Ross and attracted a large number of people from highland areas. Strathpeffer (no. 2) owes its expansion to the tourist trade attracted by the spa, as Aviemore (NH 8912) has done in recent years with the great increase in winter holidays in the Cairngorms.
Very few early buildings survive even in the early burghs. Almost all buildings, other than churches and castles, were built of timber and other perishable materials until the later 17th century. Burghs remained fairly small, and rebuilding took place on the same spot, so very few 17th or even early 18th-century houses have survived. Cromarty (no. 3) is a fine example of a small, later 18th-century burgh.

Early burghs had a public building known as the tolbooth, which served many purposes: the burgh council met there, it housed the burgh court, and it often served as the prison. An important part of an early tolbooth was often a stout tower built on the lines of a tower-house, to which a lower council chamber block might be attached. Prison accommodation was usually in the upper floor of this block or in the tower, and often overcrowded. From the 18th century onwards elegant Town Houses were built, usually with separate prison blocks, as at Cromarty (no. 3) and Dornoch (no. 60). Relatively few early tolbooths exist. The Tolbooth in High Street, Dingwall (NH 549587) is of 17th-century origin but has been substantially remodelled. The stone tower was originally entered at first-floor level from stone steps. It still has iron grilles to its windows, while an iron yett which barred a lower door is displayed outside, beside the old mercat cross. One of the latest tolbooths to be built in the early manner was the fine tower at Tain (no. 4). Inverness (no. 1) has a handsome Town Steeple.

Sir Arthur Fowler Memorial Clock, Ullapool

Town Steeple, Inverness

1 INVERNESS

NH 6645.

A royal burgh on record from the late 12th century but probably founded by David I, it was one of a group of early burghs established along the south coast of the Moray Firth. Its position was excellent, at the lowest fording point on a river opening into the Moray Firth, and at the intersection of the two great Highland routes, the natural southwest—northeast access afforded by the Great Glen, and the route from the south to the north, initially skirting the Grampian mountains and approaching Inverness from the east, and continuing along the coast to Wick. An early centre of local and foreign trade (paying customs dues in the 14th century), its continuing role as a market town and administrative centre has ensured its prominence among Highland burghs to this day.

Prehistoric and early historic occupation in the area is attested by various antiquities including the remains of a Clava ring cairn in the Raigmore housing estate (NH 687450), the vitrified fort on Craig Phadrig (no. 76) and the Pictish symbol stone from Knocknagael (no. 73). Something of the extent of the historic town can be judged from the line of the town ditch built for William the Lion around 1179. Parts of the east bank ran along the lines of Academy Street and Ardconnel Street, the ground either side of Church Street being the early nucleus together with the castle. The town ditch

Abertarff House, Inverness

(Right)

also enclosed a strip of pasture land across the river, on a line now followed by King Street.

The late 16th-century vaults of Queen Mary's House were demolished in 1969 (partly rebuilt in the hall of the HIDB office, *Bridge House, 20 Bridge Street), and the oldest surviving house in the burgh is *Abertarff House, NTS, in Church Street, a typical small 16th-century town house, built in 1594 of harled rubble with a slate roof and crowstepped gables. Its projecting stair turret was enlarged at the top into a square room with its own fireplace. The interior has been altered to form offices now occupied by the NTS, but the visitor can see the spiral stair and the ground floor with a marriage lintel dated 1681 over the fireplace. Rather confusingly, another lintel with the same initials is built into the outer wall of the adjacent building, and may have come from a house close by, owned by the same merchant family. In Inverness, as elsewhere, earlier buildings were almost all of timber.

Church Street, formerly Kirkgate, is one of the oldest streets in the burgh. Among other old houses here are the notable Dunbar's Hospital, built in 1668 with decorated dormer heads, and Bow Court, built in 1772-9 and restored in 1970 (only the central arch is original; the public may go through to view the back of the house). The High Church of 1770 is set back from the street; the vaulted lower part of its tower is thought to be 16th century and the steeple 17th century, and it stands on an early site. Alongside is the Robertson of Inshes mausoleum, an ornately decorated and pillared monument of 1660, and next to this the Gaelic Church, rebuilt in 1792 and now a Free

Church. Either side of the churchyard entrance are small 18th-century houses, now restored.

On the corner of Church Street and High Street is the fine Town Steeple built in 1791 by the architect William Sibbald of Edinburgh. The present *Town House diametrically opposite is late 19th-century Victorian Gothic, and is open to the public (booklet available). It contains many interesting portraits of people mentioned in this book. Nearby in Castle Wynd is a modern building housing the fine Inverness Museum and Art Gallery with a collection of Pictish stones.

Castle Hill is the site of an early royal castle. By 1718 this was a substantial tower-house to which bastions had been added by General Wade and others. Bonnie Prince Charlie had it blown up in 1745. The present castle on Castle Hill consists of two buildings linked by a bastioned wall. The *Courthouse at the south end was built in 1843 (architect William Burn); it has a grand stairway and a semi-circular courtroom, fitted with new seating on the old plan. The second building, also in Scottish Baronial style, was initially the prison, later the County Council Offices, and now a second Sheriff Court; it was the work of Thomas Brown in 1846-8. There is an exhibition in the Drum Tower.

Back in the 1650s Oliver Cromwell had built a new artillery fort with angled bastions further down the east bank of the river, and, despite its partial demolition under Charles II and modern industrial development, one high bastion, now grassgrown, can still be seen on the west side of Lotland Street. 'Cromwell's Tower' stands nearby in Cromwell Road, traditionally a truncated clock tower from the old fort.

On the west bank of the river is early 18th-century Balnain House, now the 'Home of Highland Music' (visit the exhibition to see the Georgian interior), and a group of 19th-century churches, including the classical West Church built in 1834, St Mary's Catholic Church built in Gothic Revival style in 1837, and the fine Episcopal cathedral, again Gothic Revival, completed in 1869 to a medieval plan with two massive west towers by the local architect Alexander Ross; interior fittings include a reredos and altar in coloured stone and tiles. Walks round Inverness might include the

banks of the Ness, its islands and bridges, and the canal complex at Clachnaharry (no. 20). Finding one's way round is easier with the OS Town Map, while various informative booklets are available from the Museum, Tourist Office and bookshops.

Pump Room, Strathpeffer

2 STRATHPEFFER, ROSS AND CROMARTY

NH 4858.

An extraordinary collection of Victorian hotels and villas set among trees on a wooded hillside, this spa settlement has been called 'Scotland's answer to the Bavarian watering place'. Far from being the usual grim granite Victorian edifices, many are enlivened with harled walls and coloured paintwork. The first record of the springs on the Cromartie estate seems to be an account of the 'Castle Leod Waters' given to the Royal Society in London in 1772, and by the end of the century Strathpeffer had become a spa. At first its fortunes fluctuated, but great expansion came after the middle of the century with the arrival of the railway: the main Dingwall-Strome Ferry line in 1869 and then the branch line from Dingwall to Strathpeffer in 1885. These in turn led to the building of some large hotels, including the Highland Hotel with 127 bedrooms, which was built by the Highland Railway as late as 1909-11. In the season there were through carriages from London and a Strathpeffer Express from Aviemore. The lines were lifted in 1948, but the weatherboarded *Railway Station building of 1881, with a glassroofed canopy supported on cast-iron columns and decorative brackets, has been restored for use as a craft centre and Tourist Information

Office and also houses a Highland Museum of Childhood.

Of the main Spa buildings the big Pump Room, begun in 1819, was demolished in 1950 when it became unsafe. The existing small Pump Room used to be called the Upper Pump Room and was built in 1839, in part as a place for the poor to have waters dispensed to them. There is said to have been an 'Institution for Poor Spa-Drinkers'. The white and green patterned tiles on the walls date to a 1901 redecoration. Water from several springs with different properties came through labelled taps. This charming building is presently neglected. Next to it stands the Pavilion, a large rather plain rectangular hall of 1879-81, which originally had an open veranda round it. Across the road from the Pump Room is Spa Cottage, a single-storey villa of 1820. The range of shops dating from the 1840s are harled and painted with attractive Dutch gables. There are several Victorian Gothic churches, the Episcopal Church of St Anne having stone, marble and alabaster altar, reredos and pulpit, together with stained glass windows. From small villas to large hotels, the rest of the buildings were designed for the summer tourist trade and the range of ornament includes towers, ornate verandas, rusticated porches, carved bargeboards, twisted columns and cast-iron roof finials.

In a field near the Railway Station is a Pictish symbol stone (no. 71), dating from about one thousand years earlier.

Court House, Cromarty (Right)

---

3 CROMARTY, ROSS AND CROMARTY

NH 7867.

Cromarty, which was a Royal Burgh from before 1264 to 1685, is now a unique example of a small late 18th-century burgh which has largely escaped later development. It stands at the mouth of the Cromarty Firth, a magnificent natural harbour, and was formerly on the main route north from Inverness, which ran along the coast, linked by ferries across the firths.

The development of Cromarty as we see it today was due to Sir George Ross, who bought it in 1765. He built the present harbour to encourage fishing and established various industries such as the hempworks and a brewery, all of which enterprises were successful for some considerable time. However, in the mid-19th century, the fishing failed, the railway arrived on the other side of the firth, and Cromarty declined. In recent times it has become a conservation area and old buildings are being restored, while oil-related industries once more provide employment.

Little is left of 17th-century Cromarty. The old castle, a fine tower-house, was demolished when George Ross built Cromarty House nearby in 1772. This elegant Georgian house, not visible from the road, is somewhat similar to the main block of Culloden House (no. 37). Its contemporary stables can be seen opposite the Old St Regulus burial ground in The Causeway. In the same road is the earliest surviving house in Cromarty, dating from around 1690; once the manse for the East Kirk, it is irregular in plan with high steep roofs. In Church Street is the East Kirk, the old parish church, of which the main east-west block may date to about 1690, but a north aisle and loft were added in 1738-40, making it a typical T-plan church. Various alterations in the late 18th century included raising the walls and adding two more lofts, one the laird's loft with its panelled front and carved cornice supported on classical columns, but little alteration has occurred in the interior since then. Most of the pews in the lofts are old, though some have been rearranged; the carved and painted pew in the north loft, opposite the pulpit, was probably once the laird's pew and has a coat-of-arms of the Mackenzies, lairds in the earlier 18th century. The bench pews in the body of the church are mostly Victorian, but some, such as the rearranged table pews, are earlier. Note the wooden bonnet pegs by the door under the laird's loft. The pulpit against the south wall was made in 1907 but is in keeping.

Also in Church Street is *Hugh Miller's Cottage, NTS, white-harled with crowstepped gables and tiny windows under a thatched roof. It shows how many of the other 18th-century cottages once looked. Hugh Miller was a local stonemason who became famous as a geologist, writer and lay leader of the Free Church. The cottage was built in 1711 by his great-grandfather, John Feddes, a sea captain, and is a substantial dwelling with six rooms. The central room was the original kitchen and has a 'hanging-lum' or chimney canopy made of wood and daub, used for smoking fish. Part of the plaster has been stripped from a wall to show the internal fabric, a mixture of rubble, clay and straw. Through a low door is the best room or parlour, with a proper fireplace and a marriage lintel over it dated 1711, now appropriately furnished, while upstairs is a display about the life and work of Hugh Miller. The house next door was built by Hugh's father in the early 19th century, and lived in by Hugh after his marriage. Up the hill is a memorial to Hugh Miller erected in 1859, and the Gaelic chapel, now roofless, built by George Ross in 1783 for Gaelic speakers who had moved into Cromarty from the Highlands.

The elegant *Court House with a dome (originally leaded) to its belfry tower and a clock by John Ross of Tain was built by George Ross in 1773. Inside, the first-floor court room retains 19th-century seating, witness box and cast-iron stoves. Behind is the prison block with three cells, one being a day-room with fireplace (originally the debtor's prison), and an exercise gallery built in 1845 by Thomas Brown, who also built the jails at Dornoch (no. 60) and Inverness (no. 1). The rest of the ground floor, one room of which was formerly a cell, was altered at the same time to provide accommodation for the jailer. There is an interesting ducted-air heating and ventilating system run from a stove in the corridor to try to combat damp. The Court House now houses an imaginative display with animated figures featuring Sir Thomas Urquhart, the eccentric 17th-century laird of Cromarty, and a 19th-century trial re-enacted in the courtroom. Open all year round.

There is a striking contrast between the houses in Fishertown, stretching west from Church Street to the sea, with small often single-storey cottages, harled and originally thatched, and the more substantial houses in other parts, stone-faced and slated. Many of these have 'cherry-pointing', tiny pieces of stone set in the mortar which helped level uneven blocks. 'An ugly fashion' wrote Southey. 'A dark slate is preferred from a vile fancy that this regular dotting improves the appearance of the building'. Happily the dotting is less obtrusive since the buildings have weathered. Of the larger merchants' houses, Bellevue and St Anne's in Church Street were built around 1800, and Forsyth House in High Street in the late 18th century.

The brewery built by George Ross stands in Burnside Place, a rectangular three-storey building with a hoist from a dormer window. Returning through Fishertown to the harbour, there is a datestone on no. 7 Braehead carved with a tailor's flatiron, scissors and the date 1727; below Braehead on the links is the mid-19th-century vaulted and turf-covered icehouse, now used as a store by fishermen. Further along is the smartly painted lighthouse, built by Alan Stevenson in 1846, with Egyptian-style doors to the lighthouse tower and adjoining keepers' cottages. Next comes the harbour, with its two piers built at the joint expense of the government and George Ross in 1785, and round the corner in Marine Terrace is another of his projects, the Old Linenworks and Ropeworks of around 1783, now converted into houses. Originally built round four sides of a yard, part has been pulled down leaving three long red

Hugh Miller's Cottage, Cromarty (Left)

sandstone ranges. The immensely long east range (and the missing west range) will have been needed for the ropewalks. There is a dwelling house in the middle of the south wing. In 1794 hempen cloth manufacture was carried on here by a company of London merchants: 'The fabrics, which are chiefly designed for cotton and coal-bagging, are in general for exportation. Within the walls are about 200 people employed—men, women and children'. Others span in their own homes. The works shut down in 1850.

Old Fishertown, Cromarty

Guide-books to the East Church and to Cromarty and tape tours of Cromarty are available from the Court House.

4 TAIN TOLBOOTH, ROSS AND CROMARTY

Early 18th century.

NH 780821. In the High Street, in the centre of Tain. Key from District Council Offices, a few doors east.

This strong tower, solidly built in Tain stone, has a medieval appearance but was begun in 1706 and its upper works completed in 1733. It replaced and probably copied closely an earlier Tolbooth of 1631 which had collapsed after a storm. The old Council House next to the tower has been replaced by a new Court House built in 1848-9 and designed by Thomas Brown in Scottish Baronial style with turrets and crenellations to match the roof of the Tolbooth. At this time the ground floor of the tower was altered to provide a main entrance to the new Court House, and a new door and window inserted. Outside the door stands the old mercat cross.

The Tolbooth, Tain (right)

A stone turnpike stair within the tower leads to the upper floors. The top room with its stone vaulted roof, small door and tiny windows was used as a prison. Above this the stair leads out onto the roof, with a central turret housing a bell made in Holland in 1630 for the old Tolbooth, and four corner turrets. The present clock of 1877 with three faces replaces an earlier one made in Tain. The turrets have conical roofs made of stone blocks pierced by curious small windows, tiny imitations of dormers. Such stone belfry roofs seem to have been a local speciality. Three others are known, all on churches, a conical-roofed tower at Kilmuir Easter (NH 757731) dated 1616, a remarkable domed belfry at Tarbat Old Church, Portmahomack (NH 914840), and a splendid turreted belfry at Kirkhill near Beauly, West Inverness-shire (NH 549457), built in 1632. Except for Tarbat, thought to be later, these may all have been built by the same mason.

Unusually for such early work the architect of the 18th-century Tolbooth is known. He was Alexander Stronach, one of a family of masons (their surname is Gaelic for mason) who worked for Lord Tarbat round the Cromarty Firth. The Burgh accounts for 1732 include this entry: 'Item: For Alexr Stronach's morning drink when he came in to see the Bartizan head—7s 6d.' Relics of Tain

as a Royal Burgh may be seen in Tain Museum, including a map of the Marches of Tain drawn in 1730, a fine set of Burgh weights and measures dated 1835, and silver marked with the Tain assay stamp. (See also St Duthac's Church, Tain, no. 59.)

5 PLOCKTON, ROSS AND CROMARTY

NG 8033. On minor road N of Kyle of Lochalsh.
NTS.

An example of a west coast planned village begun by the Earl of Seaforth, whose factor wrote in 1794 of the necessity 'to lay out the villages of Plock and Dornie'. Four years later the estate was put up for sale, and eventually bought by Sir Hugh Innes. In particulars prepared with a view to the sale, Plock is described as being occupied 'as a village and fast improving in its value and the number of its inhabitants and several good houses built and others building'. Here, as in other west coast settlements, like Ullapool, tenants were expected to combine the care of crofts with small-scale fishing. Sir Hugh Innes encouraged the new village. An advertisement in the Inverness Journal for September 16th, 1808, offered feus and ninety-nine year leases in the burgh of Plockton (now a burgh of barony, with town added to its name): 'It presents an eligible situation for a fishing station, or any branch of manufacture which requires a number of hands. . . . The proprietor is much disposed to give every facility to any undertaking which would yield employment to the rising population . . .'.

A plan of 1801 shows provision for another street of houses running behind Harbour and Bank Street, but these were never built. Nevertheless, by 1841 there are said to have been 537 residents. Plockton has a unique situation for a west coast settlement. Set on the east side of a great headland sticking out into Loch Carron, it is protected from the sea gales, and looks out onto a safe anchorage where small creeks and islets diversify the coastline. Apart from what may be an old fish- house on the shore, the buildings are domestic. The early houses built in a continuous line along Harbour Street are largely early 19th century with a few later 19th-century houses among them, and vary from single-storey cottages to two-storey and attic houses, some stone and some harled. Bank Street is a long

row of symmetrical, single-storey and attic mid-19th-century cottages, individuality being expressed in paintwork colours and the variously carved bargeboards to the dormer windows.

Plockton, a standpipe

On the small headland projecting from Harbour Street is a rare survival of a 'traditional' West Highland cottage, with low walls of whitewashed rubble, a later chimney at one end, one tiny window either side of the door and a heather-thatched roof. In Innes Street at the south end of the village is a parliamentary church (see chapter 8) of 1827-8, harled with ashlar margins; it retains the original pulpit and sloping galleries, being one of the eight parliamentary churches in which galleries were built. Opposite is the single-storey manse, no. 81, now a private house. Just down the road is the Free Church of 1845 while nos 4 and 5 Innes Street, a pair of mid-19th century, two-storey houses are the Free Church Manse and the Old Schoolhouse. The Primary School at no. 82 was built in 1889,

6 ULLAPOOL, ROSS AND CROMARTY

NH 1294.

Ullapool stands on a flat, triangular spit of land jutting out into Loch Broom, and affords an excellent anchorage. It was chosen by the British Fisheries Society for one of three planned fishing villages, together with Tobermory on Mull and Lochbay on Skye, and construction started in 1788. Before this, remarkably enough, Stornoway on

Old Parish Church, West Argyle Street, Ullapool

Lewis was the only village and customs house in the whole 1,000 miles of western coastline from the Clyde round to Duncansby Head. The advantages of the site included plenty of land fit for houses and gardens, a good anchorage, a lime quarry, and the fact that herrings regularly frequented Loch Broom. There were already curing stations for red herring operating on Isle Martin and Tanera further out in the Loch, which would help to employ the settlers and process the fish until new curing businesses were established.

Houses were to be erected by the settlers themselves, but the Society built amenity structures such as a warehouse of three-storeys and cellar, a pier and an inn. In 1790 various difficulties including trouble with the pier led to Thomas Telford being called in as 'Surveyor of Buildings', a post he held until his death in 1834. Though Ullapool was already laid out before he began work, he is known to have surveyed a herring house, a shed for drying nets with boatbuilders', coopers' and smiths' shops behind, and a storehouse for salt and casks.

Ullapool was spacious and not all of its grid of streets filled up, but many of the buildings in the streets along the shore and near the pier date to the early years of the settlement. Among the many simple but attractive harled houses is The Old Bank House in Argyle Street, with a fanlight and pillared portico to its door. By 1814 there were 72 houses, 35 slated and the rest thatched with turf, fern roots and heather; and a curing-house which had cured 5,000 barrels of herring the previous year. On the corner of Quay Street and Shore Street the building now called the Captain's Cabin, which houses the

small Ullapool Museum, is a late 18th-century warehouse of three-storeys with an outside stair to the first floor. The Caledonian MacBrayne office in West Shore Street is another former warehouse, possibly built to Telford's design about 1800, though the long stair-window in the east gable is modern.

Ullapool attracted sufficient population to warrant a parliamentary church and manse, built in 1829 to plans by Telford. The church in Argyle Street has a gallery and much of its original fittings; it now houses the Ullapool Museum and its interior can been seen. The manse in West Shore Street is now Ornsay House, a private house harled with painted margins and some alterations to the front door. Ullapool fared badly in the later 19th century when the herring failed and the inhabitants had insufficient land to maintain themselves by farming alone. However this century has seen a revival of its early prosperity due to a variety of circumstances. Though the railway never reached Ullapool, refrigeration and improved roads have made a great difference to its viability; it has again become a port for the herring and mackerel fleets, even if only as a transit point. The pier has been extended and the old fish houses reused. Tourism is important to the local economy, and Ullapool is now the terminal for the car ferry to Stornoway on Lewis.

7 WICK AND PULTENEYTOWN, CAITHNESS

ND 3650.

Pierhead Light, Wick Harbour

(Right)

Wick is called Vik in the Sagas (Old Norse *vík*, bay), and in 1140 Earl Rognvald was entertained there. It owed its existence to the river mouth, the only anchorage on the Caithness coast between Cromarty and Scrabster, though exposed to northeast gales. A small town throughout the Middle Ages, it became a royal burgh in 1589. The old town lay north of the river round the High Street, but, because of 18th and 19th century development in this area, no older houses survive. The old parish church at the west end of the High Street was replaced by the present church in 1830, but one fragment survives, the 16th-century St Fergus' Aisle, since used as a burial vault and capped with Victorian crenellations. There is some good 19th-century architecture in Bridge Street, including the Town Hall of 1828, the classical Royal Bank of Scotland of about 1830, and the Italianate sheriff court of 1862-6.

Wick depended on the fishing trade, yet there was no harbour, only jetties built against the congested north bank of the river where ships had to unload onto the shore. In the late 18th century there were nevertheless some 200 boats fishing from Wick and by 1800 some sixteen curing firms producing barrels of pickled herring.

Thomas Telford drew the attention of the British Fisheries Society and of Sir William Pulteney, one of its directors, to the advantages of Wick for a new fishing station. They agreed with him, and in 1803 acquired 390 acres of land on the south side of the river and began to build a harbour, while the land was leased to settlers who would build houses. Telford designed the harbour, a new stone bridge, the layout of the new town, and plans to which houses were intended to conform, as well as 'a healthy walk for the inhabitants with a full view of the bay and the offing'. The harbour caused trouble for many years and the Stevensons struggled with it later. It consisted of two basins with a massive breakwater now terminating in a lighthouse with octagonal tower. There is also a pilot house. Telford's bridge was replaced in 1877 by another in similar style.

Much of the new settlement, called Pulteneytown after Sir William, Telford's patron, was built within the next twenty years. It fell into two parts, the grid of residential streets on the high ground grouped

round Argyll Square, and an area for curing-houses and cooperages on the lower ground near the quayside. Telford suggested plans for the houses and stipulated sizes for walls and doors in an unsuccessful effort to ensure uniformity 'in the Elevation of Houses'. The main streets were to have two-storey houses, the lesser single-storey, all stone-faced and roofed with slate. While some of their character has been lost by unsympathetic alterations, parts of Argyll Square and its surroundings retain the attractive simplicity of Telford's original design.

Wick Harbour

Pulteneytown was intended for professional fishermen, not part-time crofter-fishers as were villages on the west coast, and the herrings which were the chief catch needed to be either pickled in salt (white herring) or smoked (red herring) to preserve them, so numerous curing-houses were essential. These were built on the low ground by the harbour, an area much altered subsequently. The best example of a curing-yard is now the Wick Heritage Centre in Bank Row. The buildings are set round an open court, some used for displays relating to old Wick and the fishing industry, which include the original kipper kiln with rows of (replica!) kippers hanging on tenterhooks and a box-vent in the roof to let out the smoke. Next to it is the reconstructed cooperage, in which were made some of the many thousands of barrels needed every year to ship out the herring. The arched entrances in the walls gave direct access for carts. Other enterprises attached to the new town were an inn, a cookshop, a boatbuilding yard, a mill, a brewery and a distillery. By 1818 some seven curing-houses, twelve cooperages and 108 dwellings had to been built, while 59,043 barrels of herrings had been shipped out the year before. Through the 19th century Wick and Pulteneytown prospered, despite the decline of the herring from the middle of the century. Pulteneytown was one the successes of the planned settlements of the 18th and 19th centuries.

---

8 THURSO, CAITHNESS

ND 1168.

Thurso was a settlement in Norse times and two characters prominent in the Sagas were killed there, Moddan in the 11th century and John, Earl of Orkney, in 1231, murdered in the cellar of a house where he had hidden. Little is heard of Thurso after this until it became a free burgh of barony in 1633. The old part of Thurso lay north of Olrig Street, where one old house dated 1687 with a round stair tower still remains at nos 16-18 Shore Street. Old St Peter's Church in Wilson Lane is the medieval parish church, much altered in the 17th century when it was filled with lofts (one loft front is preserved in St Peters and the Holy Rood). It now stands roofless (key from Municipal Offices, Rotterdam Street). The tracery window in the south gable is typical 17th century Gothic. At the east end is the apse of the medieval church, formerly walled off as a burial vault. The tower is dated 1638 or 1640, and had a session room above

reached by a private spiral stair. Later it was let out to the Town Council who used it variously as a prison and a council chamber.

In 1735 the town was described as 'A neat fashionable little town . . . with one principall street, severall wynds and sufficient buildings in it'. It was then the market for a good part of the country's produce and dealt in corn, cod and ling. Thurso expanded greatly in the early 19th century, when a New Town was laid out by Sir John Sinclair of Ulbster, the originator of the Statistical Accounts. Its grid pattern of streets is still clear, centred on Sinclair Street and Sir Johns Square. Many of the original houses still stand, and this is an attractive area to walk round, particularly on a summer evening when the traffic has stopped. The grandest houses are in Janet Street, looking out over the river, some still having stables and gighouses behind. The streets filled up gradually: thus most of Janet Street was built in 1800-10, but Campbell Street only in 1820-30.

At the end of Sinclair Street stands a classical building with portico and domed tower, the former Miller Academy, designed by W Scott of Edinburgh and donated by the Rev Alexander Miller in 1859, where boys were taught English, Mathematics, Latin, Greek and French. The Town Well in Meadow Lane is covered by a circular wellhouse

Janet Street, Thurso

with conical roof dated 1822, while the pump inside was installed in 1850. In Manson's Lane, nos 22 and 24 are the Old Brewery and the Brewer's House, part of Sinclair's planned town. The brewery is open-plan inside, the upper floors supported on wooden pillars. On the east bank of the river at Millbank (ND 115677), there is a fine group of late 18th- and 19th-century mill buildings, the miller's house with a castellated facade (now a youth centre); next to them is the old Millbank Foundry.

In the High Street adjacent to the former Town Hall is Thurso Museum. Among the exhibits is a relic of Norse Thurso, a rough stone cross intended to be laid on a grave with a runic inscription '(name missing) . . . made this overlay for his father Ingulf', perhaps 11th century in date, also two Pictish cross-slabs from Ulbster and Skinnet. On the east side of Thurso, and seen from the coastal path, is the modern Thurso 'Castle' of 1872 with a castellated gateway and lodge, replacing a mansion of 1660. Near it is the base of a concrete tower known as Lady Janet's Seat. East of Thurso (ND 135692), and to be seen only from a distance unless with permission, is Harold's Tower, a curious hexagonal mausoleum with pencil turrets at the angles, erected by Sir John Sinclair around 1790-98 to commemorate Earl Harold who was killed in battle in 1190 and buried nearby.

Miller Academy, Thurso

Old St. Peter's Church, Thurso

INDUSTRIAL MONUMENTS AND HARBOURS

Keiss Harbour, Caithness

Industrial development in the Highlands has generally been on a small scale, for the fundamental requirements of a large work force, plentiful supplies of coal or other fuel, and good communications were usually lacking. Successful industries have made use of those local resources that were plentiful, such as water, peat, barley and fish.

An early industry on the west coast was iron-smelting, which used the forests then existing for charcoal to fuel their furnaces, and local bog-iron or imported ore. At the Red Smiddy on the east bank of the River Ewe near Poolewe (NG 861797), one of the earliest blast furnaces in Scotland was started around 1610 by Sir George Hay, its bellows worked by a waterwheel; only earthworks exist today, but information is given in Gairloch Museum. In recent times the engineering shop of the Rose Street Foundry, Inverness (NH 665456), specialised in large-scale industrial iron work, such as iron footbridges for railways (no. 18). The early aluminum works at Foyers from 1896 used imported bauxite shipped down the Caledonian Canal and local hydro-electric power. Since 1943 five major hydro-electric schemes have been completed in the area covered by this book, incorporating some of the finest modern engineering, often underground (no. 9).

In Caithness the massive outcrops of flagstone lying in horizontal beds from which great slabs could easily be prised out with simple wedges, levers and hammers have been quarried since prehistoric times. James Traill began quarrying on a commercial scale in 1793 and for a time the quarries supplied slabs for pavements all over the world. Extensive remains, including the stump of a windmill probably used to drain the quarry, can be seen at Castletown (no. 15); the harbour, itself built of local flags, was enlarged with wide quay areas where flags could be stockpiled, and the village doubled in size with workers' houses. Ham Harbour (ND 240737) was also built for the flagstone trade, and further flags were shipped from Thurso. In more recent times the demand has dropped, but a few quarries are still worked on a small scale. Among the many local uses made of the flagstones were the miles of flagstone field fence still to be seen in northern Caithness.

Wherever there were outcrops of limestone, limekilns might be set up. Particularly large and fine kilns can be seen at Ard Neackie (no. 13), while there are smaller kilns also in Sutherland, near Baligill (NC 851656 and NC 855660). Another pair of kilns is in Rothiemurchus Estate, East Inverness-shire (NH 897083), close to the visitor centre.

Windmill stump, Castlehill flagstone quarries.

Wherever grain was produced, it had to be ground, whether by hand on a rotary quern or in a water-driven mill. The simplest form of water mill is often called a Norse mill but is better called a horizontal mill since examples are now known from pre-Norse times. Remains of 18th- and 19th-century mills of this kind are occasionally encountered in the north and west: they are small rectangular stone buildings, originally thatched, with two grinding-stones directly connected to a vertical shaft with wooden paddles at the bottom, turned by water from a lade flowing under the building. There is a reconstruction in the grounds of the Highland Folk Museum, Kingussie. A ruined mill of this kind with its grinding-stones still inside may be seen beside a burn at Clashnessie, Sutherland (NC 055308). In the fertile grainlands of the east coast and Caithness there are many large watermills, mostly deserted. These mills usually ground oats or barley rather than wheat, never a common crop in the north. They often have grain-drying kilns attached, as at John O'Groats Mill (no. 16) and Whaligoe (no. 14); only Golspie Mill (no. 17) is open to the public.

Another use made of grain was for brewing or distilling, and illicit distilling was for long a favourite Highland occupation. On a commercial scale, breweries were popular in the 18th century, and brewery buildings, gutted of their contents, can be seen in Thurso (no. 8) and Cromarty (no. 3). Distilleries used the local resources of barley, peat for firing the kiln and the soft water running off the hills. Distilling has continued as a Highland industry into this century, and the pagoda roofs over the old distillery kilns are a distinctive feature of the countryside. Malt whisky distilleries range from Dalwhinnie (NN 638854) in the south to Pulteney by Wick (ND 367501) in the north. Clynelish at Brora (no. 11) has a good range of old buildings. There are also a number of grain whisky distilleries making whisky used for blending. Most malt whisky distilleries now have guided tours.

Spinning and weaving wool are long established local crafts; examples of local fabrics can be seen in museums at Kingussie and Gairloch. On an industrial scale, the manufacture of woollen cloth and knitwear continues today at Pringle's Mill (NH 654431), outside Inverness on the road to

Dores; there is a ruined woollen mill at Baligill, Sutherland (NC 855656). In 1792 David Dale of New Lanark together with George Dempster of Skibo built a cotton mill at Spinningdale, Sutherland (NH 675894). This fine stone building with Palladian windows in its stair tower was gutted by fire in 1806 and is now a dangerous ruin, but visible from the A 949.

Fishing is another occupation whose origins go back to prehistory. Small fishing boats could be drawn up on sandy beaches or in rivers, but, as boats got larger, the lack of safe harbours on many parts of the coast caused problems. Piers and harbours were built through the enterprise of merchants, landowners and organisations like the British Fisheries Society (nos 3, 6, 7). Keiss (no. 13) is a fine example of such a fishing harbour, and there are many others on the east coast, including Dunbeath (ND 165293) and Lybster (ND 244349). Storehouses and icehouses are features of many harbours; the icehouses holding the ice collected in winter from shallow ponds, which was packed into boxes with the fish to keep them fresh in transit. White fishing still goes on, particularly from Kinlochbervie, Sutherland (NC 2156), where the boats come in at weekends, and herring fishing continues from Ullapool (no. 6).

The history of salmon fishing is equally ancient but has left fewer traces. Salmon netting at Bonar Bridge, Sutherland (NH 609915) may be watched from the road in the season. Before refrigeration, salmon were parboiled and salted down in barrels for sale at home or abroad (salmon were exported even in medieval times), and finally from the 19th century packed fresh in ice. There is a fine icehouse near Bonar Bridge, just before the railway at Ardgay (NH 600905): such large icehouses connected with fishing are mostly mid or later 19th century in date. There are two interesting groups of salmon processing stations in Sutherland, one inland at Invershin (NH 573966) with a dwelling house, boiling house and two enormous icehouses set round a yard, and another on the coast at Rispond, Durness (NC 451653) with pier, dwelling house and storehouse.

Lybster Harbour, Caithness

9 AFFRIC/FARRER/BEAULY HYDRO-ELECTRIC SCHEME, WEST INVERNESS-SHIRE

AD 1946.

NH 273276, Loch Benevean dam; NH 318296, Fasnakyle power station. Access by minor roads from Cannich and Struy on the A831.

This hydro-electric scheme utilizes the waters of the Beauly River basin and includes six power stations, six dams and a number of tunnels. Much of the work is underground, but the dams are dramatic examples of modern engineering.

The Glen Affric scheme was the first stage in the development of the Beauly River resources. The main power station at Fasnakyle on the River Glass, 3 km southwest of Cannich, opened in 1950, is built of stone as more in keeping with the landscape than concrete. It is faced with golden-yellow sandstone from near Burghead in Morayshire, and the decorative carvings near the top include an adaptation of the Pictish bull symbol so popular at Burghead. Beyond Fasnakyle is Loch Benevean with a dam across its mouth 37 m high; there are car park and viewpoints here. Beyond is Loch Affric, in what is generally considered one of the most beautiful glens in Scotland. Care was taken not to alter the level of water in this loch.

Extra water is brought to Loch Benevean by a tunnel, 5.5 km long, through the hills from Loch Mullardoch; to get to the latter by road requires a return to Cannich. The dam on Loch Mullardoch (NH 222313) is much larger and higher than that at Benevean, being 727 m long and 48 m high.
Further north in another section of the scheme there are dams in Glen Strathfarrar. Here there is a dam at the end of Loch Beannacharan (NH 325393), and an interesting dam on Loch Monar (NH 203393) built in a curve. Few examples of such arch dams are found in Britain because the shape of the valleys are generally unsuitable. The Loch Monar dam is some 22 km up a single track road: this is a gated private road passing through a nature reserve, open to walkers and bicyclists, but with limited access for cars in summer (tel. gatekeeper, Struy 260).

Loch Benevean dam

In the gorge of the Beauly River there are two smaller dams, both incorporating a power station, at Aigas (NH 474436) and Kilmorack (NH 494442). Both these dams and that at Loch Beannacharan incorporate Borland fish passes, which allow salmon to pass up and down stream: these are not conventional fish ladders, but work more like locks on a canal. The fish lift at Aigas dam is open to the public. All the power from the Glen Affric/Farrer/Beauly stations is fed into the Highland Grid.

10 FOYERS ALUMINIUM WORKS, EAST INVERNESS-SHIRE

AD 1896.

NH 497210. On SE side of Loch Ness; minor road from B852 to Lower Foyers; works on right before end of road. (Exterior only.)

Foyers aluminium works

This early aluminium refinery is built on a terrace above the shore of Loch Ness, and was powered by the first major commercial hydro-electrical scheme in Britain. The fine stone building has a row of eight tall gable ends to the front, with crowsteps so designed as to give a distinctly castellated appearance. Most of the interior is open-plan, with rows of cast-iron columns and girders supporting the roof, but the range at the back of the building is partly floored over, with access by a somewhat 'art nouveau' iron spiral staircase. Here was the old hydro-electric plant, where nine Swiss-made turbines were powered by water piped from the River Foyers and augmented from a reservoir in Loch Mhor in the hills above. Lord Kelvin was electrical consultant during the station's construction. One of the old turbines and generators has been kept in the factory, and these, together with another turbine kept in the new power station, are certainly the oldest of their kind still in existence in Britain.

The factory was built by the British Aluminium Company in 1896 as its first aluminium reduction works. By 1908 it employed some 600 people. At first local bauxite was processed at Larne in Northern Ireland, and the alumina brought by sea and canal to Foyers, but later the bauxite came from Ghana and was processed at Burntisland in Fife. From Foyers, aluminium ingots and rolling slabs were sent to rolling-mills in Cheshire. Sadly the works, which for long provided employment in the area, are now closed down and the building belongs to the Hydro Board (group visits can sometimes be arranged; contact the Public Relations Officer, NSHEB, 16 Rothesay Terrace, Edinburgh 3). A number of cottages in Foyers were built for the British Aluminium Company, including rows of single-storey cottages at NH 496209 and 499201, all harled and painted white, some with dormer windows.

A new hydro-electric pumped-storage scheme was begun in 1969, and a new power station built on the shore of Loch Ness east of the old works. It makes use of the old Loch Mhor reservoir with an enlarged catchment area. When generating, water flows from Loch Mhor through more than 3 km of tunnels and shafts to the new power station. At other times, off-peak energy from the Highland Grid is used to drive the turbines in the reverse

direction and pump water from Loch Ness back up to Loch Mhor. The turbines and generators are housed in huge shafts sunk in the rock below the power station. The old dam and embankment at Loch Mhor (NH 513181; close to the B 862) were retained. The dam has a small castellated structure over its sluice, similar in style to the works.

Foyers was not the earliest hydro-electric scheme on Loch Ness. As far back as 1890 a small water turbine was installed for St Benedict's Abbey, Fort Augustus, which soon served part of the town as well, and was the first public hydro-electric scheme in Britain. It was supplied by an iron pipeline from a reservoir (NH 370052) on the Connachie Burn and continued until the Hydro Board took over in 1951.

11 CLYNELISH AND BRORA DISTILLERIES, BRORA, SUTHERLAND

19th-20th century AD.

NC 897054. Just N of Brora and W of A9. Open all year, Monday to Friday: last tour 4 pm.

The old distillery was built in 1819 by the Sutherland estate with the intention of affording their smaller tenants 'a steady and ready market for their grain without their being obliged to dispose of it to the illegal distillers'. A plan of the distillery in 1819 shows that part of the buildings were given over to a piggery, for the pigs ate the spent grain discarded after mashing. A farm was attached to the distillery and given a large allocation of unimproved land 'in consequence of the command of manure which the distillery will afford the tenant'. Finally coal from the new coal mine the Sutherlands had opened at Brora was used in the furnaces. The old distillery was completely rebuilt in 1896-7 to meet increased demand, but a stone

Clynelish Distillery: the old buildings (Right)

with the Sutherland/Stafford arms is preserved in the gable end of the still house.

In this range of buildings, now disused, much of the old equipment remains. First comes the long open-plan malt-room where barley after being soaked in water was spread out on the stone floor and allowed to germinate. Iron pillars support a wooden-floored grain loft above. Part of this block is the cask-room, now the only part of the old works shown to visitors. Next comes an elevator which took grain to the kiln, where kiln-drying stopped germination at the critical point. The kiln has a peat-fired furnace at the bottom, and the grain was spread on a perforated iron grid at first-floor level. The kiln has the typical pagoda roof and ventilator above. Beside this is the mill-room where the malted grain was ground to a coarse meal; a water-wheel originally turned the grinding rolls and also the grain-stirrer in the mash tun where the sugars were removed, leaving the husks (which make animal feed, hence the pigs). After mashing, the sugar solution was then fermented in wooden vats called 'wash- backs'. The coal-fired boiler-house with its tall chimney supplied heat to work the two great copper pot stills in the still room, where the wash was converted into high-strength spirit. From the stills the spirit had to be cooled, and in the old distillery it passed down immensely long coils of tubing, gradually decreasing in size, inside huge round wooden tanks called 'worm tubs', which stand at the back of the still house. Opposite all this is the line of bonded warehouses where the whisky, under the eye of an Excise Officer, still spends at least five years in casks before it is sold. The warehouses are open-plan inside, the bays separated by rows of iron columns. One block is dated 1896 and the other block is earlier.

The new oil-fired distillery built in 1967-8 has taken over the name Clynelish. It uses malted barley already processed in a plant at the Muir of Ord, and so starts with the fermenting stage. The processes are traditional though some of the equipment, such as the condensers, are new. Inside the distillery there is a row of gleaming copper pot stills of the old pattern (each distillery has its own shape). Some of the spirit from this distillery is bottled as Clynelish Single Malt, and some goes to be blended.

12 ARD NEACKIE, LIMEKILNS AND QUARRY, SUTHERLAND

AD 1870.

NC 446596. On headland on E side of Loch Eriboll, beside A838.

Ard Neackie is a rocky promontory, virtually an island, connected with the mainland by a sandy spit. The stone pier which served the ferry across Loch Eriboll to Portnancon was built in the early 19th century by the Sutherland/Stafford family together with the Heilem Inn nearby, the simple harled and slated house which has a worn coat-of-arms over its front door. The Countess of Sutherland and her husband the Marquis of Stafford had bought the Reay estate from the Mackays in 1829, and the Marquis of Stafford built a road to connect this part of the country with Tongue. Moin House (NC 518600) beside the

Clynelish Distillery: the new stills (Left)

Ard Neackie

A 838 between Hope and Tongue was a refuge on this road; a plaque on it records 'This house erected for the refuge of the traveller serves to commemorate the construction of the road across the deep and dangerous morass of the Moin . . . in the year 1830'.

Ard Neackie, limekilns and quarry

On the promontory are four unusually large and well preserved limekilns, built around 1870 as two pairs with differently shaped draw-arches. In front of them is a boathouse and the older ferry pier which also served the limekilns. It is thought the kilns were fuelled with coal or coke brought by sea, though peat could have been used. A track leads up the hill to the top of the kilns for carts to unload limestone and coal straight into the shafts. These are still open (and deep) and the burnt brick linings to the stone shafts can be seen. After burning, the 'quick'-lime was removed through the draw-holes below. These large kilns will have supplied lime to a wide area round, much of it distributed by sea. The cart track also led to the limestone quarry conveniently sited close to the kilns, and still an impressive hole in the hillside though now flooded. Beside the ferry inn, the strange wood and concrete building with brick chimneys and a slate roof was used to house the kiln and quarry workers.

On the opposite shore of the loch where the ferry crossed to Portnancon (NC 427602), there is a corresponding long stone pier with a wood-piled extension, and a storehouse with external stair, now converted to housing.

Keiss Harbour, Caithness (Right)

13 KEISS HARBOUR, CAITHNESS

AD 1831. (Photograph p.54)

ND 351609.

The long village street winds down to the harbour with a terrace of fishermen's cottages (c 1830) following the curve of the road. The harbour, built in 1831, is enclosed with rubble breakwaters made of local flagstone. It has a good example of a stilling basin; the waves run into an outer basin with a shelving slipway on which they break, while water in the main basin is not affected. By the harbour stands a fine warehouse also built in 1831, fronting onto a quay made with the local flags set vertically. The lower floor consists of six stone-vaulted cellars, with two floors above each of two large rooms, and attics. There are small square air vents just below the slate roof. This would have been used for storing salt, barrels, nets and so on, and for storing fish prior to shipping it out. Just north of the warehouse is an icehouse backed into the slope of the cliff, with a stone gabled front. It has an antechamber which acted as a kind of air lock to help keep warm air out of the icehouse proper, which takes the form of a stone-vaulted chamber covered with turf for insulation. In the roof at the back is the door through which ice was tipped in from carts every winter. Ice was packed into the boxes with the fish as soon as they were landed. A few fishing boats still use this harbour.

In Keiss village, on the south side of the road to the harbour, there is a parliamentary church (ND 348610) and its two-storey manse (ND 346612), now a private house called Scaraben, both built in 1826.

14 WHALIGOE HARBOUR, CAITHNESS

18th and 19th centuries AD.

ND 321402. Close to A9; turn E at crossroads by telephone box at Ulbster, c 10 km S of Wick; park by cottages. The steps need a good head for heights.

Whaligoe is a fishing harbour formed out of a creek where anyone would have thought it impossible, both from the narrowness of the creek and the height of the cliff above. Telford called it 'a dreadful place' and it may indeed inspire dread. Nevertheless the shortage of east coast harbours was such that extraordinary lengths were taken to use this creek. A flight of some 330 flagstone steps descend the precipitous cliffs from the fish curing station above to the quay below, with a few resting places on the way. The steps are mid-18th century, repaired in the early 19th century when the present tiny rubble platform quay was built. Boats were hauled into the creek stern first and moored each side, or in times of storm hauled right out of the sea onto the quay. Part of a winch survives. In 1808 seven boats used Whaligoe and in 1828 some twenty-four boats.

Women had to go up and down the steps carrying nets or fish on their backs. Several travellers saw Whaligoe in use and remarked on it with astonishment. Thus Pennant in 1769 'though the height of one of these rocks is surprising yet the country people have made steps by which they go up and down, carrying heavy burdens on their backs, which a stranger without seeing would scarcely believe'. Thomas Dick Lauder wrote in 1841 'the curious enquirer finds himself on the edge of the cliffs which drop downwards above a couple of hundred feet into the wild and narrow voe of Whaligoe, his eyes at once falling from that giddy height upon the topmasts of a large schooner receiving her herring cargo'.

At the top of the steps is a former herring curing station, a two-storey building with one-storey wings on one side of a walled yard, now a private house. Further up the main road is Whaligoe Mill (ND 321404), a 19th-century mill with a former kiln to the rear backed by a lower wing. The mill has also been converted to a house.

Whaligoe steps

15 CASTLETOWN FLAGSTONE TRAIL AND CASTLEHILL HARBOUR, CAITHNESS

Early 19th century AD.

ND 193684 and 195686. The trail starts from a carpark on the road between Castletown and the harbour.

The flagstones long quarried in various parts of Caithness as building stone became more valuable when the demand for paving stones opened up an international market in flagstones or 'pavement'. Flagstones from Castletown were being shipped to Aberdeen in 1793, but the great expansion of the industry took place from 1824 when James Traill of Rattar bought Castlehill House (burnt out and demolished in the 1960s) and set about building a harbour and pavement works.

Castlehill Harbour

The flagstone trail, laid out with noticeboards, starts with a small part of the huge old quarry reopened to show the flagstone beds, and then passes the stone tower of a windmill, formerly crowned with wooden cap and sails, that pumped water into a dam. Beyond are two worker's cottages. The dam once provided water to power a waterwheel, which in turn worked saws in the cutting yard. The flagstones were then loaded onto trolleys which ran on rails to the quay, where they were shipped off in small schooners, at first to the east coast and England, later as far as Australia and South America. The Strand in London was paved with Caithness stone.

The harbour, which has a fine stilling basin (see no. 13), was built for Traill by James Bremner of Keiss in 1825 out of the local flags. Immense slabs were used both vertically as on the outside of the breakwater and horizontally, with a wide platform on the quay to provide an area for stacking the flagstones. Near the harbour can be seen an icehouse, and a little further east a large three-storey meal mill with central kiln section and enclosed grain chutes, looking out on a fine sandy beach.

Returning to the carpark, the road passes a large house with attached steading, in which one building has been restored as the Castletown Flagstone Centre with appropriate displays. Back in Castletown itself, a village which grew with the flagstone trade, note the many stoneworker's houses of single-storey and attic in the streets north of the A 836.

16 JOHN O'GROATS MILL, CAITHNESS

AD 1846 and 1901.

ND 372733. Beside the A836 between Huna and Duncansby (exterior only).

There are two mills here, and they have a somewhat complex history of reuse. The first known mill on the site was built in 1750 where the large mill stands today. The smaller mill was built beside it in 1846, and shared the same mill-lade. The new mill was then used as a grain mill and the old mill as a threshing mill. However in 1901 the old mill was completely rebuilt and the positions reversed; the

new larger mill became the grain mill once again while the smaller building was converted for threshing. It has not been used for many years. The grain mill, however, is one of the very few water-powered grain mills still working in Scotland, and mostly produces barley meal.

Of the older building, the lower block is the 1846 mill, while the two-storey block nearer the road is a store. The grain mill is a three-storey, L-plan building. The enclosed, overshot water wheel is made of wood and iron, and the mill lade derives from the Burn of Duncansby some way upstream. The external sack hoist can be seen projecting from an upper storey. There is a large kiln for drying grain before grinding, with two tall square ventilators which look somewhat like chimneys. The kiln floor is made of cast-iron perforated plates that let the heat through to the grain. There are three pairs of millstones, for shelling, grinding barley, and grinding oatmeal. An interesting feature of the mill is that the grain husks were used as fuel in the kiln, an arrangement also found at Achingale Mill (ND 240534).

An unusual amount is known of the history of this mill. The 1901 mill was designed by William Campbell Houston, nephew of the miller, then studying engineering at Glasgow University. He and his uncle travelled round Caithness looking at other mills to incorporate the most up-to-date ideas in their own design.

Beside the mill is the remains of an old rubble arched bridge traditionally dated to the 17th century; this leads now to the single-storey, early 19th-century Mill Cottage, used by mill employees. The miller, still a member of the Houston family, lives in Mill House across the road.

John O'Groats Mill (Right)

Golspie Meal Mill

17* GOLSPIE MEAL MILL, SUTHERLAND

AD 1863.

NC 841006. At north end of Golspie, beyond the bridge on the A9. Parking at Mill.

The largest mill in Sutherland, it was built for the Duke of Sutherland in 1863 to replace an older mill. It shut down in 1953 but has re-opened after careful restoration. It is a solid, L-shaped, three-storey stone building, plain but enlivened by crow-stepped gables. The large kiln with a louvred vent in its roof is in the wing behind. The mill windows have the traditional fixed glazing above and opening wooden shutters below, while much of the interior woodwork and machinery is original. The overshot wood and iron water-wheel drives three pairs of millstones and a pot barley mill. The latter (which made pot or pearl barley for soup and so on) is a large single millstone mounted vertically in a wire cage, and it polished the outer coat of the barley packed round it.

On the ground floor there is an office with fireplace and sash windows, which is partitioned off at the west end. The millstones and a rotating sieve for oatmeal are on the first floor, and on the second are the metal doors to the drying kiln, which was fuelled originally by chaff ('husks') separated from the grain, and later by coke from Golspie Gas Works. Almost all jobs, such as raising or lowering sacks, can be done by water-power and the mill can now be run single-handed.

A detailed specification exists for the erection of the meal mill in 1863. It refers to the cast iron pillars which support the upper floors, the wall stones which were to come from the Backies Quarry behind Golspie (though some stone from the old mill could be used for the inside of the walls), Caithness 'pavement' (see no. 15) for the floor, and iron latches and locks to the mill and office 'all of the best quality'. The contractor was asked to estimate for Burlington slate, Ballachulish slate and Welsh slate, and the ridge tiles were to come from Invernettie Brickworks near Peterhead. The present millwheel made by James Abernethy & Co of Aberdeen may be a later replacement. The original gears survive; one iron cog wheel has 104 wooden teeth which were repaired by a coachbuilder in Golspie.

There were two large mills here in the 19th century. The meal mill was for oats, making oatmeal, and the flour mill for wheat, making finer flour. The ruins of the four-storey flour mill are in the angle of the burn and bridge. Just by it is the old bridge of 1808, now by-passed; it has an obelisk carved with a Gaelic inscription on its parapet. Behind the meal mill are two mill-worker's cottages, probably of the same date (not open), and the mill pond, fed by a lade from higher up the burn. The various kinds of flour produced are sold on the premises. Visitors can walk round on all floors with a tape commentary while the miller works. The mill is open in the afternoon, mid-June to mid-September.

COMMUNICATIONS

Telford bridge at Helmsdale

Before 1724 there were no roads in the Highlands beyond Crieff and Dunkeld, except for a few stretches close to major towns; something it is very difficult to visualise today. To get to Inverness from the south everyone had to travel east of the Grampian Mountains through Aberdeenshire, Moray and Nairn, crossing all the rivers on the way by ferry. In 1290 it took English envoys sent to meet the Maid of Norway nineteen days to get from Newcastle to Wick. From Inverness north to Wick and Thurso there was a route round by the coast, but it involved four dangerous sea crossings over the Beauly Firth, the Cromarty Firth, the Dornoch Firth (the ferry sank in 1809 with the loss of 100 lives) and Loch Fleet. There were a few bridges in towns where burgesses could afford to build and repair them; thus Inverness had a timber bridge possibly from the 13th century, and a stone bridge from 1685, while a bridge at Wick is mentioned in 1665. Everywhere else travel was possible only on foot or on horseback, on rough tracks across country impassable for wheeled traffic, where every river and burn had to be forded. Burt wrote 'the old ways consisted chiefly of stony Moors, Bogs, rugged, rapid Fords, Declivities of Hills, entangling woods and giddy Precipices'.

In 1724 General George Wade was made Commander of the Forces in North Britain, in the aftermath of the Jacobite risings of 1715 and 1719. His task was to restore order in the Highlands, and he realised the urgent need to improve communications between the various military posts. Between 1725 and 1733 Wade built some 400 km (250 miles) of roads and about forty bridges in the Highlands, linking the four barracks at Fort William,

Kiliwhimen by Fort Augustus, Inverness and Ruthven near Kingussie (no. 42) with each other and with Crieff and Dunkeld in the south by roads passable by wheeled traffic. The contrast with the old tracks is expressed in the contemporary couplet:

If you'd seen these roads before they were made,

You'd lift up your hands, and bless General Wade.'

His road north from Dunkeld by Kingussie to Inverness took much the same route as the present A 9. The road from Crieff joined at Kingussie. From Inverness a road ran south of Loch Ness via Dores and Foyers to Fort Augustus and on to Fort William. Finally a cross road linked Fort Augustus to Ruthven and Dalwhinnie. Burt described the difficulty of building the road along the south shore of Loch Ness, much of it blasted from the solid rock with 'the Miners hung by Ropes from the Precipice over the Water' to bore holes for gunpowder.

Wade bridge at Whitebridge

Wade's roads were quite narrow, mostly about 4.8 m though narrower still in difficult places, and the bridges built of undressed stone. An exception is the elegant high-arched bridge with ashlar dressings at Whitebridge (NH 489153), south of Foyers, beside the modern road. There is a good example of a more typical bridge at Garva (no. 23).

Between 1740 and 1767, road construction was continued by Major William Caulfield, formerly Wade's assistant. Some 1900 km of military road were constructed after Wade's time, with another 938 bridges; these included the first two roads to the west coast, from Fort Augustus to Bernera barracks (no. 43) and from Dingwall to Poolewe. Other roads were built to Grantown-on-Spey and to Fort George (no. 41), also in Grampian region and in Argyll. Examples of Caulfield's bridges are Little Garve, Ross and Cromarty (NH 396628), Dulsie Bridge, Nairn (NH 931414), and the Old Spey Bridge at Grantown-on-Spey (NJ 039263) with three spans of unequal size built in 1754 by troops from Lord Charles Hay's Regiment.

The lines of the military roads are shown on the OS maps. Some parts are now bypassed and can be walked, other stretches on the line of modern roads can be driven along.

The military roads were not the final solution to communications in the Highlands, but they did show what could be done. Constructed by unskilled labour and using routes often inconvenient for civilian traffic, the problems of maintenance were never solved. By the end of the 18th century most were unfit for wheeled traffic. In 1803 the Commission for Highland Roads and Bridges was set up by Parliament to improve communications, half the cost to be borne by the government and half raised locally. Thomas Telford was engineer to the Commission. This remarkable man was responsible for not only the roads and bridges and better piers at the ferry crossings, but the new parliamentary churches and manses, the Mound embankment (no. 21) and the Caledonian Canal (no. 20), besides his work on harbours. Between 1803 and 1828 some 1,480 km of parliamentary roads and 1,117 bridges were built, many of them north and west of Inverness. Many of the roads are in use today with little alteration save to the surface. The smaller bridges were still rubble built, but the larger bridges were often multi-span structures with ashlar dressings, the cutwaters carried up to form refuges. Those that survive include Helmsdale (ND 025153), Ousdale (ND 065203) and Golspie (NC 840005) in Sutherland, the Lovat Bridge near Beauly, Inverness-shire (NH 516449) and Ferness near Ardclach, Nairn (NH 959462). Torgyle has been rebuilt (no. 22). Telford's fine cast-iron bridge at Bonar Bridge, Sutherland (NH 609915), 'a spider's web in the air', has gone, but a similar bridge at Craigellachie, Moray (NJ 285452) survives.

Since then, major road works have included the construction of the A 9 trunk road from Blair Atholl to Inverness in 1925-8, and the reconstruction of the A 9 in the 1970s to 1990s. The magnificent Kessock Bridge across the Beauly Firth at Inverness, a long embankment and bridge over the Cromarty Firth, and another over the Dornoch Firth have taken the main road north back to one of the routes used in the heyday of the ferries.

Railways reached the Highlands in the mid 19th century, first getting to Inverness in 1858 on a roundabout route via Aberdeen and Nairn, and then directly from Perth in 1863 over the Drumochter pass. Many different companies were involved with several amalgamations. In 1862 the Inverness and Ross-shire Railway opened between Inverness and Dingwall, with viaducts over the Ness, Beauly and Conon and a swing-bridge over the Caledonian canal at Clachnaharry (see no. 20). Soon after, the Highland Railway was formed. The line to Wick and Thurso opened in 1874, and Kyle of Lochalsh was reached in 1897. Among notable features of the Highland lines are the viaducts over the Findhorn at Tomatin (NH 806288) visible from the new A 9, the Shin north of Bonar Bridge (NH 578952) and the river Nairn at Culloden Moor (NH 763450), the longest viaduct in

Nairn railway viaduct

Scotland with 28 spans; the Duke of Sutherland's private station with timber waiting room at Dunrobin by Golspie (NC 849012), built in 1902 (in 1871 this Duke had extended the line from Golspie to Helmsdale at his own expense); and a most unusual wooden railway viaduct at Aultnaslanach, Moy (NH 760349), still in use on a main line. Many original features of the old Highland railways, not least the steam engines, may be seen on the Strathspey Railway (no. 18).

Sea transport has always been of utmost importance in the Highlands. While harbours are described in connection with the fishing industry, some mention must be made of lighthouses, mostly built in the 19th century by Robert Stevenson or his descendants. Many lighthouses in the area are short circular towers with domed lanterns and single-storey keepers' houses, those at Noss Head in Caithness, Chanonry by Fortrose (NH 749557) and Cromarty (no. 3) in Easter Ross having Egyptian-style doors, while Tarbat Ness, Easter Ross (N H 946875), has a tall tower painted in bands for recognition. Some of these attractive, smartly painted structures are now automated and can merely be admired from outside, but at those listed below visitors can usually be shown round in the afternoons at the discretion of the Head Lightkeeper: (east to west) Noss Head, near Wick (ND 388550), Duncansby Head (ND 405733), Dunnet Head (no. 19), Holborn Head, Scrabster (ND 106706), Strathy Point (NC 827696), Cape Wrath (NC 259747) and Rubha Reidh (NG 739918).

Wade road near Whitebridge

18 BOAT OF GARTEN STATION, STRATHSPEY RAILWAY, EAST INVERNESS-SHIRE

AD 1863; station buildings rebuilt 1904.

NH 943188.

Boat of Garten Railway Station

The name 'Boat of Garten' comes from an old ferry across the Spey. Boat of Garten railway station was opened in 1863 by the Inverness and Perth Junction Railway, later part of the Highland Railway. It has a wooden single-storey station building with slated roof and a stone station-master's house adjoining, both built in 1904 to replace others in a similar style which had burnt down. The typical iron footbridge was cast in the Rose Street Foundry, Inverness, in 1900; it comes from Dalnaspidal and replaces an identical bridge removed in 1960. Boat of Garten was a junction between the Highland Railway and a branch of the Great North of Scotland Railway joining the line to Elgin at Craigellachie, and as such had three platforms and two signal boxes. From 1863 the main line north from Perth ran through Boat of Garten and on to Grantown-on-Spey, Nairn and Inverness, until a new direct line from Aviemore to Inverness via Carrbridge was opened in 1898.

The line from Aviemore to Boat of Garten, closed by British Rail in 1965, has been reopened as an 'operating museum of steam traction' by the Strathspey Railway Company, who run a steam train service in the summer months. The line still uses semaphore signals. Their oldest locomotive was built in 1899 for the Caledonian Railway, and among the rolling stock is a Highland Railway brakevan of the 1870s. A railway museum is housed in some of the restored buildings at Boat of Garten (part of this is across the footbridge). At Aviemore,

Dunnet Head lighthouse (Right)

where restoration work by volunteers continues, a new station has been constructed in the old locomotive yard (NH 897129). The station building has been moved from Dalnaspidal and the original engine shed reopened. Locomotives are again housed and maintained there. The journey from Aviemore to Boat of Garten takes just over 15 minutes, and runs through some attractive wooded countryside with the Cairngorms in the background. The ultimate aim of the Strathspey Railway Company is to reopen the next section of line to Grantown-on-Spey.

19 DUNNET HEAD LIGHTHOUSE, CAITHNESS

AD 1831.

ND 202767. Leave A836 at Dunnet on B 856 to end of Dunnet Head.

One of the six lighthouses designed and built by Robert Stevenson with his son Alan between 1830 and 1833, and the most northerly lighthouse on the mainland of Scotland. Here a short circular tower stands on a semicircular base, with a parapet corbelled out below the light, and a circular, diamond-paned lantern with a domed top. Beside the tower are the low, white-washed blocks of the keepers' houses. A feature of the Stevenson family's work for the Northern Lighthouse Board was the attention they paid to the welfare of the lightkeepers, as well their engineering skills in providing the best possible lights. These were sometimes constructed on the most inaccessible rocks, such as the Pentland Skerries where two tall towers and a keeper's cottage were completed in 1794. Every year, the member of the family who was Engineer to the Board made a trip round Scotland to visit all the lights, even those on remote rocks or islands. Sir Walter Scott sailed on the

Lighthouse Yacht in 1814 and kept a journal of his voyage, with vivid descriptions of Cape Wrath, the dangerous currents in the Pentland Firth, and landing on the Pentland Skerries.

20 CALEDONIAN CANAL

AD 1804-22.

The canal runs from NH 644467 at Inverness to Corpach.

The canal was designed by the great engineer Thomas Telford, as a ship canal to link the east and west coasts of Scotland from the Beauly Firth to the Atlantic via Loch Linnhe and the Sound of Mull, and to save sailing vessels the dangerous passage through the Pentland Firth. The Great Glen fault offered a natural, low-lying route with Lochs Ness, Oich and Lochy providing navigable waterways for much of the way. The canal now runs from Inverness to Loch Ness, and again from the head of the Loch at Fort Augustus to Loch Oich, where it passes out of our area west of Kyltra Lock. The canal was the great engineering undertaking of its time, broader and deeper than previous canals, since it was designed to take ocean-going ships. Originally intended to be 20 feet deep, it was in the end only 12 feet (3.70 m) due to technical difficulties. It was built and has been maintained at government expense, and is now run by the British Waterways Board. The poet Southey has left a graphic description of construction going on at Fort Augustus in September 1820: 'Went before breakfast to look at the locks, five together. Such an extent of masonry upon such a scale, I had never before beheld, each of these locks being 180 feet in length. It was a most impressive and remarkable scene. Men, horses and machines at work, digging, walling and puddling going on, men wheeling barrows, horses drawing stones along the railways. The great steam engine was at rest, having done its work'. The canal employed up to 1400 men in summer, but less than half that in winter because many went home.

That part of the canal within the area covered by this volume includes, from the west end, quiet Kyltra Lock and the flight of five locks at Fort Augustus just before the canal runs into Loch Ness, where the road crosses the canal on a modern swing bridge. (The only survivor of the original

Caledonian Canal at Fort Augustus

cast-iron swing bridges that took roads over the canal is at Moy (NN 162826), south-west of Loch Lochy.)

The stretch of canal from Loch Ness to the sea runs close to the River Ness until it reaches Inverness. There is a regulating lock at Dochgarroch. On the outskirts of Inverness is another swing bridge and a flight of four locks at Muirtown, leading into Muirtown basin, designed as a second harbour for Inverness. At the north end of the basin lies Clachnaharry village, much of it single-storey houses built for canal workers, and the workshops which are the repair centre for the whole canal. Just south of these in Clachnaharry Road is a tall stone slab outside the Tilhill Economic Forestry Office. Erected in 1922, it bears a tribute in blank verse by the poet Robert Southey to his friend Thomas Telford on the opening of the canal in 1822.

Beyond the basin is the great sea-lock which projects right out into the Beauly Firth, with lock-

Caledonian Canal at Inverness, sea-lock and lock-keeper's house

gates at either end. The railway crosses the canal just north of the basin on a steel swing bridge built in 1909 for the Highland Railway, and replacing the original bridge of 1862. Beside this bridge is a small wooden signal box of standard Highland Railway pattern. There is a pleasant walk out along the side of the sea-lock to the lockkeeper's house at the far end, right out in the firth, across the lock gates and back down the other side. Tow-paths provide excellent walking the length of the canal.

21 THE FLEET MOUND, EMBANKMENT AND BRIDGE, SUTHERLAND

AD 1814-6.

NH 768977-775982. The A9 crosses The Mound 6 km S of Golspie; there is a carpark at the N end of the Mound with an information board.

The Mound is a great earthen embankment faced with stone on the seaward side, and with a bridge

Fleet Mound

at its north end, that carries the parliamentary road across the upper end of Loch Fleet. It acts as a tide barrier, stopping the sea some 2.5 km short of its natural tidal limits. The bridge has four arches planned by Thomas Telford, and two others added by Joseph Mitchell in 1837, all fitted with wooden non-return flap valves that allow the river to run out but prevent sea-water returning upriver. At certain times the flaps are opened mechanically to allow salmon to swim upriver. Above this barrier what was a salty, tidal river is now fresh water, and many acres formerly flooded at high tide have been reclaimed.

The Mound was part of the works carried out on the parliamentary road from Inverness to Wick and Thurso. Telford had intended to build new ferry piers for the Little Ferry, at the mouth of Loch Fleet. It was William Young, then factor to the Sutherland estates, who suggested a causeway across the head of the estuary, which Telford designed and which was built with local labour. It was constructed between 1814 and 1816, and took longer and cost more than expected, as with many similar projects. Young wrote on 3rd June 1816 as the last breach was about to be filled 'We are all prepared to battle the sea with 600 men. Walklate is brewing 30 hogsheads of ale and the Baker is getting 40 Bolls of Meal converted into Bread, for the people must be fed'. After many difficulties, the work was completed, and the Countess of Sutherland crossed the Mound on 26th June 1816 'carriage and all'.

Fleet Mound bridge

In 1900 Telford's embankment was utilized for the Dornoch Light Railway, a branch line from the Mound Station to Dornoch, which was closed in 1960. Two piers of the railway bridge stand in the river upstream from the road bridge. The Mound Station (NH 775983), built in 1877 for the Sutherland Railway, survives as a private house by the railway embankment near the bridge. The wooden piles in the water are to prevent ice damaging the bridge.

There are information boards in the carpark at the north end of the Mound. The road here was realigned during major roadworks in 1990. The Fleet estuary is a nature reserve and many birds can be seen.

22 TORGYLE BRIDGE, GLENMORISTON, WEST INVERNESS-SHIRE

AD 1808-11; rebuilt 1828.

NH 309129. On the A887, halfway between Invermoriston and Loch Cluanie.

This handsome three-span bridge across the River Moriston was designed by Thomas Telford to carry the parliamentary road that runs west from Invermoriston to Shiel Bridge and on to the ferries to Skye; an important link in communications to the west coast. Like other Telford bridges, it suffered in the great spring floods of 1818. Four thousand birch timbers, intended for making barrel staves for the fishing industry, had been left on the banks of the river ready to float down to Loch Ness, and thence to be shipped through the Caledonian Canal and up to the Caithness coast. These timbers were swept away by the flood and hurled against the bridge like battering rams, reducing it to ruins. A wooden bridge was erected as a temporary measure, and the stone bridge rebuilt in 1828 under the supervision of the young Joseph Mitchell, who at the age of twenty-one had just succeeded his father as Chief Inspector of Roads, responsible for the upkeep of Highland roads and bridges. He was also put in charge of constructing new fishing harbours in the Highlands, and building many of the new parliamentary churches and manses, and later on, with Murdoch Paterson, he was responsible for engineering almost the entire Highland Railway system.

Torgyle Bridge

It is not clear what alterations if any Mitchell made to Telford's original design for Torgyle Bridge. Mitchell later wrote 'I made a plan for the new bridge, which had 140 feet of waterway, with circular towers over the piers'. Both bridges had three arches. The present bridge has triangular cutwaters protecting the base of the piers which are carried up as rounded buttresses to parapet level, and decorated with cruciform arrowslits and castellations. These are almost identical to those on the grandest of Telford's bridges at Dunkeld, Perthshire and Kinross (NO 026424), whereas most of the other large Telford bridges, such as Helmsdale Bridge (ND 025153) and the Lovat Bridge at Beauly (NH 516449), are plainer and have angled buttresses.

Much of the A 887 west of Invermoriston is on the line of the parliamentary road with little alteration save for the surface. An old bridge of rubble without ashlar dressings, and now by-passed, can be seen near Invermoriston (NH 419165) and another Telford bridge, also by-passed, near Ceannacroc (NH 227106). Here the old military road from Fort Augustus through Inchnacardoch Forest (a 10 km walk with fine views) came down into Glenmoriston and took more or less the present route to Glenelg, though in places, as shown on the OS map, it ran north of the A 87.

In 1773 Dr Samuel Johnson and James Boswell rode along the military road from Fort Augustus to Glenelg, it no longer being passable for wheeled vehicles, on their way to the Western Isles. They stayed overnight in Aonach, somewhere between Torgyle and Ceannocroc: 'a village of three huts, one of which is distinguished by a chimney'; this latter was the inn. As described by Boswell it was built of turf and thatched with heather. 'It had three rooms in length and a little room which projected. Where we sat, the side-walls were wainscotted, as Dr Johnson said, with wicker, very neatly plaited. Our landlord had made the whole with his own hands.' Mitchell fared rather better in 1828 when the foundations of the new Torgyle Bridge were laid; he stayed overnight at Invermoriston House where he shared a double-bedded room and, despite his youth, as engineer he was allotted a bed to himself, while the county clerk and the factor were expected to share the other. As in army barracks, single beds were not then considered essential in the Highlands.

Garvamore Kingshouse
(Right)

23 GARVA BRIDGE, EAST INVERNESS-SHIRE

AD 1731-2.

NN 521947. Minor road W from A86 at Laggan.

A two-span bridge constructed by General Wade to carry the military road from Dalwhinnie to Fort Augustus across the River Spey. The central portion rests on a rock in midstream. The rubble construction, the narrow carriageway and low parapet are typical of Wade bridges, but it has since been strengthened with buttresses and iron braces. General Wade's accounts for 1731 include an item of £466 'For building Five Stone Bridges one of two Arches and 4 of one Arch'; the two-arched bridge being this at Garva.

The narrow road that leads from Laggan to Garva Bridge follows closely the line of the military road. Beside the road, a short distance east of the bridge, is the Kingshouse at Garvamore (NN 528943), now unfortunately in bad repair. Here, as in other places, a hutted or tented camp used for the troops who built the road was replaced by a building used both for military and civilian travellers, which later became an inn. These buildings were known as

Garva Bridge

'kingshouses' because they stood on the king's highway. This one is thought to date from around 1740. It is a long, two-storey slated range with three chimneys, the western end having stables below and a loft with fireplace above, probably for troops, while the single-storey block at the east end and the porches are later additions. Inside (not accessible) is an old wooden staircase with turned banisters and carved newel posts. A box bed removed from here is stored in the West Highland Museum at Fort William.

The military road from Dalwhinnie to Garva Bridge followed the line of the A 89 to Laggan as far as Catlodge, where it was joined by a road from Ruthven barracks to the north. It then continued south of the Spey to join the present road to Garva near the Spey dam. There is a good example of a small Wade bridge where this road crossed the Mashie Burn (NN 600935) and another bridge stands in a field beside the modern road (NN 554931). From Garva Bridge the military road went on over the hills to Fort Augustus, climbing the Corrieyairack pass by a series of zig-zags or traverses, originally eighteen but later reduced to thirteen, and each retained by a stone wall on the outside. This is one of the best known, if not the most typical, of Wade roads. It is still possible to drive to Melgarve, just past Garva, beyond which is a rough walk of some 19 km to Fort Augustus.

A contemporary traveller who crossed the Corrieyairack in 1731 recorded 'I heard the noise of many people and saw six great fires, about each of which a number of soldiers were busy . . . I found in all about five hundred men, who had this summer, with indefatigable pains, completed the great road for wheel-carriages between Fort Augustus and Ruthven . . . General Wade had given to each detatchment an ox-feast, and liquor; six oxen were roasted whole, one at the head of each party.'

24 AULTBEA, CLAPPER BRIDGE, ROSS AND CROMARTY

18th or 19th century AD

NG 873899 In Aultbea, not far from the A832 coastal road.

Clapper bridges are built from stone slabs piled into rough piers with other slabs laid across the top to form the roadway. This bridge crosses a burn running out into the sea at Aultbea. It is now bypassed by a new bridge for motor traffic, and has been carefully restored. Six rectangular drystone piers are set close together and bridged by flat stone slabs, forming seven spans of unequal length. There are low parapets either side. This very simple type of bridge construction has remained in use into recent times where conditions are suitable, and it is much easier to build than an arched bridge. The village of Aultbea has a row of attractive 18th and 19th-century cottages along the shore, and a pier at the end of the headland.

Aultbea clapper bridge

There are a number of other clapper bridges in Wester Ross and northwest Scotland, including several small clapper bridges on the old track that led round the northern coast of the Applecross peninsula, now replaced by a modern road, and a three-span bridge at NG 713398, south of Applecross; also a seven-span clapper bridge built c1835 at Achriesgill near Rhiconich, Sutherland (NC 256540)

RURAL BUILDINGS 4

Folk Museum, Caithness

Most people's idea of a Highland cottage is a one-storey thatched cottage with a chimney in the gable, white-washed walls and one window each side of the door. But this type of building, far from being ancient, only appeared in the course of the later 18th and 19th centuries and is fast disappearing again. Earlier changes are less easy to document, but certainly from the 17th century onwards rural architecture has undergone a continuing process of development.

Before the 18th century many rural buildings may have been constructed of timber, turf or mud, perishable materials which leave no trace above ground. Turf houses were particularly common in the Central Highlands. They may have been commodious and snug when new, but deteriorated rapidly. They were generally wattled inside, like the inn described by James Boswell (see no. 22); outside they had walls of turfs either built up like bricks, or pinned like slates to the wooden framework. In some more recent houses the upper part of a stone gable may be of turf, as at Culloden (no. 27).

Before the widespread changes in the 18th and 19th centuries, rural buildings were generally grouped in 'townships' or community farms, small collections of perhaps a dozen or fewer houses clustered round their arable land, then laid out in broad strips which were reallocated by lot every year. Around the townships were large areas of common grazings where the beasts were taken in summer and where the people lived in tiny shieling huts. The remains of many old townships, by no means all abandoned as a result of clearances, can be found in the Highlands (and are marked on larger scale, 1:10,000 OS maps). An excellent example is Rosal (no. 29).

These ruins are generally 18th or 19th century in date, the houses having had low stone walls which might have been heightened in turf, a central hearth and an integral byre with one door shared by man and beast. A contemporary description of the houses in Glencalvie (no. 54) from The Times of 1845 could apply to many others:

Plockton, heather-thatched cottage

'The cottages themselves are outside apparently low heaps of turf. They are grown over so as to be of the colour of the brown hills, and at a distance are not distinguishable from the hill. They are all built on one plan, and are divided into three compartments. The first you enter is a stable or cowshed; a doorway out of this leads into the family room, and another doorway beyond leads to the far room which is the bedroom and state apartment, being kept tidy and appropriated to receive visitors. The fire is on a stone in the middle of the family or centre room, and warms the whole cottage. Though the roof and sides are blackened with the peat smoke, everything within them is clean and orderly.'

As agriculture became more intensive, and more land was taken into cultivation, the lands of the lowland townships were incorporated into larger farms, while parts of the more infertile higher ground were cleared to make way for sheep. Much of the population was resettled in newly laid out crofts along the coasts, each with a long rectangular fenced strip of its own land. Other folk settled in planned villages by the sea, with their long streets of single-storey houses, for instance Plockton (no.5). Landlords made great efforts to encourage the construction of mortared stone buildings with chimneys in their gable ends and slated roofs. A few examples of an older style of building with drystone walls and thatched roofs, which less well off settlers erected in the new villages, can still be seen, as in recently deserted houses in several townships on the Applecross peninsula, for instance Fearnbeg (NG 736597), while one cottage at Plockton (no. 5) and others at Lonbain (NG 685529) and at 27 Big Sand and 11 Melvaig, both near Gairloch, are still thatched.

The older houses had a hearth in the middle of the floor, the smoke finding its way out through the thatch, or perhaps through a box-framed hole in the thatch. Later houses had real stone chimneys built into their gable walls to control the smoke. An intermediate system was the 'hanging lum', a chimney canopy of timber, mud and straw, suspended over the fire which was set against a wall. This made an excellent place to smoke bacon or fish, and was often installed in the kitchen of fisher cottages; there is an unusual one in Hugh Miller's Cottage, Cromarty (no. 3). Reconstructions of hanging lums may be seen in Culloden Cottage (no. 27), Gairloch Heritage

Museum, and the Highland Folk Museum, Kingussie. At Kingussie there is also a reconstruction of a crofthouse from the island of Lewis, and, although this differs somewhat from Highland houses, it gives an authentic glimpse of a similar interior where in summer the visitor may find a peat fire burning on the hearth and a lassie baking bannocks.

The sizes of crofts varied. The croft at Laidhay had 16 acres of arable, while the pre-clearance families at Rosal had only some 4 acres each. Crofthouses also developed in different ways. In parts of Caithness the various buildings were grouped in a long line as at Laidhay (no. 25), with more rooms, barns and stables added to an original nucleus which had been a dwelling and byre. Examples of older rural buildings may be seen all over Caithness, sometimes next to newer houses which have replaced them. A feature of the landscape in northern Caithness are the field 'fences' made of Caithness slabs.

A number of fine farmhouses, and farm steadings often built round a square, were erected on the bigger arable farms, not only near the Moray and Dornoch Firths, but right round the coast wherever patches of good agricultural land existed. Since almost all of these are working farms, it is rarely possible to visit them but some can be seen from the road. One such is the steading south of Conan House, Ross and Cromarty (NH 532535), with a dovecote beside it. Adjuncts to such steadings may include grain-drying kilns, threshing mills and large storage barns.

The Corr Latheron, Caithness, plan of 19th-century croft

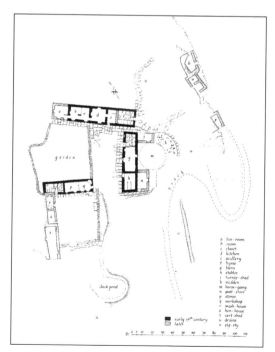

Coastal storehouses or girnals were built to serve the large estates which developed on the fertile farmlands of Easter Ross and eastern Sutherland. Agricultural tenants then paid their rents mostly in kind, in bulky materials such as oats and barley, and large stone buildings were erected as stores. Foulis Rent House (no. 30) is the best preserved, but among the others are two adjacent storehouses by the harbour at Portmahomack, Ross and Cromarty (NH 915846), of which the smaller and earlier was built by Lord Tarbat at the end of the 17th century. These have been converted into houses.

Many of the earliest known dovecots (doocots or pigeonhouses) are attached to castles, as at Urquhart Castle (no. 52), but most of the surviving dovecots in the Highlands belonged to great estates. Although they are really farm buildings, after 1617 they were confined by law to larger properties because of the damage the birds caused to crops. The pigeons were kept both for their meat, particularly useful in the winter months, and for their dung which provided valuable manure for the fields. Boath and Culloden (nos 32, 31) are the most accessible, and there are others in the park at Dunrobin (no. 33) and at Kilravock (no. 49).

25* LAIDHAY FOLK MUSEUM, LONGHOUSE AND BARN, CAITHNESS

Late 18th-19th century.

ND 173305. Beside the A9 about 2 km N of the bridge at Dunbeath.

A traditional Caithness longhouse and barn standing on a croft which comprised sixteen acres of arable land and fifteen acres of rough grazing. It was worked as a croft until 1968 when the buildings were purchased by the Laidhay Preservation Trust to be restored as an excellent example of the traditional buildings of the area. While parts of the house may date back to the later 18th century, and it shows signs of long development, the complex in its present form is thought to date from around 1842. The stable and byre were probably additions to the nucleus which now forms the house and kitchen

As seen today, the first element in the long building is the stable, its wooden partitions restored and now housing modern public toilets. The next door leads into the main living area, divided up by box beds into the 'room' on the left, a small bedroom at the back, and the 'middle room', the general living area on the right. This once had four box beds ranged along the back wall. Through a stone wall is the kitchen and beyond that the dairy with its stone flagged floor. This is now separated from the byre by a wooden partition, but earlier the kitchen door led straight into the byre, the near end of which may have served as scullery or dairy. The old stone slabs which formed stalls in the byre have gone, but it has cobbled paving, a drain and a small 'shot-hole' in the south gable, covered by a timber

shutter, for shovelling manure through onto the midden outside.

The walls are of stone bonded with mud mortar. The roof was formerly carried on small crucks, one pair of which survives in the kitchen, but the others have been replaced by dressed timbers. The roof is straw-thatched, bedded on heather divots and fastened down with wire netting weighted with anchor stones. All the rooms are furnished with a collection of appropriate plenishings and tools; there are churns, pails, butter pats, cheese press and cream scoop in the dairy.

Laidhay Folk Museum, interior of barn (Left)

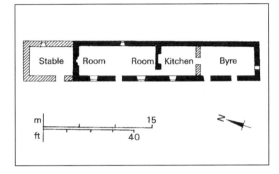

Laidhay Folk Museum, plan of longhouse

Beyond the longhouse, and in line with it, is the remains of the cartshed and a small pig- and hen-house. Behind the house is the thatched barn with flagstone floor, now containing a collection of agricultural tools. Its roof is supported on crucks and rafters made of any wood to hand, including local birch branches and many re-used ship's timbers, including part of an oar. The barn originally had two doors opposite each other to assist winnowing.

Laidhay Folk Museum

26* MARY-ANN'S COTTAGE, DUNNET, CAITHNESS

19th and 20th centuries.

ND 211715. From Dunnet take B855 to Dunnet Head; after 90 m go straight ahead on minor road to T-junction at West Dunnet; the cottage is then opposite on the left. Open in summer.

Mary-Ann's Cottage, interior

This is a particularly well preserved croft complex, with many features typical of the last century which on other crofts have been altered out of all recognition or destroyed. In the centre of a line of buildings is the stone house built by Mrs Mary-Ann Calder's grandfather around the middle of the last century. She was born there as the youngest of five children in a crofting family. As the croft land was only 11½ acres, her father also fished (she helped salt down the catch) and sailed on the schooners shipping flags out of Castletown. Mrs

Mary-Ann's Cottage (Right)

Calder left the croft in 1990 at the age of 93, and the local trust which has taken it over, complete with furniture and tools, has been able to learn from her in detail how the croft worked and the family lived. It has thus kept its lived-in atmosphere; indeed you feel the owner has just stepped outside.

The house has the typical 19th-century lay-out of two larger rooms, each with one window and a chimney in the gable, a central front door opening into a lobby, and a tiny mid-room behind. The kitchen fireplace has no grate but a peat fire laid directly on the hearth, where Mrs Calder baked beremeal bread, oatbread and scones, while a kettle hangs from the swey above. The furniture ranges from box-beds to a television. A more up-to-date back kitchen was added in 1960, but there was never a bathroom or privy—men used the stable, women the byre.

The outbuildings provide separate accommodation for all needs; a henhouse, workshop and store, byre with slate partitions, stable, cartshed, turnip store (these under a roof of huge Caithness slabs), a threshing barn which was the last building erected on the croft in 1906, a thatched pighouse, and a small milk-house (dairy) by the front door. The adjacent flagged enclosure was first a duckhouse, later the dogkennel. The animals on the croft, typically four horses, two cows and six sheep with their lambs, were kept tethered, a practice that reflects older, pre-improvement farming methods. The croft land lies behind the buildings; the land in front is communal and used to be cultivated by the township in strips on the run-rig system.

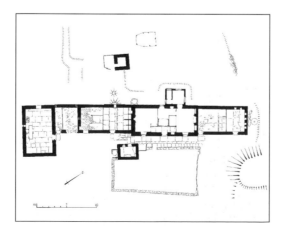

Plan of Mary-Ann's Cottage

27 CULLODEN COTTAGES, EAST INVERNESS-SHIRE

18th century AD.

NH 745450. At Culloden Visitor Centre, Old Leanach, 14 km E of Inverness on B9006.

NTS.

Old Leanach Cottage and King's Stables Cottage are two surviving early buildings from a series of scattered settlements spread out along the eastern edge of Culloden Moor above the River Nairn, which are known to have existed in 1745 and are shown on contemporary drawings. Whether these two actual cottages were built before 1745 is less certain, but it is possible.

Old Leanach Cottage can be reached only through the new NTS Visitor Centre building. It is a small rectangular cottage with low stone walls, a massive buttress on one side, an extra room attached on the other, tiny windows and a heather thatched roof held down by netting weighted with stones. From outside its appearance is quite authentic, but the interior was unfortunately altered and the roof raised to provide more space when the cottage was the display centre for the Culloden Battlefield. There is one pair of what seem to be original crucks in the wall behind the hearth, showing the lower line of the old roof. A hanging lum has been reconstructed against this gable, and new, massive crucks put in to support the roof, of the sort more often found in turf-walled houses. An interesting feature of the cottage is the turf walling in the top of the east gable, technically known as a turf gablet. The cottage is now furnished somewhat as it might have been in the 19th century, with box bed and so on. In the 18th century it most probably had a central hearth, earth floor and turf gablets at each end.

A little further west along the B 9006, on the north side of the road where the woods stop, is another very similar old cottage, now called King's Stables Cottage (NH 733448). It also belongs to the NTS, and is presently closed, but the exterior can be seen at all times. It has low stone walls, tiny windows, heather thatched roof, turf gablets and a reconstructed box-framed smoke-hole in the thatch; no original features are left inside.

Culloden Battlefield, where the Duke of Cumberland defeated Bonnie Prince Charlie's Highland army in 1746, is now laid out with paths for the visitor. Information on the battle is displayed in the Visitor Centre.

Culloden, Old Leanach Cottage

28 BADBEA, DESERTED CROFTS, CAITHNESS

19th century AD.

ND 087199. On the coast 5 km S of Berriedale. Signposted public footpath from layby on the A9, 1.5 km N of Ousedale Bridge.

Small groups of ruined crofthouses and outbuildings are dispersed at intervals along the clifftop for a distance of some 2 km. The path leads to a monumental stone pillar set on the ruins of one longhouse. This was erected in 1911 by Donald Sutherland from New Zealand, in memory of his father Alexander Sutherland, who was born at Badbea in 1806 and left for New Zealand in 1839. It also bears the names of some other early inhabitants. The history of the settlement is

Badbea

obscure, but traditionally it was founded by tenants evicted in some of the earliest clearances. People from Langwell in Caithness are said to have arrived in about 1793, followed by others from Berriedale and Ousedale. Some stayed temporarily before accepting free passages to America, others permanently. The site is very exposed, though not infertile, and the population gradually left for other parts

The crofthouses are strung out along the flattish ground on the clifftop, each with its own patch of cultivated ground still showing as grassy islands in the heather. The separate crofts which now seem so typical to us, contrast with the older layout at Rosal (no. 29), where the houses were grouped round the common infield. The buildings are very similar, with longhouses set running down the slope, the lower end a byre, and other small structures, barns, stables and kailyards arranged haphazardly. The houses may originally have had central hearths, but latterly at least they had chimneys in the gable walls, as seen in the building south of the monument. The large slabs in its gable were to reduce the weight on the lintel over the hearth.

Most of the other crofts lie north of the monument and were once linked by a track. In 1871 the settlement was described by the Ordnance Survey as 'a district of some six crofts of a few acres each'; by then it had perhaps already diminished. Originally there were rather more houses, but it is difficult to reconcile the surviving remains with traditions that there were some 28 families at Badbea in the early 19th century, and some 60 to 100 people living there in 1847.

Rosal, plan of a longhouse and its outbuildings
(Right)

29 ROSAL, PRE-CLEARANCE TOWNSHIP, SUTHERLAND

18th century AD.

NC 689416. In Strathnaver, some 20 km S of Bettyhill. At Syre take B871 over River Naver, turn immediately S down signposted forestry road to carpark; track and path to site, about 1.5 km.

Forestry Commission.

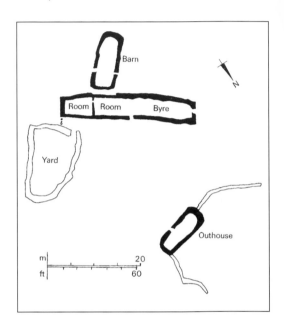

An example of the layout of an 18th-century farming township, from which the inhabitants were moved to coastal settlements in 1814-18. The site has been preserved by the Forestry Commission as a grassy island within the surrounding forest, and

Rosal, pre-clearance township

is laid out with wooden walkways over the wettest areas (gumboots still advisable) and explanatory noticeboards. The site was planned and a few buildings excavated in 1962.

A few traces of prehistoric occupation were found, such as some hut circles (all outside the fenced area and now under trees) and a souterrain (see chapter 10) near the centre, now filled in again though one or two of its lintels still show; there is a plan beside it. The remaining structures relate to the township and comprise the ruined stone walls of buildings, enclosure walls, clearance cairns and broad cultivation strips known as rigs in the ploughed 'infield'. The area now fenced is this infield of some 50 acres enclosed by a stone ring-dyke; the far larger area of common grazing outside this, where the all-important black cattle, sheep and goats were grazed in summer, is now under trees. Even within the enclosure wall only about two-thirds of the land had been ploughed. In Upper Strathnaver arable land was not continuous, and Rosal and the other contemporary settlements would have appeared as green patches in a wide expanse of brown moor.

The 1962 survey noted some twelve to fifteen exceptionally long buildings which were probably houses; this agrees well with a record of thirteen families living here in 1808. The buildings were scattered in clusters round the perimeter of the enclosure, the longhouses set on slopes with the byres at the downhill end to assist drainage. The house excavated in 1962 had low stone walls less than 1 m high, which would have been heightened in turf, and slots in the walls for the wooden crucks that supported the thatched roof. There was only one door at the junction of house and byre, and no partition between the two, a central hearth in the main room, and one separate room with its own hearth divided off by a stone and mud partition. By the house was a separate barn with two opposed doors, a kail or stack yard, and another outbuilding. There were also several corn- drying kilns at Rosal, generally attached to barns; one has been moved and rebuilt at the carpark.

Strathnaver was cleared in 1814 and the inhabitants given new lots on the coast at Bettyhill and Farr, where they were expected to take up fishing. The agent Patrick Sellar was brought to trial on charges of brutality over their eviction, but acquitted on the evidence presented. Later accounts refer to wholesale burnings of houses in Strathnaver. The excavated buildings at Rosal were certainly not burnt; but it emerges that Rosal was part of a new sheep farm which Sellar leased himself, where he was able to leave the old tenants of one half (including Rosal) in possession for an extra four years after 1814, so they were able to move out slowly to their new allotments.

Rosal with thirteen families was one of the largest settlements in Strathnaver, and only two were larger. Indeed of the 49 'settlements' listed in 1806 many were very small, eleven having only one or two families. It has been suggested that some of the small settlements were the result of people settling permanently on shieling grounds and starting to cultivate small patches. Such a population must have been particularly vulnerable in times of famine.

30 FOULIS RENT HOUSE, ROSS AND CROMARTY

Mid 18th century AD.

NH 599636. Beside the A9, some 3 km S of Evanton. Signposted 'Foulis Ferry. Restaurant and Picnic Area'; large carpark and picnic area by shore. (Exterior only.)

The Old Rent House at Foulis Ferry Point stands on the shore of the Cromarty Firth just above the high

Foulis Rent House

tide line, where boats could beach on the shingle. It was built around 1740 as an estate storehouse or girnal for the Munros of Foulis, at a time when rents were largely paid in kind. Oats and barley were stored here, and some portioned out to farm servants as part of their wages; the rest went off by ship to be sold to the army at Fort George (no. 41), or in the markets at Inverness or further south. Various accounts survive relating to the Rent House; one is a 'Note of Barley and Oat Meal given into the Store House of Fowlis' in 1795, which also lists issues of meal or barley to various folk including widows, the schoolmaster, and the Minister who got 38 bolls (a boll of barley weighed around 160-170 lbs). By the early 19th century most rents were paid in money, but the Rent House remained in use as a storehouse for goods moving in or out of the estate by sea well into the 20th century. Next to the Rent House is a low cottage, now a restaurant, where the ferryman used to live.

The Rent House is a large rectangular building of two floors and an attic, constructed of harled rubble masonry bonded with mortar under a slate roof. One gable has a chimney, the other a decorative ball finial. Dressed stonework frames the doors and windows. There were three original ground-floor entrances on the seaward side. A massive external stair was added early on, giving access to doors to the two upper floors. These doors may formerly have been served by hoists, or an outside wooden stair. The windows are noticeably small, those on the ground floor mere slits to provide the necessary ventilation for the grain. They were provided with both shutters (recently replaced on the old pattern) and bars. Some doors and windows have been altered or replaced in the course of time.

Inside, most of the ground floor was one open room, with the wooden floor of the room above supported on a central row of wooden pillars, and the attic floor above similarly supported. Downstairs there may have been a small room at the west end, next to the chimney, for the man in charge of the store. At the east end two small rooms were partitioned off before 1817 to serve as lockup stores. One has had wooden meal bins built round its walls. On the wooden panelling of the partitions, and on some beams upstairs, are a series of scribbled notes of amounts of grain; one

Culloden dovecote (Right)

mentions a schooner loading oats in 1817, another the schooner Euphemia of Berwick (registered at Berwick 1849) and there are later references to steamships.

The Rent House was the scene of a meal riot in 1796 when the townspeople of Dingwall marched on it at a time of food shortage to prevent the export of grain they believed to be held there, but they eventually dispersed without incident.
It is hoped to open the Rent House to the public some time in the future.

31 CULLODEN HOUSE DOVECOTE, EAST INVERNESS-SHIRE

Late 18th century AD.

NH 720462. Between Smithton and Balloch, on minor road off A96 some 3 km E of Inverness.

The dovecot stands beside the road outside the gates of Culloden House Hotel. It is a fine octagonal stone building with a slate roof. There is a plain doorway facing south, a round ventilation hole above this, and a single stone ratcourse, a horizontal line of stone slabs partway up the wall primarily intended to stop rats climbing in to steal the eggs. Three dormer windows projecting from the roof have wooden fronts fitted with flight holes and landing ledges. The interior can be seen through an iron grille; there are 640 nestboxes built against the walls, and a tall revolving wooden ladder, called a potence. These ladders were fitted in many dovecotes to reach the nests.

The dovecote belonged to the Forbes family of Culloden House (no. 37). Near the dovecote are the late 18th-century stables and an estate barn which has been converted into a church hall. In a housing estate south of the road, but not visible, is an unusual cottage of 1802 with Gothic windows, incorporating an earlier round dovecote similar to that at Boath (no. 32). Behind it are the ruined kennels.

Culloden, dovecote converted to cottage

much overgrown with bushes. The 12th-century castle may have consisted of wooden buildings within the earthwork, which would have been crowned with a stone wall or timber palisade. It became ruinous in medieval times. Later a historic battle was fought closeby: Montrose, fighting on behalf of King Charles I, raised his standard here before the battle of Auldearn on 9th May 1645, at which he defeated the Covenanting forces. There is an explanatory notice on the site with a plan of the battlefield.

32 BOATH DOOCOT, NAIRN

17th century AD; within 12th century earthwork.

NH 917556. In Auldearn, 3 km E of Nairn; signposted from A96.

NTS.

The dovecote which served an earlier Boath House stands on a hill above the town of Auldearn. It is a small circular dovecote built in the later 17th century; the exterior is harled, with a single ratcourse, and the conical roof slated with a circular entrance for pigeons at the apex. Above the door are six flight holes in a framed stone panel: a similar set of flightholes to the rear are now blocked and harled over. The inside is lined with nestboxes for the pigeons.

The dovecote stands within a much earlier earthwork, all that remains of the old castle of Eren built about the middle of the 12th century from which Auldearn (Old Eren) takes its name. This was one of a number of fortifications built to maintain the authority of the Scottish kings in Moray, then a centre of revolt. In this castle in the 1180s William the Lion issued his second charter to the burgesses of Inverness. At present a circular earthen bank of some 28 m diameter can just be made out, running round the edge of the hill and

Boath dovecote

MANSIONS AND MEMORIALS

Dunrobin Castle, aerial view

Castles dominated the Highland landscape for many centuries. Not until the early 17th century did the Scottish nobility feel sufficiently secure to live in undefended houses, such as were then beginning to appear in lowland Scotland. In the Highlands, however, many people just added a wing of more domestic appearance, and certainly more comfort and convenience, to an existing tower-house, as at Cawdor and Kilravock (nos 48, 49). Such new wings were generally still several stories high with crowstepped gables and dormer windows in steeply pitched roofs, though they now had many fireplaces and scale-and-platt stairs (with straight flights and landings) as well as spiral stair turrets. Nevertheless some large houses were now built in the Highlands, even if few survive today. In the north the main block of the House of Tongue (NC 591587) is dated 1678, while old Thurso Castle, built in 1660 and demolished around 1875, was a purely residential structure. Nor were such houses necessarily behind the times. The great mansion at Miltoun of Tarbat in Easter Ross, built by Lord Tarbat in 1685-7 and demolished in 1787, had plasterwork by George Dunsterfield, who had just completed work at Holyrood Palace, and incorporated sash windows within a decade of their appearance anywhere in Britain.

There are in contrast many surviving houses of various sizes built by the nobility and lairds in the 18th century. Many of these are particularly tall buildings in the vernacular style, harled and painted but otherwise rather plain. Among them are Balnakeil House (NC 391686) built in 1720-44 and

Calda House of around 1720 (no. 46) in Sutherland, and Dundonnell in Wester Ross (NH 112859), built 1767. Forse House Hotel, Caithness (ND 212353) was built in a similar vernacular style in the early 19th century. However, from the middle of the 18th century there appeared a number of elegant classical mansions clustered round the Moray Firth which show the influence, and sometimes the actual handiwork of the celebrated Adam brothers, Robert and James, who frequently visited their brother John, then working on Fort George (no. 41). These mansions include Culloden House (37), Foulis Castle (no. 34) and Cromarty House (no. 3). One of the most elegant of them, the second Tarbat House built in 1787 in Easter Ross (NH 769736) is presently derelict. At the same time other clan chiefs stayed in the family castle and added yet another wing or two in Georgian style, as at Dunrobin Castle (no. 33), Kilravock (no. 49) and Castle Grant, East Inverness-shire (NJ 041301). The influence of these great houses spread down through the lower ranks of society to laird's houses and farm houses; thus bow windows were added to many smaller houses in Easter Ross in the course of the century.

Mansions built in the 19th century tend to hark back to earlier styles, and versions of the Scottish baronial style pioneered by the Adam brothers (who called it 'the castle style') in the 1780s became highly popular. It was even used on bridges, as at Torgyle (no. 22). Its most charming expression is at Dunrobin (no. 33), a variation in château style, where the new mansion with its soaring roofs and slender turrets totally enclosed the original tower-house. Many of the other Victorian and later houses seem rather gloomy with their dark stone walls and towers, eg Ardross Castle, Easter Ross (NH 611741; 1880-1), Duncraig Castle, Lochalsh (NG 814333; 1886), Carbisdale Castle, Sutherland (no. 38) and Aigas House, West Inverness-shire (NH 459414), a shooting lodge of 1877, now a field centre, garden open. Since most private houses, particularly the smaller ones, are not accessible to the public, it is worth looking out for those whose exteriors can be seen occasionally under Scotland's Gardens Scheme, which include the House of Tongue and Dundonnell, mentioned above, and the small Georgian house at Allangrange in the Black Isle, Ross and Cromarty (NH 554524), built in 1760.

Monuments or memorials were often erected in the Victorian era and earlier. Around Dunrobin (no. 33) there are several including the Gothic memorial to Duchess Harriet in the park, and the statue of the first Duke of Sutherland on top of Ben Bragghie above Golspie, visible from many miles away. A more grisly memorial is the Well of the Heads beside Loch Oich (NN 304991), while the most unusual is certainly Fyrish (no. 39). At Cromarty, Hugh Miller's Monument can be seen (no. 3), above Dingwall is a tower monument (NH 549584) erected to General Sir Hector Macdonald who died in 1903, and in Quay Street, Ullapool, a handsome cast-iron clock on a column, dated 1899, is a memorial to Sir J Arthur Fowler and his son Sir John.

33* DUNROBIN CASTLE, SUTHERLAND

14th to 20th centuries AD.

NC 850008. Just N of Golspie on A9. (House open May-September.)

Dunrobin Castle

Dunrobin Castle, by William Daniell, 1821

Viewed from a distance, a fairytale castle floats above the trees; close to, it is a vast baronial mansion. 'A mixture of an old Scotch castle and French château' wrote Queen Victoria in her Journal. She saw Dunrobin after the massive extensions of 1845–47, designed in complex collaboration by Sir Charles Barry, architect of the Houses of Parliament, working in his 'château style', William Leslie of Aberdeen and the second Duke of Sutherland himself. Severely damaged by fire in 1915 when used as a naval hospital, extensive repairs and alterations were made in 1919 by Sir Robert Lorimer, the notable Scottish architect associated with the Arts and Crafts movement, which included altering some of the roofs, replacing soaring spires by dumpy domes and redesigning most of the principal rooms.

A wide stone staircase leads from the hall to the principal rooms on the first floor. As redesigned by Lorimer, these have elaborate plaster ceilings and several are panelled, all the work being of the highest quality. From the windows there are extensive views over the Moray Firth. The furniture, tapestry and paintings in the house are in keeping with the magnificence of their setting, and include works by Canaletto, Reynolds, Ramsey and Michael Wright. A contrast to the grandeur of the main rooms is provided by such items as a charming glimpse of the children's nursery, a display of Wemyss ware, and a steam- powered fire-engine in the subhall.

William Lord of Duffus became the 1st Earl of Sutherland around 1235, and Dunrobin, first mentioned as a family stronghold in 1401, still belongs to the Sutherland family. The Victorian mansion envelopes an earlier house of several periods grouped round an interior courtyard which can be best seen when touring the house from the windows of the Cromartie passage and the stair leading down to it. In one corner of the courtyard is a square 14th century tower with an iron yett outside its entrance door. Next to this is a round stair tower with pedimented windows, added in the 17th century to give access both to the old tower and to a new wing with angle turrets. Another wing was added at the end of the 18th century.

Early travellers frequently mention Dunrobin. 'A house well seated upon a mote hard by the sea, with fair orchards wher ther be pleasant gardens, planted with all kynds of froots, hearbs and floors' wrote Sir Robert Gordon around 1600. Bishop Forbes commented in 1762 'It makes a grand appearance, like a King upon his throne, being beautifully situated upon the Top of a little green Hill, . . . with fine gardens below, high-walled, and close up the Highway, which is along the shore. It has a most commanding prospect to Murrayshire and as far as the eye can stretch.'

The formal gardens lying below the castle and linked to it by a series of stonewalled terraces, steps and balustrades, were designed by Sir Charles Barry, who believed that gardens near houses should have an architectural character. To one side stands a garden pavilion built in 1732, which houses a museum with a collection of Pictish stones (no. 74). Trails have been laid out through the extensive wooded park, and west of the house can be seen the round icehouse, used as a cold store for perishable food, and an 18th-century dovecote with some 500 nest boxes inside. The trails are open all the year round.

Foulis Castle

34* FOULIS CASTLE, MANSION, ROSS AND CROMARTY

18th Century AD.

NH 589641. 2.5 km SW of Evanton; signposted off road from Evanton to Foulis. (View by appointment only; tel. Evanton 830212.)

Foulis has been one of the principal seats of the Clan Munro since Robert Munro first held Easter Foulis of the Earl of the Ross in the mid 14th century. The present house replaces an old castle, probably a tower with outbuildings, burnt down by the Mackenzies in the '45.

The rebuilding was begun by Sir Harry Munro, whose portrait hangs in the dining room.

Incorporating some surviving fabric from the old house, he constructed a simple domestic courtyard but gave his new house a highly original semi-octagonal tower with the main door at the foot and, at the top, a prospect room originally used as a library. It was from a balcony here that Bishop Forbes in 1762 saw 'an extensive prospect of Cromarty Bay and a commanding view of a rich country of Corn Fields'. In 1777 a more fashionable formal range was created on the southwest, again incorporating exisiting material at the southern end. It has a pedimented centrepiece with a central door at the head of a double flight of steps and, on the short end elevations, elegant full-height angled bays. This range is in the manner of John Adam, who used more traditional designs than his better-known brothers, Robert and James. The stairhall fills the width of the house and is entered both from the courtyard and the garden front. In the left wing is the drawing-room, formerly the ballroom, one and a half storeys high, and in the right wing is the panelled dining-room, both lit by long sash windows. Some rooms have late 18th century plaster cornices and friezes, and there is a fine cast-iron stove in the lower hall.

On the lower ground floor are the service rooms, and the old kitchen which retains some of its Georgian and later fittings. Just beyond is a stone spiral stair. The narrower northeast wing may be earlier 18th century and predate the burning in the '45. In the Clan Munro room is a clay-and-straw partition wall, partly dismantled to show its internal wooden structure. There are similar walls in the attics. The outbuildings in the courtyard

Foulis Castle, courtyard view (Left)

served various domestic purposes, one being the bakehouse, while the courtyard wall with its three arched entrances dates from the 1790s. Gun-loops of an 'inverted keyhole' type recently discovered in the stone vaulted basement of a building in the courtyard date to around 1500 and suggest this was a corner tower on the enclosure wall of the old castle.

35 POYNTZFIELD, ROSS AND CROMARTY

18th century AD.

NH 710642. In the Black Isle, 8 km SW of Cromarty, off B9163. Follow signs to herb nursery.

Poynztfield House

This charming 18th-century house is a more modest affair than the great mansions of Foulis and Dunrobin, and it is representative of other laird's houses on the east coast and a few on the west. It was built in 1720 as a two-storey house with wings and heightened to three storeys in 1757 when a new room was added above the stair tower. The latter date is on the corbel heads below a tiny pediment on the west front. Once known as Ardoch, it was formerly the seat of the Gordons of Ardoch, but later belonged to the Munros in the late 18th century and was renamed Poyntzfield, when a Munro married a Poyntz heiress. Itspartial resemblance to Foulis Castle (no. 34), also a Munro house, is curious, and one wonders if the pediment, and the view room on top of the tower, were incorporated in deliberate imitation of the other house.

Poyntzfield has a main block of three storeys with two lower wings forming a courtyard in front, and is harled and painted. At the back is an octagonal stair tower, the view room at the top having an attractive ogee-domed slate roof. A drawing-room with decorative plaster frieze and an angled bay was added in the late 18th century; this is now the dining-room. Outside the front door are two carved stone pediments, formerly above dormer windows, one dated 1673, which have come from some other house.

There are two old sundials in the garden, one either side of the house. Along the north drive is a simple one-storey mill building with the crowstepped miller's house beside it. There is a herb nursery in the walled garden, open all year, from which the back of the house can be seen.

36* MONIACK CASTLE, NEAR BEAULY, WEST INVERNESS-SHIRE

17th–20th century.

NH 552435. Signposted off the A862 some 11 km W of Inverness. Carpark and Winery, open all year except Sundays. Outside only: chapel can sometimes be seen, ask at Winery.

This is a house of the Fraser family, showing alterations and additions over a long period, with the various elements united by the traditional harled walls and slated roofs. The prominent tower belongs to the oldest part of the house, though here it is not a medieval residential block, but the stair-tower of a small L-plan house of around AD 1600. It contains a wide wheel-stair. The main entrance at the bottom has a heavily nailed plank door, and at the top the tower is corbelled out to contain a square room reached by a turret stair in the corner. The cannon-shaped spouts drained water from the wall-walk behind the original parapet, until in 1804 new battlements with corner turrets were built on top. Substantial change followed in 1807–8, when a new entrance front was built on the north; the front door is framed by a columned portico between the sash-windowed bays of the new drawing and dining rooms, all in the Georgian manner but still harled and with stone margins to the windows and chimneys.

The old house is linked by 19th- and 20th-century additions to what was formerly a free-standing two-storey house with dormer windows in the roof. This may be the farmhouse built here in 1760, and there are further outbuildings.

South of the house is a rockery with six upright stones on it. The second from the right, looking from the house, is a Pictish symbol stone known as the Balblair stone and brought from near Kilmorack. This is one of the very rare stones with a single male figure on it, in this case a man in a short kilt holding something like a baseball bat (sword or truncheon?). The head is most strange, and the figure may be either bird-headed or wearing a helmet with a prominent noseguard. The stone is very worn, so little can be made out save the legs and tunic, and then only in a good light.

37* CULLODEN HOUSE, EAST INVERNESS-SHIRE

c. AD 1780.

NH 721465. Between Smithton and Balloch on minor road off A96 some 3 km east of Inverness. Now a hotel.

Entering through stone gate piers crowned by urns, you see the house across the lawn, a mansion in the classical manner with no concessions to vernacular tradition. It is built in a warm red sandstone that from a distance looks like brick, with soft yellow sandstone for the basement, the door and window surrounds and other dressings. The double pile centre block is linked to pavilions each side by passages hidden by screen walls with columns and arches. On the other side of the house these walls have niches with classical statues representing Cato and Scipio, Odenatus and Zenobia, the last two a king and queen of Palmyra in Syria, an odd choice. The front door between two columns has a broad round-headed arch above; on entering, the shape is repeated in the screen at the far end of the hall with painted columns and Venetian arch. Behind is a coved passage and the four principal rooms: breakfast room, library, drawing room and dining room, the latter two still in use for their original purposes. The kitchen was in the south pavilion, set apart to avoid cooking smells in an age when hot food was not an important consideration. The basements contain a series of vaulted storerooms, stone under the main house, brick under the wings.

The interior decoration of this house is in a restrained, neo-classical, Adamesque manner. The drawing room has plaster decoration on walls and ceiling; on the walls are roundels depicting classical scenes depending from swags, while between the windows are delicate vertical motifs incorporating urns and sphinxes. The dining room has similar plasterwork on the walls and a handsome recess for the sideboard flanked by Corinthian columns; both rooms have carved white marble fireplaces. Details

Culloden House

such as original fireplaces, window shutters, doors and simple plaster friezes are found throughout the house. This is a splended example of a late 18th-century house complete in all details and surviving almost unaltered. As a hotel, there is public access to the outside and to the principal rooms.

Outside the gates are the contemporary stables, now ruined but to be restored as housing, and a dovecot (no. 30), and an icehouse further along the road at NH 724464.

The present house was built for Arthur Forbes of Culloden around 1780. He had succeeded his father John at the age of 12, and when he married an English heiress, Sarah Stratton, in 1779 they used part of her large fortune to build the new mansion. One or two illustrations survive of the old house which stood at the time of the battle of Culloden. It was then the home of Arthur Forbes, Lord President of the Court of Session and Government supporter, having been in the Forbes family since they acquired it from the Mackintoshes in 1625. The Jacobite army captured old Culloden House, and Bonnie Prince Charlie stayed there the night before his defeat on Culloden Muir.

The architect of Culloden House is unknown, though various names have been suggested, including John Adam, one of the family working on Fort George in the 1750s and 1760s. However, he virtually gave up designing houses around 1769. There is a tradition current in the Forbes family that John Forbes and one of the Adam brothers were friends, and dined alternately at Culloden and Fort George. One day John Forbes said how much he wanted a new house, and Adam seized a linen table napkin from the table and drew on it the plan and facade of a house. As John then had no money, this was carefully put away. Years later when his son Arthur married, the new bride burst into tears on seeing old Culloden House (it is not clear if this was because it was not a castle, or because it was an old and inconvenient house), so they got out the cherished napkin and the Adam plan was built. While there is at present no documentation to support this story, it fits many of the known facts and would in particular make sense of the problem that the design of Culloden is rather old-fashioned for 1780, whereas its plasterwork is right up to date for that time.

The exterior of Culloden House is so similar to Cromarty House (see no. 3) that they are considered to be by the same architect. Cromarty was built in 1772, but there are reasons why it also may well have been designed in the 1760s.

38 CARBISDALE CASTLE, CULRAIN, SUTHERLAND

AD 1906–17.

NH 674963. Leave A9 at Ardgay and follow minor road up west side of Kyle of Sutherland. Carpark inside gate for forest walk. Now a Youth Hostel, view outside only.

Carbisdale Castle stands imposingly on a wooded bluff overlooking the Kyle and the railway bridge, and is well seen from the A 836 to Lairg on the other side of the valley. The stone gate piers are like miniature towers with arrowslits and battlements, and they support attractive cast iron gates. Proceeding up the drive past the equally battlemented service block, note the astonishing female figures on the rainheads to the downpipes, also to be found on the castle but less easy to see. At the top of the drive are more gates, and a courtyard overlooking the Kyle with the house to the right. Built of a local dark stone, it has a sombre appearance and is a strange amalgam of styles of different dates. The clock tower was said in 1912 to show 'the stern strength which belongs to the Scottish Baronial style' but the wing opposite is English Tudor with stone mullioned windows and fancy gables, and between the two is a hall block with three curved bays. All this is on the north side: the gardens lie to the south with a view down to the Dornoch Firth.

Inside (only accessible to youth hostellers) is a long, imposing hall full of 19th-century white marble statues by various noted European sculptors, a carved wooden staircase copying one by Grinling Gibbons, and some other original fittings. The rooms were decorated by periods, such as Tudor, Jacobean and Queen Anne.

Carbisdale was built for 'Duchess Blair', the mistress and second wife of the 3rd Duke of Sutherland, who spent six weeks in Holloway Prison as a result of a wrangle over his will. He died in 1892, leaving her his personal fortune and the estate for life, but his son and heir contested this and the Duchess, while examining papers in front of lawyers, threw one on the fire. For this, a judge sent her to prison. Soon after, she relinquished her claims in return for a large sum of money, which she used to build a castle to rival Dunrobin. Refused land in Sutherland, she built on the border of Ross-shire (as it then was), but the house was not finished when she died in 1912.

Carbisdale was later the home of the Salvesen family, and King Hakon VII of Norway lived here during World War II. Carbisdale is also connected with the Covenanting Wars; at the top of the drive a marked Forest Trail leads west over the hill to the site of Montrose's last battle, where he was defeated in 1650.

Fyrish Monument

39 FYRISH MONUMENT, ROSS AND CROMARTY

AD 1783.

NH 607697. Near Alness. From A 836 take minor road W to Boath; after 1.5 km carpark in wood on left. Signposted footpath (a walk of about 1 hour uphill).

A pleasant walk leading uphill through trees onto open moorland with magnificent views over the Cromarty Firth from beside the monument on the top of Cnoc Fyrish (453 m OD). This simulated ruin consists of nine massive circular columns built of mortared rubble, the centre four columns being linked by pointed arches, above which the wall finishes in curious stumpy battlements. The outer four columns are offset and incomplete, while a smaller and shorter column blocks the centre arch. The monument is set on the edge of the hill and can be seen from many miles away, looking like tiny teeth on top of the hill.

This unusual monument was erected by General Sir Hector Munro of Novar around 1783 as a relief work in a time of famine, and is believed by long-standing tradition to be a copy of the gates of the fortress of Negapatam on the Coromandel coast of India. 'There are . . . some odd edifices on the summits which he is said to have designed as imitations of the hillforts in India' wrote the poet

Southey in 1819. Sir Hector served in the army in India with distinction for many years. During the war between the British and Haidar Ali, the British attacked the Dutch settlement of Negapatam, then garrisoned by some thousands of Indian troops. It fell on the 11th November 1781 to a combined force of soldiers commanded by Major-General Sir Hector Munro and a naval detachment under Sir Edward Hughes, an event which destroyed Dutch power in the area, while the British captured much needed supplies of currency, artillery and horses. The monument is loosely based on Indian architecture in the shape and arrangement of its three arches, which resemble those in the gateway at Seringapatam, though not in the battlements above, and it is entirely plausible that Sir Hector designed and built it to commemorate his great victory.

Sir Hector also repaired the chapter house of Fortrose Cathedral (no. 61) and as MP for the Inverness group of burghs helped to build the Town Steeple (no. 1).

40 CAISTEAL GORACH, DINGWALL, ROSS AND CROMARTY

c. AD 1790.

NH 544611. From Tulloch Castle Hotel, on N side of Dingwall, walk on up the drive to the steading, where ask permission to proceed; thence straight uphill to folly (about 30 minutes up).

A folly-ruin in the form of a castle, placed as an eye-catcher on the side of Tulloch Hill above

**Caisteal Gorach
(the Gaelic name
means
'Silly Castle')**

Tulloch Castle. A perfect expression of the mania for ruins which seized so many 18th-century landowners, it is one of the most attractive and has an impeccable pedigree, being designed by the great Scottish architect Robert Adam. Several sketches by him survive, dated 1789 and 1790, and inscribed 'sketch of an old tower for Duncan Davidson Esqr....' or the like. These are more elaborate than the folly as built. It is a round tower flanked by angled, ruined walls, as if at an angle of an enclosure. Stunted pine trees, probably planted there deliberately, perch on the tower, which has a round-headed doorway and windows on the ground floor and mock cruciform arrowslits and a worn quatrefoil opening above. The flanking walls are pierced by narrow round-headed embrasures, and part of each wall is thickened, though still solid, to suggest a square tower. Quite a lot of stonework has fallen off. From behind, the structure appears as a screen, the tower being hollow and incomplete at the back. It may have had two wooden floors. The design is in Robert Adam's late Picturesque manner, and it made a charming object for Mr Davidson's guests to drive out to view.

**Sketch for
Caisteal Gorach
by Robert Adam**
(Right)

Return to Tulloch Castle through the steading, dated 1774 and arranged round a courtyard. The short square tower over the entrance has crowstepped gables and a dovecot on the roof.

Tulloch Castle belonged to the Bains from 1542 and later to the Davidsons. It retains its 16th-century tower though with later crenellations and windows, but an earlier east wing has been engulfed by 19th- and 20th- century alterations and additions, including an attic storey and a plaster ceiling to the first floor hall by Sir Robert Lorimer.

ARTILLERY FORTS AND BARRACKS

**Fort Augustus
by T Sandby, 1746**

Medieval castles proved no obstacle to later artillery. Once big guns could knock down stone castles from a distance, military engineers in Europe turned to new designs. It was realised that successful defence depended on scientific planning of the fortifications and in particular on the provision of solid bastions projecting from the corners of the curtain walls to provide lateral and diagonal fire. The first artillery forts in the Highlands with earth-backed ramparts and projecting corner bastions echoing European developments were Inverlochy (NN 120754) and Inverness, built for Cromwell at either end of the Great Glen. Oliver's Fort at Inverness (no. 1), built in 1652 by Major-General Deane, was a regular pentagon with a three-pointed bastion at each corner, but it was mostly demolished under Charles II in 1661.

The next phase of fort construction came immediately after the Jacobite rebellion of 1715, when four barracks were built by the Hanoverian government, three in the Highlands and one in Stirling District at Inversnaid (NN 348096). Of these Ruthven (no. 42) is the best preserved, while the shell of Bernera (no. 43) still stands in Glenelg. The third of these barracks was Kiliwhimen (NH 377090), just outside Fort Augustus, of which one wall stands in the backyard of the Lovat Arms Hotel. These barracks were intended to house infantry garrisons and, although well provided for defence against infantry (a handful of men held Ruthven against 200 Jacobites in the '45), they had no defence whatsoever against artillery. General Wade had some doubts about the barracks: in his first Report to George I in 1724 he wrote 'It is to be wished that during the Reign of Your Majesty and Your Successors, no Insurrections may ever happen to experience whether the Barracks will answer the end proposed'. The two new works he constructed, a remodelling of the outworks that had been added to Inverness Castle around 1690, and an entirely new fort at Fort Augustus, were both provided with angled bastions for artillery. Nevertheless his forts proved no more effective than the barracks, for both forts fell to artillery in the '45, Fort Augustus after a siege of only two days when a shell exploded the power magazine. The remains of the fort are incorporated in *St Benedict's Abbey, Fort Augustus (NH 381091; exhibition open all year, check times).

The culmination of artillery fort design in the Highlands was the new Fort George at Ardersier (no. 41), built after the '45 as a great garrison fortress that could withstand siege cannon, and incorporating the most up-to-date ideas of fort design. Fort George, 'so powerful that it has no history', remains virtually unchanged as a unique example of Georgian military architecture.

**Fort George,
aerial view**

Fort George, the Lieutenant Governor and Fort Major's House

41* FORT GEORGE, ARDERSIER, EAST INVERNESS-SHIRE

AD 1748-69.

NH 762567. On the coast 18 km E of Inverness: from the A96, take the B9039 or the B9006 N through Ardersier.

Historic Scotland.

When the 1745 rebellion exposed the inherent weakness of the small Highland forts and barracks, the Duke of Cumberland called urgently for new works, and Fort George was planned in 1747 as a new impregnable northern base. The site finally chosen was a flat, barren spit of land jutting out into the Moray Firth at Ardersier. William Skinner, newly appointed military engineer for North Britain, designed the fort and largely on the strength of its success rose to be Director of Engineers with the rank of Lieutenant-General. The new stronghold was a bastioned artillery fortress designed to the highest European standards. Within the defences were extensive ranges of buildings to accommodate the Governor and other officers, an artillery unit and a garrison of sixteen hundred infantry, together with a magazine, ordnance and provision stores, a bakehouse, a brewhouse and a chapel. The contract for the masonwork and brickwork was held first by William Adam, and on his death in 1748 by his sons John, Robert and James.

Though the fort is still in use by the army today, the visitor may see all the defences and inside many of the buildings. The fort is defended by a sophisticated system of ramparts and angled bastions, huge earthworks faced in stone, with projecting sentry boxes at intervals. The bastions are provided with cannon embrasures and musketry firing steps, and a number of old guns have been installed.

At the landward end of the promontory is a complex outer earthwork called the Ravelin, where the outer ditch and the main ditch are crossed by wooden bridges. Within the fort there are various displays, those in the guardroom and barrack blocks recreating life in the fort at different periods in the fort's history. There is a private soldiers' barrack room of 1780, when eight men shared the room, two to a bed, and cooking was done over the

**Fort George,
the main gate**

A feature of the fort are the casemates, underground bomb-proof barrack rooms dug into the back of the ramparts, each meant to hold up to forty men so that the whole garrison could be accommodated there in times of siege. An unaltered casemate is usually open to visitors. On the south side of the fort is the Grand Magazine, a squat building with immensely thick walls designed to withstand a direct hit from a mortar bomb; inside there are replica powder barrels mounted on racks and a video programme about the fort. Also housed here is the remarkable collection of late 18th-century arms and equipment long kept at Castle Grant, used by militia and other regiments raised by Sir James Grant; these include not only 190 India pattern muskets and 134 pikes, but most unusual survivals like ammunition pouches and knapsacks. At the far end of the fort stands the chapel with a castellated west tower and flanking stair turrets; inside a two-tiered arcade of timber columns supports a gallery on three sides. The original three-decker pulpit, once in front of the chancel arch, has been moved to one side and its splendid domed canopy stored away.

fire; an officer's room of the Napoleonic war period; and an enlisted ranks' room of 1868, when five men lived in a room in single beds. An opportunity to see inside the Lieutenant-Governor and Fort Major's House, the elegant building with simple pedimented facade that balances the Governor's House at the opposite end of the main block, is provided by its use as the Regimental Museum of the Queen's Own Highlanders (Seaforth and Cameron). The building has a plain wooden staircase but some elegant Adam fireplaces remain.

42 RUTHVEN BARRACKS, EAST INVERNESS-SHIRE

AD 1719-21.

NN 764997. On the E side of the River Spey; approached by B970 from Kingussie.

Historic Scotland.

Ruthven is the best preserved of the four infantry barracks that were built by the Hanoverian government after the Jacobite rebellion of 1715. It can now be seen to good effect to the east of the new A 9 road as it passes Kingussie. The barracks stands on a prominent hill, perhaps in part artificially scarped, rising from the flat floor of the Spey valley, which had earlier been the site of a 13th century stronghold of the Comyns and a stone castle of the Earls of Huntly. In 1745 Sergeant Molloy and twelve men heroically resisted a besieging army of some 200 Jacobites, only to be forced to surrender when the rebels returned with artillery the following year. Later some of the defeated Jacobites rallied here after Culloden. Thereafter the barracks fell into ruin.

**Fort George,
sentry box**

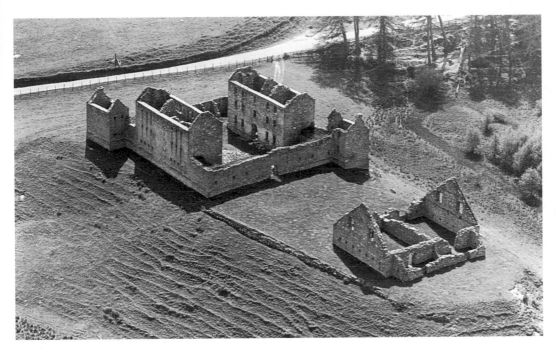

Ruthven Barracks

The original Board of Ordnance plans survive, and though some modifications were made during construction they help to interpret the existing structure. The tall buildings are the barrack blocks, each having a central timber stair leading to six rooms, one either side of the stair on each floor. The timber stairs and floors are long gone. Each room had a fireplace intended for cooking as well as warmth (there was no mess hall), and would have contained 'five beds for ten men in as little space as can well be allowed', though it is doubtful if Ruthven ever housed its full complement of 120 men. The lofts and basements were for stores and powder magazines. The inner walls had windows, two to a room, while the outer walls had musket-loops on each floor. The enclosure walls round the parade ground had a wall-walk above a series of open-ended vaults, but each of these was provided only with one musket-loop. There was no provision for mortars or cannon. One angle tower seems to have been a guardhouse, with rooms above, and the other a bake- and brew-house, where part of the oven remains. Latrines were built in the two remaining corners of the fort.

In 1734, at the recommendation of General Wade, a guardhouse and stable for thirty dragoons was built, of which the attic floor was probably used as a hayloft. A postern gate was inserted in the west wall of the barracks to give access to the stable block. The dragoons were 'to serve as a convoy for money or provisions for the use of the Forces as well as to retain that part of the country in obedience'.

Historic Scotland guidebook is not available on site but is obtainable from the Highland Folk Museum, Kingussie.

43 BERNERA BARRACKS, WEST INVERNESS-SHIRE

AD 1720-3.

NG 815197. At the mouth of Glenelg; minor road from A87 at Shiel Bridge to Glenelg, then road to Kylerhea ferry. When opposite fort, take footbridge over river and path across plain. View from distance; no close access.

Bernera Barracks, like Ruthven, was one of the four barracks built after the '45, its main purpose being to control the narrow crossing from the mainland to Kylerhea on the Isle of Skye. Bigger than Ruthven, the barracks is now more ruinous, and it stands in splendid isolation on the flat plain at the mouth of Glenelg looking across to Skye.

The design is similar to Ruthven (no. 41) except that the barracks are double blocks with a chimney

Bernera Barracks

decorative detail was used at Bernera, unlike the other three barracks; thus dressed stone was used for the corners of the buildings and the chimney stacks, and all round the windows and doors, and there were also dressed mouldings round the arched head to the main doorway in the enclosure wall, now fallen. Like Ruthven, Bernera has open-ended vaults round the perimeter wall, again provided only with small gun-loops for use by infantry with muskets.

Before 1745 Bernera regularly housed one or two companies of infantry. Thereafter the garrison was reduced and in the later 18th century was often only a few soldiers under the command of a sergeant or corporal. Johnson and Boswell rode past in 1773 on their way to take the ferry to Skye, and Boswell recorded 'As we passed the barracks at Bernera I looked at them wistfully, as soldiers always have every thing in the best order, but there was only a serjeant and a few men there'. The military garrison was finally withdrawn in about 1800.

in each gable, with four rooms on each floor instead to two, making a total of 24 rooms in all. There are also windows facing outwards as well as inwards over the parade ground, the outer windows having been protected by iron bars. The barracks thus had accommodation for over 200 men. The angle towers served for guardhouse and brew- and bake-house, rather than protecting the main wall with enfilading fire as their projecting position would have allowed. The entrance to each angle tower was protected by a pistol-loop built into the wall of the adjoining vaulted chamber. Some slight

The present road from Shiel Bridge over Ratagan to Glenelg follows the line of the old military road from Fort Augustus built by Major Caulfield in the 1750s, and rebuilt by Telford. Earlier it was a drove route from Skye to Falkirk.

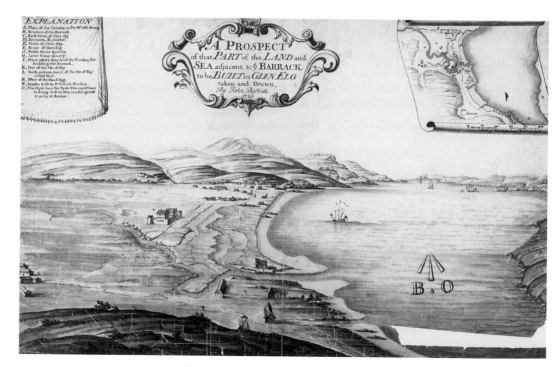

Bernera Barracks, Board of Ordnance perspective drawing, 1720

7 CASTLES

Urquhart Castle

The Highlands, for so long a region of disorder and unrest, have a rich heritage of castles, often sited in dramatic positions on rocks jutting into the sea, or by the side of lochs. Many of the early castles in the north of Scotland were royal or baronial and were linked with the attempts of the Scottish kings to establish their authority in that area. They were generally 'castles of enclosure', a strong curtain wall enclosing a space which might contain other stone or wooden buildings, including a tower or keep. The larger castles were intended to house a garrison if need be as well as the lord's own household on his occasional visits, and were often in the charge of a resident Constable.

The first surviving stone castles date from the 13th century. The great fortress of Urquhart Castle (no. 52) is unusually large and had a stone keep within it. Smaller castles of early date are Castle Roy (NJ 006219) and Lochindorb (NH 974363), both in East Inverness-shire. Other early castles, now much less obvious, consisted simply of an embanked enclosure with timber buildings inside, as did the castle at Auldearn (no. 32). From the 14th century onwards the favourite building form was the tower, and for the next 300 years or so many typically Scottish tower-houses were built, with the living space increased by building upwards, not outwards.

These towers have been compared to iron-age brochs in their concentration on passive defence. At their simplest the towers had a room on each floor; at the bottom a vaulted store, then a hall, solar or lord's chamber, and bedroom, a spiral stair in one corner of the massive walls, and an overhanging parapet from which missiles could be dropped on attackers. The entrance was sometimes on the first floor and reached by a moveable wooden stair or ladder which could be pulled up if necessary. In some of the larger and more elaborate towers, wings were added to the central block to produce plans of L, Z and U-form, while in the 16th and 17th centuries upperworks were often corbelled out at the top of the building so that the roofs positively bristled with turrets. Though some tower-houses now stand in isolation, all originally seem to have had courtyards and outbuildings attached. When James IV granted the lordship of Urquhart to John Grant of Freuchie in 1509, he was to 'repair or build at the castle a tower, with an outwork of stone and lime, for protecting the lands and the people from the inroads of thieves and malefactors; to construct within the castle a hall, chamber and kitchen, with all the requisite offices such as a pantry, bakehouse, brewhouse, oxhouse, kiln, cot, dovegrove and orchard, with the necessary wooden fences'.

Castle Leod, Ross and Cromarty

Few domestic details survive to enable us to visualise the interiors of these towers. Iron yetts, strong wrought-iron gates used to reinforce wooden entrance doors, can be seen at Cawdor and Dunrobin Castles (nos 48 and 33), both with a smaller door set within the large gate, and at Eilean Donan (no. 50). Some castles had seats in window embrasures, as at Rait (no. 51), and several had hooded fireplaces though few survive; there are traces of one at Rait. Later carved stone chimneypieces can be seen at Cawdor (no. 48), and there is an unusual painted fireplace lintel at Castle Leod (NH 485593), a fine 16th-century tower (open by appointment, tel. Cromartie Estate Office, Strathpeffer 421264). The hall at Kilravock still has its wooden-beamed ceiling. The bare rooms we see today would have been enlivened with painted walls and ceilings, embroidered wall-hangings and carved wooden furniture, all long vanished.

Early towers can be seen at Kilravock and Cawdor (nos 49, 48) and late examples at Ballone and Keiss (nos 45, 44). Ruined tower-houses are found all over the Highlands, and examples further to those described include Fairburn Tower (NH 469523) and Castle Craig (NH 631638) in Easter Ross; the courtyard wall of the ruined tower of Strome Castle, NTS (NG 862354) in Wester Ross; the tiny roofless tower of Castle Varrich (NC 860567) and the grassgrown remains of Borve Castle (NC 725641) in Sutherland; and Bucholly Castle (ND 382658) in Caithness. A number of tower-houses were either never ruined or have been restored; those which can be seen from the road include the splendid Castle Stuart (NH 741498) and the smaller tower of Muckrach (NH 985250), both in East Inverness-shire. The exteriors of three well-restored later tower-houses, not normally accessible, can be seen occasionally under Scotland's Gardens Scheme: the Castle of Mey, Caithness (ND 290739), Kilcoy Castle, Ross and Cromarty (NH 576512) and Dalcross Castle, East Inverness-shire (NH 778482).

From the 17th century onwards, the nobility and the lairds looked more to comfort and convenience than defence. They either added new domestic wings to their old towers, as at Dunrobin, Cawdor and Kilravock, or they built completely new houses such as Calda House (no. 46) and the new Keiss Castle (no. 44). Ballone Castle (no. 45) was deserted when its owners moved to New Tarbat House, and Cromarty Castle was pulled down to build Cromarty House in 1772 (see no. 3). After the Cromwellian period, fortifications in the Highlands were either artillery forts or barracks erected by the Crown. 'Castles' were still built into the 19th and even the 20th century, but they no longer served any defensive purpose and are noted under mansions.

Keiss Castle

Keiss Castle, stair turrett

44 KEISS CASTLE, CAITHNESS

Late 16th-early 17th century AD.

ND 357616. Park at Keiss harbour, 13 km N of Wick; walk N along shore and clifftop to castle.

This ruined tower-house stands dramatically on the very edge of a sheer cliff falling to the sea below. Most of it survives to its full height of four-storeys and an attic, but one corner has fallen away completely, so that one can see the interior without going inside, which is unsafe.

Two round towers, one containing rooms and the other the principal wheel stair, are attached to the main oblong block at curious angles, perhaps to conform to the shape of the clifftop. The ground floor was vaulted and the hall was on the first floor; the entrance was on the ground floor at the northeast corner which has fallen away. Keiss is a late tower-house, and has the characteristic proliferation of upper works, such as a number of extra stair turrets serving the upper floors, the main stair tower corbelled out to form a square room at the top, and a generous provision of fireplaces necessitating several chimney-stacks. Though the walls are made of local flagstone, dressed and moulded imported sandstone frames the doors and windows, and there are a number of purely decorative carved features such as the chequered corbelling below some of the turrets, and a panel at the top of the south gable.

Ballone Castle
(Right)

The castle belonged originally to the Earls of Caithness, and later to two other branches of the Sinclair family. It was finally abandoned when the new Keiss Castle was built in 1755 (ND 355617). This white-harled building stands inland from the old castle and was originally a simple three-storey house, until altered and extended in Scottish Baronial style in 1860. It now has a four-storey tower and circular corner turrets.

On the way back to the harbour the path by the shore passes close to the remains of two iron-age brochs (ND 353610 and 354612; see chapter 10). These were excavated at the turn of the century but have decayed badly since; both have outbuildings round them. There is yet another excavated broch on the A 9, next to the cemetery by the war memorial (ND 348615). For the harbour, parliamentary church and manse see no. 13.

45 BALLONE CASTLE, ROSS AND CROMARTY

16th century AD.

NH 928837. From Portmahomack, 11 km E of Tain, take minor road E to Rockfield village. Walk N along path by shore to castle.

The impressive ruined tower stands on the edge of the cliff. It is gradually being restored, but can be seen from the shore below. The rectangular block of three-storeys and an attic is flanked by a square south tower and a round north tower, forming a typical Z-plan castle.

Built in the 16th century, traditionally by the Earls of Ross, it belonged to the Dunbars of Tarbat when first recorded as the 'fortalice of Easter Tarbat' in the early 17th century. In 1623 it was purchased by a branch of the Mackenzies, but they seem to have left it unoccupied by the end of the century.

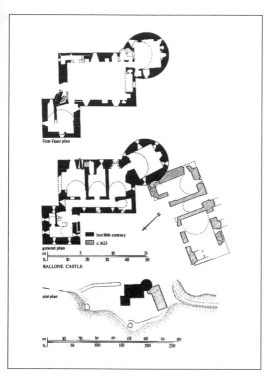

Ballone Castle, plan (Left)

The main entrance is a round-headed doorway on the north side of the square tower. This gave onto a spiral stair in the tower leading to the hall on the first floor of the main block, with a large fireplace and a private room in the round tower. From opposite corners of the hall two small stair turrets set in the angles of the walls led to upper rooms; perhaps family accommodation at the north end and visitors' rooms at the other end. A feature of the castle are the turrets set on the angles of the main block, carried on unusual decorative corbelling and having numerous shot-holes angled for downwards fire pierced through their walls and floors. There was also an ample provision of gun-loops round the base of the castle. The lower floor of the main block consisted of a kitchen, two storerooms and a passage, all stone vaulted. The adjoining northeast range, of which only the vaulted service basement survives, was added in the 17th century. Together with other walls, it enclosed a small courtyard between the castle and the cliff.

46 ARDVRECK CASTLE AND CALDA HOUSE, SUTHERLAND

Castle 15th-16th century AD; house c 1720.

NC 239236 and 243233. Beside Loch Assynt, just N of Inchnadamph on A837.

Standing in empty countryside against a backdrop of loch and mountains, Ardvreck Castle and Calda House must be counted amongst the best romantic ruins. The castle stands on the neck of a promontory jutting out into Loch Assynt. It seems to be of two phases, probably built in the 15th century and altered in the 16th. An old record of a 1591 or 1597 date-stone may relate to the alteration. The circular angle tower was an addition to the original oblong block, once four-storeys high, of which one end remains. The basement of the main block contained two stone-vaulted rooms and a passage with several gun-ports, while above it would have been the hall, originally also vaulted. The lower part of the tower is round and held a spiral stair communicating with the first-floor hall, while its upper part is corbelled out to the square in typical 16th-century fashion to form rooms, one of which can be seen to have a fireplace of its own. A stair turret built across the angle between the tower and the hall gave access to the upper floors. This castle was the residence of the Macleod Lairds of Assynt, and here Montrose was held prisoner after his capture in 1650.

The ruins of Edderchalder or Calda House stand beside the road a short distance south of the castle. Built for the Mackenzies in the 1720s, its domestic style of architecture is in complete contrast to its predecessor. The house was a double block two storeys high with an attic, each half having a pitched roof, and it probably had a central staircase. There were chimneys in each of the four gables and another chimney stack, now fallen, in the centre of the house, so some sixteen rooms had fireplaces. It was gutted by fire in 1737. It has been suggested that this commodious house, which has some resemblance to contemporary barracks such as Bernera (no. 43), may have served as a garrison post, if need be, as well as a domestic residence. Beside Loch Assynt and near Elphin are outcrops of limestone rock and the soil is unusually fertile, a fact appreciated by farmers since prehistoric times. Neolithic chambered cairns can be found scattered along the line of the A 837 from Loch Assynt south to Loch Borrolan.

Ardvreck Castle

47 CASTLE GIRNIGOE, CAITHNESS

15th-17th century AD. (Photograph p.27)

ND 378549. On the coast 4.5 km NE of Wick.

From Wick take road on north side of harbour out to Staxigoe and on to Noss Head. Stop at carpark and follow clifftop path west.

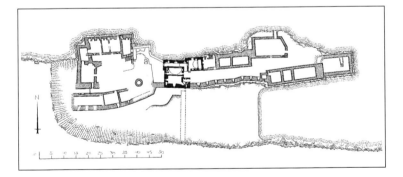

Plan of Castle Girnigoe

This imposing ruined castle, once the seat of the Sinclair Earls of Caithness, is set on a precipitous promontory, one side facing out to sea, the other looking over a narrow sea inlet (a 'geo' or 'goe'), and it is defended by two rock-cut ditches with an outer ward between them. Within the inner ditch stands the tall tower built in the late 15th century by William, Earl of Caithness, and behind it are lower buildings occupying all the available space. In 1607 a whole new structure was built in the outer ward, a fortification of some architectural pretension judging by the finely carved corbels

which once supported angle turrets and windows. Sometimes known as Castle Sinclair, this building was an addition to the earlier castle, not a replacement. It is possible that it is built over, or incorporates, an earlier gatehouse. It is now very ruinous save for one fragment standing three-storeys high. The castle was besieged and captured in 1690 in the course of an inheritance dispute and never occupied again.

Both ditches must have been crossed by some sort of removeable wooden bridge. A vaulted passage with portcullis slot leads through the buildings in the outer court to the second ditch; this slopes down to the sea at a dangerous angle and is best approached, not from the outer court, but through the small postern gate in the south wall. The original access to the tower was by a wooden bridge to a door on the ground floor, but present entry is by a breach in the wall of a vaulted basement store or dungeon, from which a straight flight of stairs leads up.

The main tower is an irregular L-plan block with an extra stair tower. It is built of thin grey Caithness flagstone with imported red sandstone dressings for the window frames and the corners. On the ground floor is a dog-leg entrance passage with two guard rooms beside it, one with a small fireplace and a stone seat. There is a kitchen in the wing behind with wall cupboards and a large fireplace, with a seat in it, filling one wall. Below the central guard chamber is another basement, perhaps once the well room, reached by a stair in the wall. All these rooms are vaulted. Food from the kitchen had to be carried across the open court to reach the stairs to the great hall. This was on the first floor, and had a fine oriel window looking west and a private room in the wing behind. In the floor of this room was a trapdoor to a hidden room above the kitchen, with a window looking out to sea. Above were bedrooms and then attics, their wooden floors and the roof long vanished.

Considerable attention was given to defence, and the wall above the sea inlet had a regular row of gun-loops. Projecting from the seaward face of the castle are a line of stone corbels that held a covered wooden balcony from which defenders could rain down missiles on anyone below (or haul up the furniture: lords often carried their furniture from castle to castle, and it might not go up spiral stairs). Traces of a similar balcony exist higher up on the south face above the geo. Beyond the tower a passage leads down the narrow promontory between ruined buildings, in two of which one comes suddenly on steep stairs or shafts giving access to the sea, one halfway along and one at the far end.

The castle and the cliffs are dangerous and unsuitable for children.

48* CAWDOR CASTLE, NAIRN

15th-17th century AD and later.

NH 847498. On B9090 about 7 km SW of Nairn.

(Open May—September.)

Dominated by its great 15th-century tower, Cawdor is an outstanding example of a fortified house which has evolved over many centuries. Whether or not the site was occupied in the 11th century at the time of Macbeth, the Calders are documented as Thanes of Calder or Cawdor from the late 13th century on. The present tower dates from 1454 when William, Thane of Cawdor, was granted a royal licence 'to erect his castle of Cawdor and fortify it with walls and ditches, and equip the same with turrets and means of defence'. By the forced marriage of an heiress in 1510 the succession passed to a cadet branch of the Campbells of Argyll.

The central tower has a blocked entrance (now a window) to the first-floor hall, and the usual vaulted basement reached only by a stair in the wall. From this there is a modern opening to a newly discovered pit-prison with its own latrine chamber, formerly reached only from above through a trapdoor. The iron yett at the foot of the stair is said to have been taken from Lochindorb Castle, which was destroyed in 1457. Access from the hall to the upper floors was by a spiral stair in the thickness of the wall. The early tower may well have been surrounded by a walled courtyard with outbuildings on the present lines, but these ranges have been extensively rebuilt.

To the south and south-east are two-storey ranges of the mid to late 19th century, but built to match the style of the earlier castle; in the east wall is a central drawbridge over the dry moat. On the west and north are long three-storey ranges, 16th century in origin but largely rebuilt for Sir Hugh Campbell of Cawdor between 1639 and 1674 by local masons from Nairn. These ranges have vaulted lower rooms with slit windows and thick walls, crowstepped gables, and projecting attic stair turrets with attic chambers above, and they are linked to the old tower by a new scale-and-platt stair tower. The north-east range is early 18th century (contract signed in 1699) but its roof, dormer windows and turret were added in the 19th century, when some alterations were also made to the north range.

Over the entrance to the 17th-century wing is a date-stone of 1672. On the first floor is the new Great Hall with wooden ceiling beams, a musicians' gallery at one end, and its original chimneypiece. Above this on the bedroom floor is the Tapestry Room, its walls still hung with tapestries made for the room in Flanders in 1682. All the rooms are filled with family furnishings and pictures collected over many years. Passing through other rooms the visitor reaches the present dining-room, with its curious chimneypiece carved around 1670 to commemorate the Calder-Campbell marriage of 1510. Past the modern kitchen is the old kitchen with a rock-cut well in the vaulted basement of the west range. This room was used as a kitchen from at least the 17th century to 1938, and retains much of its old equipment. Beyond were the bakehouse, now a larder, and the vaulted stables, later used as wine cellars.

Cawdor Castle fireplace

Round the castle are three different gardens, and there is an attractive 17th-century church in Cawdor village.

Kilravock Castle

49* KILRAVOCK CASTLE, NAIRN

15th and 17th centuries and later.

NH 814493. 10 km SW of Nairn, signposted off B9091. (Open one day a week, April to September.)

The early tower dominates the later, more domestic additions to this attractive castle, which stands on the edge of a cliff above the River Nairn. The lands of Kilravock have belonged to the Rose family since the 13th century, and the family still live here.

Hugh Rose received a licence to build 'a tour of fens' from the Lord of the Isles, then also Earl of Ross, in 1460. This 'defensive tower' has a corbelled wall walk, open turrets called bartizans at the corners (similar open bartizans at Cawdor (no. 48) were given conical roofs in the 17th century), and a gabled attic roof. Inside the tower a wheel stair in the wall gives access to single rooms on four floors and to the wall walk. The first-floor hall has its old wooden beamed ceiling, blackened by smoke or fire. A chimney lintel carved in 1666 for the wedding of Hugh Rose and Margaret Innes has been moved from this room to the entrance hall, and replaced by a modern fireplace. The upper room has the usual vaulted roof.

In the 17th century a large domestic wing was added to the tower, linked by a square stair tower. Its harled walls contrast with the bare stone of the old tower. The passage and storerooms on the ground floor are all vaulted, with the main rooms on the floor above. Here two turrets for spiral stairs are corbelled out giving extra access to the rooms above. Four dormer windows break the line of the high pitched roof. On the north side of the castle two service wings of varying height and later date form a small entrance court. Much of the interior was remodelled in the later 18th century. The present drawing-room now has a corniced and coved ceiling, a Venetian window in the end wall, and an Adam style chimneypiece. There is an 18th-century staircase with carved balusters, and the castle is furnished with family furniture and pictures.

Below the castle on the river side is a small 15th/16th-century corner tower with a later stone-seated privy in the ground floor chamber and a

Eilean Donan Castle

dovecot above, accessible only by ladder. Around the castle are woodland, a tree garden and nature trails.

50* EILEAN DONAN CASTLE, WEST INVERNESS-SHIRE

14th century AD; restored 20th century.

NG 881258. At the head of Loch Duich, just S of Dornie. (Open May—September.)

The castle stands in a spectacular setting on a small islet at the junction of Loch Duich, Loch Alsh and Loch Long. Originally accessible only by boat, it is now linked to the shore by a modern bridge. From the old road above the A 87 there are splendid views over the castle to the hills of Skye beyond.

Fragments of vitrified stone found on the shores of the island show that there was once a prehistoric or dark-age fort here. In historic times, the site may have been fortified in the 13th century, but the present tower was built in the late 14th century and belonged to the Earls of Ross. It passed to the Mackenzies of Kintail in the early 16th century, when the MacRaes became Constables of the castle.

In 1719 the castle was occupied by a small Spanish garrison, part of a force supporting an unsuccessful Jacobite rising on behalf of the Old Pretender, James, the son of King James II. Three English frigates sailed into Loch Alsh and bombarded the castle, which lay in ruins for the next 200 years. It was restored between 1912 and 1932 by a descendant of the MacRaes, so what is seen today is almost entirely modern; though not correct in every detail, it give an excellent idea of the original appearance.

Within the great tower, the stone-vaulted basement would originally have been for storage, reached only by an internal stair from the hall above. The great hall on the first floor had a large canopied fireplace, a wooden ceiling carried on heavy wooden beams, deep window embrasures, and stairs in the thickness of the wall leading to the bedrooms above. The main entrance on this floor would have been reached by an outside wooden stair. Note the two massive wooden bars that secure the door inside and the square bar-holes in the wall that they slide into; brochs had much the same arrangement. In the hall is a fine iron yett, which originally must have reinforced the main entrance door.

The buildings round the tower were reduced to little but the stumps of their walls before restoration, but the hexagonal structure near the bridge is mostly original masonry and appears to have been a large and unusual cistern for storing rain-water.

51 RAIT CASTLE, NAIRN

Late 13th or early 14th century.

NH 893525. On B9101 Auldearn to Cawdor road, some 4 km W of Auldearn, turning marked 'Raitcastle Farm'; track continues past farm to castle.

Rait Castle

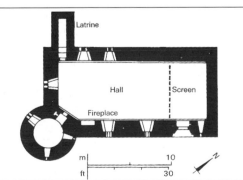

Rait Castle, plan of first floor

This interesting hall-house contrasts with the numerous surviving tower-houses in the Highlands. Built in the late 13th or early 14th century, it now stands roofless and floorless, but apart from a modern breach in the east wall the stonework is almost complete to roof height and in good repair.

The main structure consists of the rectangular hall and a round tower. Only fragments remain of a narrow latrine tower which projected from the north wall. The roof was pitched, with gables at either end set back behind overhanging parapets, for which corbelling survives at the east end. The walls are rubble, with dressed sandstone framing the doors and windows. The ground floor, reached by a wooden stair from the floor above, was used for storage. Tiny windows secured by iron grilles supplied ventilation, while the room in the base of the tower had defensive arrowslits. The hall on the first floor had a wooden floor supported on a scarcement ledge. It was entered through an imposing arched doorway in the south wall, reached by an outside wooden stair. The door was defended by a portcullis (the slot can be seen from below), and a wooden door inside it secured with a drawbar. The small lancet window by the door was for the porter. The hall is lit by large pointed windows with benches either side, and part of the simple window tracery survives. The windows had both iron grilles and wooden shutters, which have left traces in the stonework, and the roofs of their embrasures have ribbed vaulting.

Urquhart Castle
(Right)

At the west end of the hall was the raised dais for the high table, lit by two windows, with a hooded fireplace in the south wall flanked by brackets for lamps. Doors led to the latrine and to a private chamber in the tower. The tower room has two arrowslits and one large window with bench seats, together with a fine domed roof built in concentric courses of stone. The joist holes for the floor have disappeared in the course of modern repairs.

The hall stood on the north side of a courtyard with other buildings round it, some vestiges of which remain. One must have been the kitchen, another may have been a chapel of St Mary recorded in the late 12th century. There were magnificent views from the site before the trees grew up, though it is in a poor defensive position, with its courtyard bounded by higher ground. The

castle belonged first to the de Raits, who took their name from the manor and may actually have been Comyns, later to the Mackintoshes and to the Campbells of Cawdor.

---

52 URQUHART CASTLE, WEST INVERNESS-SHIRE

13th-17th centuries AD.

NH 530285. Beside Loch Ness, on the A82 near Drumnadrochit.

Historic Scotland.

This great castle stands on a low promontory jutting out into Loch Ness, beside the strategic northeast-southwest route along the Great Glen, a promontory which had been used earlier for a vitrified fort, possibly of dark-age date. As a royal castle, Urquhart played its full part in the power struggles in the area, both in the Wars of Independence and later in the conflicts between the Kings of Scotland and the Lords of the Isles. During these centuries 'Urquhart was continually taken and retaken, pulled down and rebuilt, sacked and replenished'. Since a detailed guidebook may be bought at the site, only a brief survey is given here.

Urquhart Castle in the late 16th century: reconstruction drawing by David Walker

If there was a castle here in the 12th century, nothing of it can be identified; what exists today originated as a great 13th-century fortification, held by Alan Durward from 1229. This castle consisted of a citadel, the stone-walled enclosure on the top of the highest mound with buildings at each end, and an outer walled courtyard or bailey perhaps with other buildings in it. Except for the citadel, most of the buildings we see today are of 14th century or later date, including the gatehouse, the massive foundations of domestic buildings in the Nether Bailey, and the great tower-house.

The castle was defended to landward by a huge dry ditch, crossed by a stone causeway and, originally, a wooden drawbridge. The gatehouse with tumbled fragments lying round it was blown up, perhaps by royal troops after the accession of William and Mary to prevent the Jacobites making use of the castle. This strong gatehouse may have been built in the 14th century and possibly housed the lodging of the constable or keeper of the castle. The gateway was flanked by two half-round towers and defended by a portcullis and double doors. The buildings against the old curtain wall on the south

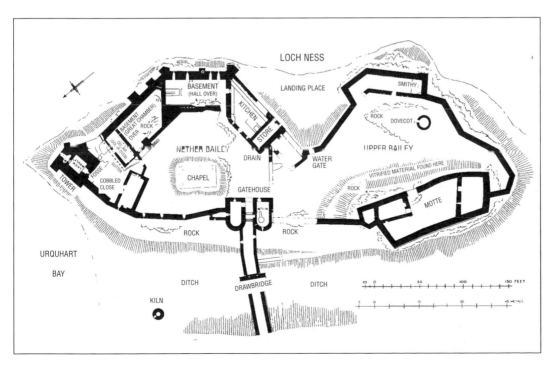

Urquhart Castle, ground plan

of the Nether Bailey have immensely massive walls, but only the vaults survive of what was once a substantial structure several storeys high. On the first floor of this range was the great hall and chamber of the 14th-century castle, and perhaps also the lord's private apartment, used on his periodic visits.

A more or less self-contained tower-house stands at the end of the promontory, thought to have been built for the Grants to whom James IV gave the lordship of Urquhart in 1509. This tower stands on an earlier basement, and its upper works were repaired in 1623. Although the south wall has fallen, the visitor can still climb to the wallwalk by the original spiral stair. At the top of the tower were four square gabled corner turrets, each containing a small room with a fireplace, a tiny window with gun-loop below, and a privy. Over the main door, and again over the postern on the other side, platforms were corbelled out from the parapet from which missiles could be dropped on any enemy below.

From the later 17th century the castle decayed, and was plundered for its stone, lead, timber and other building materials. Finally in 1912 it was put in the custody of the then Office of Works, and today it is once again maintained by the State.

Castle of Old Wick

53 CASTLE OF OLD WICK, CAITHNESS

Possibly 12th or 13th century AD.

ND 369489. In Wick take road S of harbour to coast, carpark and signed footpath.

Historic Scotland.

A ruined tower, known to seamen as the Old Man of Wick, stands on a rocky promontory jutting out into the sea, cut off on the landward side by a ditch. What survives is the ruined shell of a simple tower keep, so simple that it has no diagnostic features by which it can be accurately dated. Most probably it was built in the 12th or early 13th century AD, the time when the Norse Earls of Orkney held Caithness from the King of Scotland, and thus it has some claim to be called a Norse castle.

The ditch was originally spanned by a drawbridge, and has the remains of a rampart and gatehouse outside it. The tower had four floors and an attic under a pitched roof, with one room on each floor, and the floor beams carried on scarcement ledges built into the walls. The only entrance was a door to the first-floor hall on the seaward side, but this part of the wall has collapsed, and entry is now through a breach in the wall into the storeroom below. As there are no stairs in the thickness of the wall, all access up and down from the hall must have been by internal wooden ladders. There are no fireplaces or chimneys either, so the rooms may have been heated by braziers set on stone flags let into the wooden floors. Each room had two tiny windows. The only feature built into the walls of this tower was a small chamber on the first floor in the southwest wall, possibly a latrine, of which the last traces can still be made out.

Beyond the tower a passage led down the middle of the narrow promontory past two rows of buildings, now grassed over, to a small courtyard at the end. These buildings will have housed the kitchen, bakehouse, stables, servant's quarters and so on. Down the coast at Forse (ND 224338) is another promontory castle with a small tower of rather similar design, whose date is also uncertain. Both castles belonged to the Cheyne family in the 14th century.

ECCLESIASTICAL 8 MONUMENTS

Cromarty, East Church

Christianity was brought to the Highlands largely by Irish missionary monks, including St Columba who visited the Pictish King Bridei in his fortress near Inverness, and St Maelrubha who founded a monastery at Applecross (no. 64). No visible traces of their monastic buildings remain, because the tiny churches and the few huts were commonly built of timber and wattle, often on sites which were altered by centuries of later use for worship and burial. Tangible evidence for the early spread of Christianity is, however, provided by Gaelic placenames in cill ('church') with an early saint's name such as Kildonan and Killearnan, and by the remarkable series of carved stone cross-slabs which extend from the Moray Firth right up the east coast and into Caithness (chapter 9).

The first surviving stone churches in the Highlands are a few simple structures of the 12th century, which date to the reorganisation of the diocesan system by David I and the subsequent founding of many parish churches and their dependant chapels. One of these is St Mary's, Crosskirk (no. 63), while the ruins of another, with a 9th-century cross-slab in its graveyard, may be seen at Skinnet, Caithness (ND 130620). Few recognisable medieval churches survive in the Highlands. The ruined church at Barevan near Cawdor, Nairn (NH 836472) is a typical elongated rectangular church of about AD 1300, while the restored church at Tain (no. 59) shows the comparative wealth of the burghs. Substantial portions exist of the medieval cathedral of the diocese of Caithness (which included modern Sutherland) at Dornoch (no. 60), and rather less of the cathedral of

Cromarty, interior of East Church

Ross at Fortrose (no. 61). There was no early cathedral at Inverness, then part of the diocese of Moray. Few religious houses were established in the Highlands, and only two monasteries, Beauly Priory (no. 62) and Fearn Abbey, Ross and Cromarty (NH 837772). Of the Dominican Friary at Inverness, Blackfriars, only one pillar remains. In general, the architecture of medieval ecclesiastical buildings reflects the fact that there was less money to spend than in most other parts of Scotland.

After the Reformation of 1560 many of the larger medieval churches decayed because they were too large for the parish to maintain, while others were altered out of all recognition to suit new modes of worship. There were other hazards too; the old church of Dingwall with its thatched roof and thatched steeple was burnt down in 1731 by a burgess shooting pigeons. Medieval churches had focussed on the altar and the celebration of mass; now the emphasis was on the preaching of the Word. 'Every kirk was to

Fort George, garrison chapel

have a bell to convocate the people together, a Pulpet, a Basen for Baptising, and Tables for the Ministratioune of the Lordis suppar' ordered the First Book of Discipline in 1560. The interiors of churches were reorientated to face the pulpit on the south wall, and lofts were added to accommodate the large congregations. Long communion tables ran down the axis of the church, and the body of the people sat on their own stools in the nave until fixed pews were built. At Cromarty (no. 3) in the 18th century, some of the heritors complained 'that they were incommoded in going to their seats by the stools in the kirk floor'; again at Cromarty Hugh Miller records that, a few days after the Disruption Assembly in 1843, 'all the poor bodies that used to occupy the passages' came to take away their stools, many of them in tears.

Fort George, interior of garrison chapel

A north aisle with laird's loft above and sometimes a burial place below might be added to an earlier church, giving rise to the characteristic T-plan to which many new churches also conformed. The use of the term 'aisle' to describe a projecting wing is a particularly Scottish usage. No churches now exist with their 16th- or 17th-century arrangements unaltered. Old St Peter's Church, Durness (NC 391636), built in 1619 with an aisle added in 1698, is now roofless. However, from the 18th century there stem a number of typically Scottish kirks of particular charm, many of them with their interiors little altered, including Cromarty (no. 3), Golspie (no. 56), Reay (see no. 57) and Tongue, Sutherland (NC 590570). Different in style, but equally attractive, is the garrison chapel at Fort George (no. 41). As time went on it became possible to span larger open spaces, and larger rectangular kirks were built to various plans, including Farr (no. 66), and, in Ross and Cromarty, Loch Broom (NH 177847) with its original lofts, pulpit, pews and long communion tables, Rosskeen (NH 688692) and Dingwall (NH 549589).

Plockton, parliamentary manse

Between 1823 and 1835 thirty-two churches and forty- one manses were built for the Church of Scotland in the Highlands and Islands, paid for by a special Government grant and thus known as parliamentary churches. They were needed since in some parishes the population had increased dramatically, and others were too large for one minister to service. Thomas Telford provided standard designs for a simple T-plan church, to which galleries could be added if necessary, and a choice of manses. The latter had lean-to outbuildings including byres, stables and poultry houses. Many churches remain, a few with fairly unaltered interiors, but the existing manses have been considerably

altered. Among the 12 churches built in the area covered by this volume are those at Berriedale (ND 121232) and Keiss (no. 13) in Caithness, each with a two-storey manse, Poolewe (NG 856809) with a single-story manse, since altered to two storeys, and Kinlochbervie (NC 220563) with an unaltered but derelict two-storey manse, both in Ross and Cromarty. The least altered church is Croick (no. 54), while those at Plockton and Ullapool (nos 5 and 6) on the west coast retain much of their interior layout.

Plockton, parliamentary church

After the Disruption of 1843 many churches of new denominations were built, particularly Free Kirks with their associated schools and manses. One such group may be seen at Migdale by Bonar Bridge (NH 626921), and another at Strathy (NC 843652) both in Sutherland. Later on, when the Church of Scotland and the United Free Church were reunited in 1929, the congregation generally chose to use the new, better maintained Free Kirk and the old parish church, often of greater architectural interest, was disused. The growth of population in towns and burghs led to the erection of large Victorian churches, no longer conforming to any particularly Scottish idiom but built in Gothic Revival or occasionally Neo-Classical style. There are several such churches in Inverness and Strathpeffer (nos 1 and 2).

There are few 20th-century churches, but one impressive example is the new church of *St Benedict's Abbey at Fort Augustus (NH 381091). Begun by E W Pugin, this was largely designed by Reginald Fairlie; it is plain outside, and inside has a Neo-Norman nave with vaulted roof, a wooden hammerbeam angel roof in the monk's choir, an interesting leather baldacchino and unusual stained glass in the windows.

evicted 18 families from Glencalvie, 92 people in all, to make way for a new sheep farm. Unlike those cleared in Sutherland, they were not given new crofts. Unable to find accommodation despite a desperate search, some 80 people of all ages took refuge in the churchyard at Croick, where they camped in a crude shelter covered with tarpaulins and blankets. Their plight was vividly recounted in a Times report (of which a copy is displayed in the church). Their further history is uncertain, though some at least were settled near Edderton, and others in Ardgay and Shandwick where their descendants now live.

Scratched on the glass of the east window are poignant references to this event: 'Glencalvie people was in the churchyard here May 24th 1845; Glencalvie is a wilderness below sheep' and the like. It seems unlikely that these were written by the evicted people themselves, who spoke only Gaelic as the Times reporter records. A possible candidate is the 'John Ross, shepherd, Croick' whose name appears four times, twice with the date 1869.

Croick, parliamentary church (Left)

54 CROICK CHURCH, SUTHERLAND

AD 1827.

NH 456914. Minor road up Strathcarron from Ardgay.

One of the parliamentary churches designed by Thomas Telford, but better known for its connection with the Clearances, the church shelters in a belt of trees in the empty strath. It is still in use, but the single-storey parliamentary manse just up the road is now a private house.

The harled church is built to the usual T-plan with a small belfry, cast-iron latticed windows and two doors, but with no provision for galleries. It is one of the very few parliamentary churches with its original fittings intact, the pews with a long communion table in front facing the pulpit and the reader's desk, which are flanked by the box pews for the elders and the manse.

One of the best documented Clearances took place here, witnessed by a Times reporter. Already in 1840 a number of families had emigrated from the district to Pictou, Canada, in a ship chartered by their minister, the Rev R Williamson, so that the new minister found 'ruined homesteads and a depopulated parish'. In May 1845 James Gillander, factor to Major Charles Robertson of Kindeace,

55 ST MARY'S CHURCH, ESKADALE, WEST INVERNESS-SHIRE

AD 1826.

NH 453399. On the S bank of the River Beauly: minor road from A833 at Kiltarlity through Culburnie to Eskadale

The impressive interior of the Roman Catholic church of St Mary is unexpectedly reminiscent of an English parish church. Built in 1826 by Lord

Eskadale, St Mary's Church

Lovat in Neo-Norman style, it has side aisles separated from the nave by round Norman columns which, together with the walls and roof, are painted in a variety of colours. An elaborately carved stone altar with reredos behind, and the Lovat tomb to one side, are later additions in Gothic Style. Above the entrance door is a gallery used by the Lovat family. The whole is a striking contrast to the austerity of so many post-Reformation Protestant kirks (compare Croick, no. 54, built in 1827).

Golspie,
St Andrew's
Church, laird's loft
(Right)

There are two graveyards, one the family burial place of the Frasers. An interesting and unusual survival is the stable in the trees west of the church, where those who rode to Mass could leave their horses during the service. This has a cobbled floor and tying posts, but not the usual long-term stable furnishings such as loose-boxes. The group is completed by the former priest's house of about the same date just across the road, now called Chapel House (where the key to the church may be obtained if it is locked).

56 ST ANDREW'S CHURCH, GOLSPIE, SUTHERLAND

AD 1736-7 and 1751.

NC 837002. In the main street, Golspie.

Golspie,
St Andrew's
Church

The church with its pleasant white-harled exterior and neat belfry stands on a knoll above the street. The site may be early, for a Pictish cross-slab stood here (now in Dunrobin Museum). There was a 'chapell of Sanct Andrew' at Golspie from at least the 14th century, and in 1619 this became the parish

church. Whether the old chapel was used as such or a new church built is not known. By the mid-18th century the church had become unsafe; 'both the gavils (gables) were broke off from the side walls' and it was all pulled down and rebuilt in 1736-7 on a T-plan, with the main east-west block probably set on the old foundations. The new north aisle faced the pulpit on the south wall, and housed the handsome Sutherland loft. The church was also provided with fixed seating at this time, and the communion table pews opposite the pulpit may be of this date. The south wall soon became unsafe again, and the south aisle was added to prop it up in 1751. The east and west lofts were originally rather simple, and the present stepped lofts were only made about 1849. Most of the pews were replaced in 1954 but resemble the originals.

The pulpit with its carved backboard and canopy is dated 1738 and the Sutherland loft 1739. The loft has panelled walls, and three slender columns support its carved entablature with painted details, including the Sutherland coat of arms. Behind the loft was a comfortable retiring room with a fireplace, reached by an outside stone stair. Here the Sutherland family could retire to eat a meal between the morning and afternoon services.

The interior of the church is an admirable example of the layout and furnishings of an 18th-century kirk. Only in the south aisle have there been changes, where an organ and seats for the choir have replaced the elders' pew, the precentor's desk and the stool of repentance.

57 ST DROSTAN'S CHURCH, CANISBAY, CAITHNESS

Medieval origin; 17th century and later alterations.

ND 343728. On N side of A836 at Kirkstyle, 4 km W of John o'Groats.

This white-harled parish church has a history spanning many centuries, starting as a long narrow medieval church perhaps with a western tower. As usual, considerable alterations were made after the Reformation. The north aisle with its crowstepped gable may have been added in the 17th century, while the south aisle, used as a porch, is dated 1724. The lower part of the tower may be medieval though details are hidden by harling, but the saddleback roof with ball finials on the gables is dated 1720. Further renovations took place in 1833 and in 1891 when long windows were inserted in the south wall. The interior is laid out on a T-plan with seats in three aisles facing a later 19th-century pulpit on the south wall, and galleries at the east and west ends. The former Sinclair of Mey gallery in the north aisle has been removed, though the reeded pilasters and corniced lintel that framed it remain. At the back of this aisle is a worn stone mural monument of the 17th century with fluted Corinthian columns.

In the porch is a tombstone commemorating various members of the Grot or Groat family. Part of the inscription (unfortunately recut late last century) reads 'Donald Grot sone to Johne Grot laid me heir April XIII Day 1568'. A Dutchman call Jan de Grot is said to have settled in Caithness, where in 1496 John Grot held one pennyland in Duncansby from the Earl of Caithness. His descendants in the 16th and 17th century ran the ferry from Huna to Orkney, and John o'Groats is called after him. There are a number of interesting tombstones from the 17th to the 20th century in the walled graveyard (some recut by the local sculptor John Nicolson).

There are two other attractive harled churches with belfry towers on the north coast of Caithness. That at Reay (NC 967648) is a post-Reformation church dating from 1739 with its original pulpit, while Dunnet (ND 219711) has a similar history to Canisbay with a medieval west tower.

Ardclach Bell Tower

58 ARDCLACH BELL TOWER, NAIRN

AD 1655.

NH 953453. From A939 at Redburn, 14 km S of Nairn, take minor road signposted to Ardclach Bell Tower. Check with HBM at Fort George for key: tel. Ardersier 462777.

Historic Scotland.

The tower is set on a hillock reached by a long flight of steps. It is like a tiny square keep only two storeys high, with a chimney in one gable and a belfry on the other. In the south gable is a stone dated 1655. The ground-floor room is stone vaulted with a tiny door and no windows (a torch is useful); there may have been a latrine under the stone stairs. Upstairs is a single room with tiny windows facing east and west and three shot-holes. Over the fireplace is a stone with the initials MGB. There may have been another latrine in the corner over the stair. The timber of the roof has been restored but the slates and stone coping are old.

It seems that the tower was built as a combined prison (downstairs) and watchtower (upstairs) after a period of considerable unrest during the wars between Royalists and Covenanters. The tower was on the estate of Alexander Brodie of Lethen, a Covenanter, whose house was attacked at least four times, once by Montrose, and twice plundered. The initials MGB may stand for

Margaret Grant Brodie, his second wife. The battle of Auldearn took place not far away (see no. 32).

Since the parish church stood down below in the deep ravine of the river Findhorn, a belfry was incorporated in the tower to take the church bell. The church, rebuilt in 1832, is now disused. Detached belfries are unusual, but two still exist at Latheron, Caithness and Clyne, Sutherland. These were built solely as bell towers and are quite different to Ardclach.

59* ST DUTHAC'S CHURCH, TAIN, ROSS AND CROMARTY

Late 14th-early 15th century AD.

NH 780821. In the High Street, Tain, near the Tolbooth.

Tain, St Duthac's Church.

Restored 16th-century pulpit

A well-preserved medieval church built at the turn of the 14th and 15th centuries as the parish church of Tain. There are three medieval churches in Tain and some confusion as to their purpose. All are dedicated to St Duthac (or Duthus), a saint said to have been born in Tain around AD 1000. His relics were kept in the ruined 13th-century church which stands close to the sea, and they were a focus for medieval pilgrimages. A second ruin of the later 13th-early 14th century, close to the existing church, may have belonged to a community of priests who served St Duthac's sanctuary. In 1487 this community acquired collegiate status and by then had a provost, five canons, a sacrist, an

assistant clerk and three boy choristers. From then on the college seems to have used the choir of the parish church for their services, while the townsfolk used the nave.

The church has large windows with restored tracery in three walls and lancet windows in the fourth. In the west wall is a niche with a cast of a statue of a bishop, perhaps St Duthac (the original statue is inside the church). The interior has been stripped of most of its furnishings, medieval or later, and the roof is a restoration. In medieval times the church, now so quiet and empty, was full of colour and sound and incense. It was divided into choir and nave by a wooden screen with a central door and an altar either side. The position of the screen is shown by the piscina in the south wall. The eastern end was the choir, later used as the collegiate church, with the high altar under the window and wooden stalls for the canons along the walls. A fine triple sedilia (built-in stone seat) for the clergy celebrating mass survives in the south wall. There was probably no fixed seating for the lay folk in the nave.

The Stuart kings had a special attachment to St Duthac and to Tain. James II and James III endowed chaplaincies there: later accounts speak of 'the man who singis (masses) for the King at Tain'. James IV made some 18 pilgrimages to Tain between 1493 and 1513, the last the month before he fell at Flodden. The royal accounts show that on various occasions he lodged with the vicar, provided new silver relics for the church, and bought new bonnets for himself 'the time he passed to St Duthus'.

The church survived the Reformation intact, but the interior was altered to make it suitable for Protestant services by removing the screen and altars. The fine 16th-century pulpit is said to have been presented by the 'good regent Murray' (James Stewart, Earl of Moray, Regent for James VI 1567-70). Lofts were built to serve a larger congregation, but all are now gone, and only the painted front of the Trades Loft with craft emblems and inscriptions dated 1776 now survives, set up on one wall. In 1815 a new church was built and this one fell into disrepair. Later on the roof and windows were repaired, and the pulpit restored from a few surviving fragments.

Church, museum and 'Pilgrimage' visitor centre are signposted 'Tain Through Time'. Tape tours are available at the visitor centre.

60* DORNOCH CATHEDRAL, SUTHERLAND

13th century and 19th century AD.

NH 797896. In Castle Street, in the centre of Dornoch.

Much of the 13th-century cathedral survives, though heavily restored in the 19th century. It was founded by Gilbert of Moravia, bishop of Caithness from 1223 to 1246. His two predecessors had been murdered at Halkirk, and he moved south to Dornoch. The cathedral was constructed on the usual cruciform plan, with a choir, transepts, a massive tower over the crossing and an aisled nave. Drawings show that round pillars with pointed arches separated the nave from the aisles; these dated from a 15th-century alteration. In 1570 the cathedral and much of the town were burnt by the Mackays of Strathnaver and the cathedral remained a roofless ruin until 1616 when the choir and transepts were reroofed for use as the parish church. The present steeple was begun in 1726.

The building as seen today is the result of a thorough 'restoration' in 1835-7 by William Burn, the architect who restored St Giles Cathedral in Edinburgh. The ruins of the nave were demolished and rebuilt without the aisles; only two of the old nave pillars escaped, and can be seen recessed in the walls close to the piers of the tower. The clustered columns of these piers, the tower arches and most of the choir and transept walls are medieval, as are the lancet windows in the choir, but the vaulted roof dates from the 1835 restoration. The coffin of Richard of Moravia, brother of Gilbert, with his mutilated effigy in mail lies at the end of the nave. There is a fine collection of 19th- and 20th-century glass in the windows.

Opposite the cathedral stands part of the old bishop's palace (now a hotel). The tall tower-house at the west end was built around 1500 and substantially repaired after it was burnt in 1570. The building east of the tower was added in about 1813-14, but the tall chimney behind it belongs to the original 16th-century vaulted kitchens, parts of which survive. In the late 19th century the roof of this block was raised and the east tower built. Close to the palace is the Town Jail, built in 1840-50 in Scottish Baronial style (now a craft centre); part of the interior with its vaulted cells and passages has been laid out as an unusual jail museum.

61* FORTROSE CATHEDRAL, ROSS AND CROMARTY

13th century and late 14th/early 15th century AD.

NH 727565. Near centre of Fortrose, signposted from High Street.

Historic Scotland.

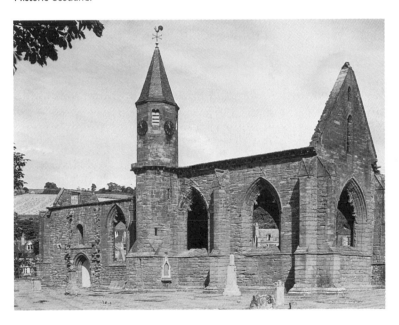

Fortrose Cathedral

Of the medieval cathedral of the diocese of Ross only the south aisle and chapel and the chapter house now remain as separate buildings, but the plan of the foundations is laid out in the grass.

The bishopric of Ross was originally at Rosemarkie, but Bishop Robert (1214-49) moved to Fortrose and started to build a new cathedral. The choir, chancel and chapter house may have been finished by the end of the 13th century, but work probably ceased during the Wars of Independence, and the building was only completed in the early 15th century. After the Reformation the Regent Moray allowed the lead to be stripped from the roof, while Cromwell is said to have taken the fallen stones, as he did at Beauly, to build his fortress at Inverness.

The cathedral was a long rectangle with heavily buttressed walls and a west tower. The most important surviving structure is the south nave aisle, added in the late 14th-early 15th century, of which the eastern section was traditionally erected as a chantry chapel and burial aisle for Euphemia, Countess of Ross in her own right, who died in 1395. Her first husband was Sir Walter Leslie, whose arms appear on a roof boss. Ironically, her second husband was that Alexander Stewart, Wolf of Badenoch, who with 'wild Wykked Heland-men' burnt Elgin cathedral and burgh in 1390. The tracery of the windows in her chapel at Fortrose is similar to that of the new windows put in the choir aisles at Elgin after the fire. The ribbed vaulting of the aisle roof is particularly fine. Between the aisle and the nave are three arched tombs: from east to west, these are traditionally those of Countess Euphemia herself, Bishop Cairncross (1539-45) and Bishop Fraser (1489-1507). It is curious that a bishop's head is carved on the Countess's tomb. Halfway along the south aisle is an octagonal stair

tower and bell turret with a Victorian pointed roof. Only the chapter house preserves any portion of the original 13th-century cathedral: the vaulted undercroft of this building, located next to the chancel, was probably a combined chapter house and sacristy (where the priests prepared for the services), while the room above may have housed the cathedral library and a treasury.

62* BEAULY PRIORY, WEST INVERNESS-SHIRE

13th century AD and later.

NH 527464. In the centre of Beauly.

Historic Scotland.

Only the roofless church of this 13th-century priory still stands. Said to have been founded by Sir John Bisset about 1230, it is one of only three houses of the French Valliscaulian order in Britain, the other two being Pluscarden in Moray and Ardchattan in Argyll. The church was laid out on a cruciform plan, having a long narrow nave without aisles and no tower, and it was considerably altered in the later Middle Ages.

Beauly Priory

**Crosskirk,
St Mary's Church**

The west front with its tall lancet windows was rebuilt by Robert Reid, Prior from 1530 to 1558. The nave has windows of several dates, including the three eastern windows in the south wall which are of a rare trefoil design of 13th century date, and it was once divided from the choir by a wooden screen west of the transepts. Between the nave and the south transept is the arched tomb of Prior Mackenzie, built in an odd mixture of styles and perhaps a 16th-century reconstruction. The north transept was heightened and its stair turret added in the 15th century; it contains the monument of Sir Kenneth Mackenzie of Kintail dated 1491, and was restored in 1901 as the Kintail burial aisle. The chancel has early pointed windows framed in arcading, and the great east window, once filled with tracery and coloured glass, was inserted in the 15th century.

The priory buildings all lay south of the church. The monks' dormitory was next to the south transept, and the door to the night stair down which the monks passed from their dormitory to the nave can be seen in the south wall. Next to the transept stood the cloister, and in the south wall of the church are the projecting stumps of the walls of the west cloister range with traces of a first-floor fireplace. This building may at one time have contained the prior's lodging.

After the Reformation the priory passed to Commendators, or Lay Priors. By 1633 the church was said to be 'badly decayed'.

63 ST MARY'S CHAPEL, CROSSKIRK, CAITHNESS

12th century AD.

ND 024700. About 8 km W of Thurso, minor road signposted N to Crosskirk; then signposted path to chapel on W side of Crosskirk Bay.

Historic Scotland.

This simple chapel on the cliff near the sea is one of the oldest ecclesiastical buildings in Caithness and was probably built in the 12th century. It is now roofless, but the rubble-built walls stand almost complete. There is a short nave and a small square-ended chancel which may be a later reconstruction on early foundations. The gable ends of the nave show it had a pitched roof, probably thatched. The present entrance in the south wall is modern; the two original doors are in the west and east walls, the latter connecting the nave with the chancel. The sides of the doorways converge towards the top where they are crossed by a flat lintel; such inclined jambs are also found in early Irish churches. There are now no windows, but the new entrance may have destroyed one in the south wall.

The footings of an early chapel of similar plan have been excavated at The Clow, near Watten, (ND 233524), and there is a similar chapel at Skinnet (ND 130620). These small chancelled churches are unlike others in the Highlands at that time, but are familiar in the Northern Isles, and their design was probably derived from Orkney, then ruled by the Norse Earls who also controlled Caithness.

DARK AGE CARVED STONES

Deer head symbol, part of a Pictish stone, from Ardross (Inverness Museum)

The Highlands have an incomparable heritage of dark-age carvings, particularly in the Pictish area along the east coast and round the Moray Firth. The slabs of Old Red Sandstone so readily obtainable were an ideal medium first for incised and later for relief monuments, huge cross-slabs covered with the most intricate carvings, not unlike pages from the painted Gospel books of the time translated into stone. Over the centuries their significance was lost: some fell, others were built into nearby churches, and after the Reformation, even the old veneration for the cross-slabs faded to the extent that the cross on the Hilton of Cadboll slab was hacked off to convert it to a 17th-century tombstone. More recently there has been a revival of interest in these carvings and an effort made to preserve them, but sadly damage from the weather and industrial pollution means that the best of those still standing in the open may have to be moved under cover.

Symbol stones were erected by the Picts all over their kingdom, most probably in the later 7th and first half of the 8th century by which time the population was generally Christian, though some have suggested the symbols started earlier. A symbol stone is an unworked slab or boulder with two symbols (or very rarely one) cut into one face, to which a mirror, or a mirror and comb may be added, probably implying a woman. Several symbols are recognisable animals, often male (boar, bull, eagle, snake, fish) and a few are objects (mirror, tongs), but others are abstract designs to which modern names are given for identification, such as 'double-disc and Z-rod', or 'crescent and V-rod'. There is also a non-realistic animal known as the 'Pictish beast'. Some stones were reused; the worn stone by the gate of Dingwall churchyard, Ross and Cromarty (NH 549589), has three symbols on one face and two on the other. No totally convincing explanation of the symbols or of their placing on the stones has yet been offered, but there is a strong possibility that they are gravestones. Sometimes several are found in one area, often more or less convincingly linked with dark-age slab-lined graves.

Wolf symbol, part of a Pictish stone, from Ardross
(Inverness Museum)

Overlapping in date with the latest symbol stones are cross-slabs with symbols of the later 8th and 9th centuries AD. Of unique quality are the large relief-decorated monuments at Shandwick, Nigg and Rosemarkie (nos 68-70) and the damaged stone from Hilton near Shandwick (now in NMS), all dating from around AD 800 or a little later. Other fine slabs are those from Ulbster and Skinnet in Caithness, now in Thurso Museum, and from Golspie, in Dunrobin Castle Museum. The symbols are in pairs or multiples: two, four, six or eight on a stone. Many cross-slabs come from sites which are still graveyards attached to churches. They are carved on both sides, generally with an emphatic cross on one face and the symbols on the other, though the stones from Ulbster and Skinnet also have crosses on the back with the symbols.

Cross-slabs without symbols may have been erected at the same time, and probably continued after the union of Picts and Scots in c AD 843. Fine cross-slabs still stand at Farr (no. 66) and Creich (no. 65). There are others in Caithness in the old church at Reay (NC 969648), and beside the ruinous 12th-century chapel at Skinnet, where the cross-slab with symbols was also found (ND 130620). Some isolated cross-slabs could have been preaching crosses, used by travelling clergy where there was no church. On early monastic sites, large cross-slabs may have served the same functions as the free-standing crosses of Iona and Ireland, sanctifying areas of special significance and acting as focuses for communal processions or private meditation. Small slabs with simple incised crosses were used as gravemarkers. Large cross-slabs can be seen at Applecross (no. 64), where the Scottish monks may have called in Pictish stone-carvers, and at Rosemarkie (no. 70) there are several simple cross- slabs besides the great slab with symbols, and also what may be part of a stone shrine. Fragments of cross-slabs from the churchyard at Tarbat, Ross and Cromarty (NH 914840), now in NMS, may indicate another early monastic site there.

In the northern and western isles there are a few Norse gravestones, but only one is known from the Highlands, a stone cut in the shape of a crude cross with a Norse runic inscription on it, found in Thurso near St Peter's Church and now in Thurso Museum (no.8).

**Rosemarkie
cross-slab,
Pictish symbols**

64 APPLECROSS, CROSS-SLABS, ROSS AND CROMARTY

8th or 9th century AD.

NG 713458. One cross-slab in old churchyard at Applecross, on N side of bay, 1.5 km from village. Others in church.

The cross-slab standing by the gate is almost three metres high. Incised on one face is the outline of a large, plain ringed cross. The stem of the cross expands into a wide base, imitating the sort of base that supported free-standing crosses. The top of the cross seems to be partly carved into shape, but may have broken along the carved lines.

Inside the church, at the west end, are three more carved fragments kept in display cases. The largest is part of a broken cross-slab decorated in relief. The design and execution of the complex patterns are of a very high standard. To the right of the ringed cross is a panel of whirling triple-spirals with varied terminals including birds' heads, closely related to designs in gospel books of the period. Other patterns include interlace and key

pattern. The other two smaller pieces belong to one or more cross-slabs decorated with interlace. They were found at the east end of the graveyard.

The cross-slabs are the only surviving physical evidence of an Early Christian community founded here in 673 by St Maelrubha, who came from the abbey of Bangor in Ireland. He chose a well sheltered and fertile spot for his new monastery, of which he was abbot until his death in 722. From historical sources we know little more about it than the names and dates of the first two abbots. No trace remains of the monastic buildings, which may have been a few thatched huts and a little stone chapel within an enclosure bank, and only the cross-slabs give us some idea of the artistic capabilities of these early monks.

The church is next recorded in 1515 as the parish church of Applecross in the diocese of Ross. The existing church, now disused, was built in 1817. Most of the furnishings have been removed, but a west gallery survives, and a fine pulpit with reader's desk. The ruins of a small 15th-century chapel stand in the graveyard.

65 CREICH, CROSS-SLAB, SUTHERLAND

9th or 10th century AD.

NH 636891. Stone in field E of graveyard beside A949 at Creich, 4.5 km E of the bridge at Bonar Bridge.

This is a tall stone over 2 m high, which seems to have been used with little or no shaping. The outline of a large cross with expanded arms and base is incised on one side, rather irregularly in places. The coarse-grained stone was probably too hard to carve in relief. The stone is known as St Demhan's Cross, after St Devenic to whom the medieval parish church was dedicated. The medieval church stood in the graveyard on the site now occupied by the ruins of a later parish church built in 1774. The presence of the cross-incised stone suggests an ecclesiastical use of the site before the medieval church was built, and it could be that the stone was a preaching cross rather than a gravestone.

Applecross cross-slab (Left)

Creich, cross-slab

The church at Farr was built in 1774 as the parish church, on an old site, and is now the Strathnaver Museum. Its unusually large and handsome pulpit with a reader's desk in front, dated 1774, is still in position between the long windows. Among the exhibits, mostly connected with crofting life or the Clearances, are a collection of fine 18th-century tombstones from the churchyard and from Bighouse in Strath Halladale, and a small dark-age cross-slab from Grumbeg in Strathnaver. (If the museum is closed, ask at the Tourist Office for the key-keeper.)

66 FARR, CROSS-SLAB, SUTHERLAND

9th century AD.

Farr, cross-slab
(Right)

NC 714622. Outside church at Farr, less than 1 km E of Bettyhill, on N side of A836.

A fine cross-slab, 2.3 m high, stands in the graveyard outside the west end of the church at Farr. It has no Pictish symbols and is carved in relief on one side only, an unusual feature which may indicate it originally stood close to a wall so the back was not seen. It is best seen at midday (1 pm summertime) when the sun is sideways on to the stone and shows up the detail. A ringed cross in high relief occupies the greater part of the carved face with panels of key pattern above and below, much of the lower pattern being hidden in the ground. The cross and its ring, and the background, are decorated with tight interlace and curvilinear patterns. On the central boss is carved a triple spiral, and in the curved base of the cross is a pair of birds with their necks crossed.

67 EDDERTON, CROSS-SLAB, ROSS AND CROMARTY

8th or 9th century AD.

NH 719842. In graveyard of old church beside A836, 1 km E of cross-roads at Edderton.

The cross-slab is near the entrance gate, in the fourth row of graves. It is carved in high relief on both sides. On the east side is a cross set on a curved frame, and within the frame a rider on a horse: he is apparently unarmed, and sits on what may be a saddle cloth. Below him are two incised figures on horseback, partly hidden in the ground;

they carry round shields and spears and are also armed with swords. On the other side of the slab is a large ringed cross on a tall stem, with low bosses in the angles of its arms. There are no Pictish symbols on this stone, but the riders are similar to those on stones with symbols, such as Shandwick (no. 68), and must be close in date to them.

The white-harled T-plan church built in 1743 was originally the parish church, but became the Free Church when a new parish church was built in Edderton in 1842. It has three galleries, the two at each end now blocked off, and a 1794 pulpit together with ingenious late 18th-century pews which unhinge and fold down to become long communion tables. Outside at the east end is the remains of an earlier church, and at the west end is a roofless burial aisle built in 1637.

Shandwick, cross-slab, east face

68 SHANDWICK, CROSS-SLAB, ROSS AND CROMARTY

Late 8th or early 9th century AD.

NH 855747. From A9 about 4 km S of Tain follow signs to Balintore and Shandwick. Stone stands on hill beside road SW of Shandwick.

This great cross-slab, known as the Clach a' Charridh, is one of the most impressive of all Pictish monuments. It stands in its original position on a hill overlooking the little fishing village of Shandwick, and is a landmark which can be seen from far out to sea. The stone blew down in 1846 and broke in half, but it has been carefully restored. It is now covered by a glass conservatory to protect it from pollution, necessary but unsightly.

The stone stands 2.7 m high. On the face which looks out to sea is a prominent cross formed of protruding bosses, which are covered with a complex relief pattern of interlocking spirals. Below each arm is a small angel with two pairs of wings, then a beast each side of the stem, and then

Edderton, cross-slab (Left)

two contrasting groups of interlaced creatures, animals with ribbon-like bodies on the left and snakes on the right. Below the cross is a damaged pattern of large low bosses surrounded by snakes' bodies meeting head to head, and covered with a mesh of interlace.

The other side of the stone is divided into five panels and decorated in rather lower relief. At the top is a damaged double-disc symbol with spiral patterns on it, and below this a 'Pictish beast' symbol, its body left quite plain, but tiny animals squeezed in below. The next panel has a positive menagerie of people and animals, including men on horseback, a man with a drinking horn, a stag being hunted, two men with swords and small shields fighting, and a kneeling man shooting a crossbow at a stag. The fourth panel has a most beautiful circular composition of interlocking spirals. The fifth panel carried four patterns, but parts of only two can now be seen.

Long after the Pictish origin of the cross-slabs had been forgotten, a local legend grew up around this stone and its neighbours at Nigg and Hilton. In brief, the story is that the stones were erected to mark the graves of three Norse princes who were wrecked on a reef off Shandwick Bay while pursuing the Earl of Ross, because the Earl had ill-treated his wife, their sister, and banished her to Ballone Castle. The reef is called the King's Sons or the Three Kings.

Close to the stone is an ancient graveyard, now under the plough, used in recent centuries only for the burial of unbaptised children, and in 1832 for cholera victims.

Nigg, cross-slab
(Right)

69 NIGG, CROSS-SLAB, ROSS AND CROMARTY

Late 8th or early 9th century AD.

NH 804717. Stone inside old church at Nigg.

B9175 to Nigg and Shandwick, follow signs to Pitcalnie and Nigg village; go on past school to church.

This great stone, which once stood outside the east end of the parish church, has been cleaned, repaired and re-erected inside a room at the west end of the church. The cross face of the stone has bossed

ornament, as at Shandwick, but here the Pictish carvers have set the bosses on the background, not on the cross itself. At the top, in a triangular pediment, are two robed human figures bowing down their heads; representing St Paul and St Anthony in the desert, as recounted in the Lives of the Saints. The bird between them with a round object in its beak is the raven which usually supplied St Paul with half a loaf, but cannily brought a whole loaf when St Anthony visited him. The two animals may be the lions which helped St Anthony bury St Paul.

The great cross is covered with key pattern and interlace, some of it formed by the threadlike bodies of pairs of animals. Part of the top is missing, and has been left blank in the restoration. Either side of the cross are elaborate bossed patterns in six panels, all different but balancing. In the central panels the bosses are covered with meshlike interlace and surrounded by the bodies of snakes. In the lower panels are swirling peltas.

The back of the stone is framed by a wide border, within which at the top is an eagle symbol. It is known from old drawings that a 'Pictish beast' symbol filled the space beneath. The rest of the back is badly damaged, but has traces of various figures and animals connected with Biblical accounts of David as shepherd, warrior, king and psalmist. At the top left is a man standing holding spear and shield, with two beasts in front of him; centre left, a sheep with a very curly coat and a harp below; to the right David rending the jaws of the lion (what looks like a wing is drapery); bottom left, a man holding two cymbals, following a man on horseback hunting a deer.

The white-harled Nigg church was built in 1626 probably on the site of an earlier church. It was originally rectangular, but has been altered several times and a north aisle added.

70* ROSEMARKIE, CROSS-SLAB, ROSS AND CROMARTY

Late 8th-early 9th century AD.

NH 737576. In Groam House Museum, High Street, Rosemarkie.

This stone is some 2.6 m high, and was found built into the floor of the old church. The top of the stone is missing, and probably part of the bottom too. One side is carved in shallow relief, with a small cross defined by sunk panels towards the top, the rest of the surface being covered with a variety of elaborate interlace. The other side, now turned to the wall, has four symbols at the top; three crescents and V-rods and one double disc and Z-rod, all elaborately ornamented in contrasting styles. Above the lowest crescent is a comb and below it two mirrors, or perhaps one mirror and a mirror-case. The central panel on this side has an equal-armed cross of a type used in manuscript decoration. The lowest panel is filled with key-pattern. Both edges of the slab are also decorated with elaborate interlaced ribbon patterns, some with animal heads.

Another dozen or so fragments of carved stones which may date to the 9th century AD are also kept in Groam House, some found in the churchyard. There are simple cross-slabs, a stone with tree-scroll ornament and two casts with parts of figures. Five other fragments with flat, all-over key patterns

may all be part of a stone shrine that housed the relics of a saint or important cleric. Historical sources hint at a Christian establishment at Rosemarkie from the early 8th century, and the number of carved stones suggests a wealthy church or monastery flourishing in the later 8th and 9th centuries AD. Most probably illustrated manuscripts and metalwork were also produced here. The museum has information on other Pictish stones and a video on the Picts.

71 STRATHPEFFER, SYMBOL STONE, ROSS AND CROMARTY

Late 7th or 8th century AD.

NH 85585. In Strathpeffer, near the A835 to Dingwall. From old railway station go E 60 m on A835, then turn left up path between hedges to gate on right into field with stone.

A stout slab, somewhat damaged at the top, which has been re-erected in a concrete base in its original position. It bears two symbols: a 'horseshoe' decorated with a curvilinear pattern and below this a realistic eagle with long wing feathers, hooked beak and strong claws. The stone is often called simply 'The Eagle Stone', but its Gaelic name was

Rosemarkie, cross-slab

Strathpeffer, symbol stone.

Knocknagael, symbol stone
(Right)

'Clach Tiompan' or sounding stone. It is a good example of a Pictish symbol stone and the symbols are deeply incised and easy to see.

72 EDDERTON, SYMBOL STONE, ROSS AND CROMARTY

2nd millennium BC and 7th or 8th century AD.

NH 708850. At cross roads in Edderton turn N on minor road to Ardmore; stone is in field on left of road past houses.

A tall pillar-like stone some 3 m high, this can be approached closely when there is no crop. There are two symbols, a fish cut obliquely at the top, and below this the double-disc and Z-rod, set vertically to fit onto the narrow stone. The carving is worn, and best seen in a sideways light in the early morning. Only two of the fish's fins can now be made out. Other marks on the stone are the result of weathering and of parts of the surface having flaked off. It is probable that this tall pillar, an unusual shape and size for a symbol stone, is a bronze-age standing stone to which the symbols were added some 2,000 years later. There are several other known or suspected instances of Pictish symbols added to prehistoric stones.

Edderton, standing stone with Pictish symbols

Almost directly opposite the standing stone, in the gorse bushes on the other side of the road and close to the fence, is part of a rough circle of low boulders, probably the kerb stones of a bronze-age cairn now robbed away. Within the circle is a cist grave or stone coffin which has been dug out.

73 KNOCKNAGAEL, SYMBOL STONE, INVERNESS

Late 7th-8th century AD.

In Highland Regional Council Offices, Glenurquhart Road, Inverness.

Historic Scotland.

This huge slab of stone, known as the Boar Stone, is over 2 m high. It formerly stood in the countryside 3 km south of Inverness, but it was moved to protect it from vandalism. It is now visible through a large window at the south end of the building.

About the centre of the slab is a finely carved boar facing right with a bristly spine. It has decorative joint spirals where the legs join the body, as do other Pictish animal symbols such as the Burghead bulls and the wolf from Ardross (now in Inverness Museum). The same feature occurs on the Evangelists' animal symbols in some Dark Age Gospel books and is one of the few good pointers to the date of the symbol stones. Above the boar is the so-called 'mirror-case' symbol, a circle with a rectangle below it: the identification is only guesswork and the design may be another abstract symbol. The irregularly weathered surface of the stone can make the symbols hard to see.

74* DUNROBIN CASTLE MUSEUM, PICTISH STONES, SUTHERLAND

Late 7th-9th century AD.

NC 850008. In grounds of Dunrobin Castle, N of Golspie, access through castle.

The museum is in a garden pavilion, the front part of which was built in 1732 as a summerhouse, and the back part added in 1878 when it became a museum. As well as Pictish stones, it houses local archaeological finds, objects from brochs, and hunting trophies from all over the world, all within a Victorian setting.

The collection of local Pictish stones is outstanding and includes almost all those found in Sutherland, which were concentrated in the narrow, fertile strip

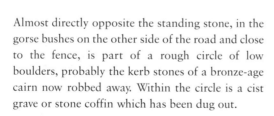

One side has a cross in relief, both cross and background decorated with a great variety of interlace patterns and other patterns. This was much defaced when the slab was used as a gravestone in the 17th or 18th century and an inscription cut round the edge. The other side of this slab is carved with a series of what may be eight symbols, including a figure of a man in a tunic holding a knife or short sword in one hand and an axe in the other. It is not certain if the paired snakes, or indeed the man himself, are symbols in the same sense as the others, which are all familiar from symbol stones. The symbols at the top, known as a rectangle and a Pictish beast, are shown more prominently than the others, apparently deliberately. Both edges have a pleasing design of spirals in high relief.

On the rounded angle between this face of the stone, and its right and top edges is incised an ogam inscription. The ogam alphabet was introduced to the Picts from Ireland, but Pictish inscriptions are mostly unintelligible: here the letters include the word 'meqq', which seems to be equivalent to the Gaelic 'mac' meaning 'son of', so the inscription may correspond to the usual ogam formula in Ireland '(the monument of) A son of B'.

of land along the east coast. Most numerous are the symbol stones, of which there are nine more or less complete examples and several more incomplete. Many have a mirror, or mirror and comb, probably indicating a woman, added to two other symbols and the different types represented can be compared. Notable for their fine drawing and execution are the symbol stone from Dunrobin with a male salmon, 'tuning-fork' (its real identification is unknown) and a mirror and comb; one from the Dairy Park south of the castle with a double crescent, snake and Z-rod and mirror and comb; and another found in Golspie with a crescent and V-rod, 'Pictish beast' and mirror and comb. These three stones were all found associated with graves, but two may have been reused.

A large cross-slab with Pictish symbols was found in the graveyard of St Andrew's Church, Golspie.

Part of symbol stone from Clynemilton

FORTS, BROCHS AND SETTLEMENTS

Dun Telve broch, Glenelg

Those later prehistoric and early historic monuments in the Highlands which are stone built, and so have survived, consist for the most part of places where people lived. Many of these monuments are fortified, but there are also extensive traces of open settlement generally connected with hut circles.

Forts

Forts of various sizes occur all over the Highlands, but are noticeably fewer north of the Moray Firth. Their ramparts are generally stone, loose rubble retained front and back by stone walls. As in other parts of Britain, some forts had layers of timber in their stone ramparts, giving extra stability. If such timber-laced ramparts were burnt by an enemy to destroy them, some types of stone softened or melted, and on cooling solidified, fusing other stones together in great lumps which remain, though most of the rampart simply collapsed (burning is not a method of construction!). These so-called vitrified forts have been thought to be iron age, but more recently it has been found that some vitrified and other timber-laced forts were dark age, while scientific dating methods suggest other vitrified forts are much earlier. Vitrification may be seen at Craig Phadrig, Knock Farril and Dun Lagaidh (nos 76, 77 and 79).

The inhabitants of forts lived in round, thatched timber houses, though only one or two huts would have fitted inside the smallest forts. Very small stone walled forts are called duns, but there is no precise distinction between duns and forts. 'Dun' is a Gaelic word meaning fortress, castle, heap or mound, and it may occur in placenames applied to forts, duns or brochs. Some duns were built in the 1st millennium AD.

Garrywhin fort, slabs at entrance

Only a small selection of iron-age fortifications can be described here in the space available. There are many small forts west of Inverness, among then Dun a Chliabhain (NH 447460) and Ashie Moor (NH 600316). In the north the fort on St John's Point, Caithness (ND 310751) is one of many promontory forts, but bigger than usual.

Some forts were built or re-occupied in the first millennium AD, as were Craig Phadrig (no. 76), the vitrified fort under the citadel at Urquhart Castle (no. 52) and possibly Dun-da-Lamh (no. 75).

Brochs

Brochs are a specialised form of defensive structure, a tall round tower with hollow stone walls, and stairs and chambers within the walls, an astonishingly sophisticated construction to build without mortar. The broch at Mousa, Shetland, which still stands some 12 m high, is almost complete. While other brochs may not all have been quite so tall, Dun Telve and Dun Troddan (nos 83, 84) are still 10.10 m and 7.6 m high respectively. The double wall construction, the two walls tied together with bands of horizontal slabs which formed a series of so-called galleries in the wall, as seen so clearly at Dun Telve, seems to be a technical device to lighten the immensely heavy wall, which might otherwise collapse under its own weight. The lowest gallery was useable, but the others too small to get into. The stairs which curve up within the wall probably led, as at Mousa, to the wall head, and the chambers in the base of the wall served as an adjunct to the main living space in the central court. This varied from 7 m to nearly 10 m in diameter. There was usually a wooden floor at a height of some 3 m, supported on the specially provided ledge or scarcement built into the wall. Two brochs described here have doors leading out onto this floor, Totaig and Rhiroy (nos 85, 86). A thatched roof probably covered the whole interior of the broch, with a vent or two for smoke. Some people suggest there was a large hole in the middle of the roof, and wooden galleries round the walls, but this would have made the interior very wet and cold and wasted valuable living space.

Many brochs were surrounded by exterior settlements of stone-walled huts, defended by a stone rampart and a ditch. Carn Liath (no. 83) is a good example, Nybster (no. 92) another. A few, such as Kilphedir (no. 93), have an outer rampart but apparently no settlement.

While the date at which brochs began is unknown, many brochs seem to have been built and lived in during the first century BC and the first century AD, or thereabouts. The broch towers fell after a century or two, or were pulled down before they fell (many were extensively buttressed), but such huge masses of building stone attracted settlement for long after. Often a house was constructed within the remains of the tower, as at Carn Liath and Yarrows (nos 90, 105), and the exterior settlements were rebuilt as well. Brochs occur in great numbers in Caithness and Sutherland, with many in Ross and Cromarty, but thin out towards the south of the area, where forts and duns predominate. Many brochs are now only shapeless overgrown mounds, though still impressive in size. Some of the more interesting brochs are a long way from the nearest road, such as Carrol Broch, Sutherland (NC 846064). Kylesku (NC 217341) is an example of a west coast broch set on a tidal islet, probably for reasons of defence. A series of brochs on the Caithness coast north of Wick were excavated in the last century, but allowed to decay afterwards. These include three at Keiss (no. 37); Nybster (no. 92); and Skirza Head (ND 394684). Two brochs where the structure is better preserved are Sallachy, near Lairg, Sutherland (NC 549092; off an estate road); and Ousdale, Caithness (ND 071188; below a layby on the A9, but involves climbing a gate in a deer fence).

A few small duns of irregular shape which can never have been towers contain broch-like features such as wall chambers, stairs or galleries. The dun at Dun Lagaidh (no. 79) is one of these. Another called Dun Grugaig lies up Glen Beag beyond Dun Troddan (NG 851159).

Wags

Forse Wag, one of the later buildings

Unique houses found almost exclusively in southern Caithness are long or round buildings with stone pillars to support their roofs. These have been called 'wags' after their local Gaelic name, but pillar houses would be a better name for them. Examples can be seen at Forse Wag and at Yarrows (nos 94 and 105), and about a dozen others are known. They are later than brochs, and date to the early centuries AD. They may be contemporary with the wheelhouses of the northern and western isles.

Hut Circles

Hut circle near Drumnadrochit

Hut circles occur in great numbers in the Highlands. They are the low stone walls of capacious round huts, which now appear as a ring in the grass or heather, generally from 9 m to 13 m in diameter. They had thatched roofs supported on an interior ring of posts, and most belonged to the 2nd and 1st millennium BC or the first few centuries AD. Good examples can be seen at The Ord and Kilphedir (nos 95 and 93). Many of these hut circles are above the limits of modern cultivation and thus have survived, but they represent only the margins of iron-age settlement, and others on the better land below have been destroyed by modern cultivation.

Traces of cultivation are often found near the hut circles, in the form of stretches of old field walls, part buried in peat, and the more obvious clearance cairns. The latter are simply heaps of stones, usually around 2 m to 3 m in diameter, gathered off fields, to make them easier to cultivate. They are not always of the same date as the hut circles and may be bronze age, iron age, or even related to modern cultivation (modern ones are generally larger).

Some remarkable stretches of ancient landscapes exist in the Highlands, but these are under threat from modern development and in particular from forestry.

**Suisgill souterrain,
Caithness**

Souterrains

Souterrains or earth-houses are underground passages attached to huts, and were used as cold stores where perishable produce could be stored at an even temperature. They were dug into softer patches of ground as an open trench, and then lined with stone walls, roofed with stone lintels and covered over with earth. The entrances are small and often led down steps from a trapdoor in the house. Often the huts have been destroyed and only the souterrain remains. Usually it is simply a curved tunnel, but sometimes extra chambers were added. Highland souterrains are fairly short, usually only 9 m or 10 m in length, and nothing like the size of the massive examples known in Angus. Their owners were probably farming on a smaller scale.

Souterrains may be seen at Laid and Kilphedir (nos 96, 93), and another is inserted into a large round mound at Ham, Caithness (ND 238738); a torch is essential and preferably two torches to light the length of the passage. Souterrains seem to have much the same date range as hut circles.

Burnt Mounds

Burnt mounds have only recently been recognised in the Highlands, though long known in the Northern Isles. They are heaps of burnt stones, generally covered in grass, piled up in circular or kidney-shaped mounds beside a slab-lined trough and a hearth which are not now visible. They were always sited near water. Stones were heated in the fire, thrown into the water in the trough to bring it to the boil, and then large joints of meat boiled in the trough. The stones cracked and had to be discarded. Burnt mounds are often difficult to recognise, and only the examples near Forse Wag (no. 94) and at the Ord (no. 95) are noted here. These communal cooking places may have been used through much of the 2nd and 1st millennium BC.

75 DUN-DA-LAMH, FORT, EAST INVERNESS-SHIRE

1st millennium AD.

NN 582929. About 9.5 km NNW of Dalwhinnie. On A86, about 3 km SW of Laggan, park behind cottages. Walk N 1 km along track, then left into trees (notice on gate admits walkers), and 1st turn right. At end of track, go uphill through heather; fort on right in trees. (About 45 mins).

The fort is built on a knoll at the east end of a long, steepsided ridge known as the Black Craig, and is divided from the main ridge by a saddle. Standing some 200 m above the valley floor, it has extensive views over upper Strathspey and Strathmashie. The knoll has two craggy summits with a lower area between, now overgrown with tall grass and heather: its Gaelic name (pronounced 'dun da larve') means 'fort of the two hands' and may refer to the two summits. The rampart does not follow a level contour round the hill, but climbs up and down with the crags, and it was unusually massive, varying in width from four to six metres or more; it is now tumbled and lichened. The inner face of the wall has been exposed at the northwest and southwest corners by the removal of tumble, showing the fine quality of the masonry built with small slabs (however, unless covered over soon, this face will itself deteriorate). Because of the odd shape of the hill, the fort has pronounced corners, with angles skilfully constructed on the inner side of the wall. The original entrance may have been in the middle of the north wall where there seems to be a gap.

The position of the fort on such a craggy knoll and the use of rock outcrops suggest that this fort may be of early historic date, perhaps contemporary with fortifications on crags in the south of Scotland, such as Dumbarton Rock near Glasgow, Dunadd in Argyll and Dundurn, Perth and Kinross District.

76 CRAIG PHADRIG, FORT, INVERNESS

1st millennium BC and 6-7th centuries AD.

NH 640452. About 2.5 km W of Inverness. A862 over canal, left at roundabout (King Brude Road), 3rd right (Leachkin Road), 3rd right (Leachkin Brae), shortly track on right into carpark for Craigphadrig Forest. Steep path to fort on top of hill.

Forestry Commission

The fort occupies the summit of a prominent wooded hill. It has two more or less concentric ramparts enclosing a grass-grown subrectangular area some 80 m long. The fort and its ramparts are clear of trees, and there are glimpses of the originally extensive views over Inverness and the Beauly Firth.

Dun-da-Lamh fort

Craig Phadrig

The fort occupies the summit of a ridge standing high above Strath Peffer with steep slopes to north and south but a gentler approach at the west end where the ridge continues. It is covered in grass which is a pleasant change from the tough heather of so many Highland forts.

The fort is subrectangular in plan, and its stone rampart is heavily vitrified. Great masses of vitrified rock outcrop along the south rampart in particular, where in places stones can be seen to have partly melted, started to run out like thick treacle, and then solidified again. An unusual feature of this fort is that lines of vitrified rampart lead out east and west from either end. These may have been ramparts with breastworks each side, built to prevent attack along the narrow spine of the ridge. There are traces of an outer rampart round part of the circuit. Modern scientific tests (thermo-luminescence dating) of the vitrified stone suggest the main rampart may belong to the bronze age, but more evidence is needed. The plan of the fort is confused by three later ditches which cut across the fort from side to side: one ditch cuts across the vitrified wall east of the fort, one across the fort itself and the other across the western wall, each with a bank on its west side. These were trenches excavated by the engineer John Williams in the 1770s as part of an early attempt to understand vitrified forts. He suggested that there was a gap between the main rampart and the end walls, so that they could be cut off if necessary by removing a drawbridge.

Excavation in 1971 showed that both ramparts had been constructed of timberlaced stonework and subsequently burnt, and contained large masses of vitrified material. The inner rampart is particularly massive, and good examples of vitrification can be seen under the roots of a pine tree at the north end. There is a steep slope down to the outer rampart which is a slighter affair. No original entrances can be identified. Radiocarbon dates from the ramparts suggest they were built in the 5th or 4th centuries BC.

A small excavation in the interior produced unexpected evidence for recoccupation of the fort in the 6th or 7th centuries AD. The finds included a few small scraps of imported pottery, and a clay mould for casting a metal fitting for a hanging-bowl (in NMS, replica in Inverness Museum). There is some suggestion that the ramparts were refurbished at this time. An historical king of the Picts, Bridei son of Maelchon who ruled around AD 555 to 584, had a royal house near the river Ness where he was visited by St Columba. The description would fit Craig Phadrig well, though other sites such as Inverness Castle Hill are also possible.

77 KNOCK FARRIL, FORT, ROSS AND CROMARTY

Late 2nd or 1st millennium BC.

NH 504585. West of Dingwall. Approach from S on A835 via Maryburgh and Ussie to Knock Farril crofts, then road and track to W end of hill.

Knock Farril

(Right)

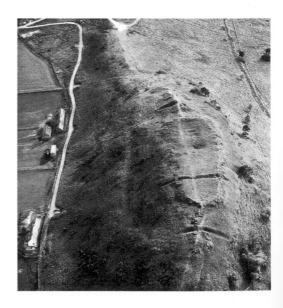

Inside the fort, a pond in the western half was probably a rock-cut cistern to hold rain water. West of the pond are the foundations of two more recent structures.

78 AN DUN, DUN, GAIRLOCH, ROSS AND CROMARTY

Later 1st millennium BC/early 1st millennium AD.

NG 802753. On headland S of Gairloch. Park by golfcourse beside A832, walk S along beach to dun.

A small narrow promontory with steep sides projects abruptly into the sea from the headland of An Ard, providing splendid natural defences. A narrow rocky path gives access from the shore to the small stone-walled dun which occupies the first part of the promontory. The farther end is cut off by a rocky chasm with the sea flowing through it.

The dun comprises two enclosures. The inner enclosure occupies the highest part of the promontory, making use of the steep slopes either side. On the landward side, which was most vulnerable to attack, there is an outer wall, probably contemporary, providing both an outer line of defence and a second small enclosed area. There is hardly room for more than one hut in either enclosure. The stone walls are largely overgrown with grass, but parts of the wall-faces are visible, particularly the inner face of the inner enclosure and the outer face of the outwork wall on the landward side. The position of the entrance is not known.

79 DUN LAGAIDH, FORT AND DUN, ROSS AND CROMARTY

Fort, 1st millennium BC; dun, early centuries AD.

NH 142913. Turn off A835 about 12 km S of Ullapool on minor road which follows W side of Loch Broom to Loggie; continue by track to fort.

Three successive fortifications have been built on a hogback ridge on the western shore of Loch Broom: a vitrified fort, a dun and a medieval castle. They have been partly excavated and the finds are in the Hunterian Museum, University of Glasgow.

On the highest part of the ridge are the tumbled remains of a small dun; piles of loose stones round the dun have fallen from the walls, but the outlines of the wall-faces can be distinguished. West of the dun is a pile of stones cleared from the interior and retained by a modern wall, not to be confused with the wall of the dun. The entrance to the dun was on the east but is now blocked, as is a chamber which opened off it to the north in the thickness of the wall. On the west a doorway gives onto a little lobby and a stair leading upwards within the wall. There is some question as to whether this small round structure is a dun or a broch, but the fact that the wall is thin in relation to the overall diameter suggests that it is more likely to have been a dun.

The dun was not the first defence on the site but overlay an earlier fort occupying the whole west end of the hill, an area of some 90 m by 35 m. Its western end was defended by a massive stone rampart, now vitrified: good patches of vitrification can be seen at the western corner, and part of the outer wall-face on the northwest. There are no traces of ramparts on the precipitous north and south sides of the hill. Another stretch of rampart crossed the hill under the east end of the dun, with an entrance in the middle, and east of this there was a narrower outer wall, now obscured by later banks and ditches with trees growing on them. A rushy hollow within the fort may be the site of a well or cistern.

The third fortification on the hill was a small and extremely simple medieval castle, probably built in the 12th century AD. The ruins of the dun were

An Dun, Gairloch

(Left)

Dun Lagaidh

**Dun Lagaidh,
stairs in dun**

Dun Canna (Right)

80 DUN CANNA, FORT, ROSS AND CROMARTY

Later 1st millennium BC/early 1st millennium AD.

NC 111008. On A835 about 10 km N of Ullapool, park in layby, and walk down road to Blughasary. At end of road, continue N on path by river, cross river three times, about 300 m after third crossing take track on right to its end at dun. (About 60 mins.)

This stone-walled fort is built on a promontory projecting into the sea at the north end of a long sandy beach, and the walls for the most part follow the high rocky cliffs of the promontory. There are two enclosures, both defended by thick stone walls now badly collapsed. The inner enclosure at the end of the promontory is long and narrow, and the outer enclosure is larger and has a thicker wall. Parts of the original wall-faces may be distinguished amid the mass of tumble.

The modern path across the outer wall passes the ruin of a recent stone house built into the fallen wall. This is not the line of the original entrance, which was on the steep northeast side of the promontory where the ends of the wall overlapped to form a short entrance passage, now overgrown with heather. This would have been provided with wooden gates. The approach to the entrance was thus along the side of the hill, where it would have been more difficult to rush the gate. The position of the entrance to the inner enclosure is unknown.

Back near Blughasary, on the south side of the River Runie and some 100 m west of the bridge is a small mill of the 18th or 19th century AD, with the two millstones still lying in the ruins.

cleared out to serve as a motte tower, while the western end of the hill, the old fort area, formed the bailey. Short stretches of mortared wall, much narrower than the fort rampart, run north and south from the dun to the edges of the hill.

Abandoned crofthouses from the village of Newton Loggie can be seen south of the hill, and cultivation ridges and clearance cairns west of it.

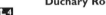

81 DUCHARY ROCK, FORT, SUTHERLAND

1st millennium BC.

NC 850048. Leave A9 about 2.5 km S of Brora on any of three side roads to Doll, which join into one. Park before ford, and take track W opposite house 'Tigh na Rosa'. Follow track, keeping right at fork, through wood into open moorland, then uphill until fort is reached on the right. (About 40 mins.)

A finely sited fort with an impressive, though tumbled, stone rampart, set high up in open moorland with views to the north and out to sea. The fort occupies a flat-topped ridge some 300 m long, with steep precipices on either side. The easier approaches at the north and south ends are each defended by a single stone wall, originally nearly 4 m thick but now tumbled. Large blocks and slabs as well as smaller ones were used in the construction of both ramparts. These have unfortunately been considerably disturbed by shepherds making sheep shelters among the tumbled stone. The shorter southeast rampart makes some use of natural rock outcrops in its layout. There is a narrow entrance near the centre, unusual in that it is only 1.3 m wide. Perhaps it was a postern gate which could admit people but not carts or sledges.

The longer northern rampart cuts off the ridge from the hills behind. Parts of the outer face of this rampart are exposed among the general tumble. About the centre of the rampart is an entrance nearly 5 m wide, now partly blocked with fallen stones. Some very large stone slabs line the entrance passage, and the wall-face east of the entrance is constructed of particularly massive blocks. There are some straight building-joints crossing the line of the wall; it has been suggested that these represent further blocked entrances, but it seems more likely that they are simply a local building trait, also to be seen in the apparently unfinished fort at Cnoc an Duin, Ross and Cromarty (NH 696768).

At its east end the northern rampart runs into a well defined precipice. To the west, it continues as a slighter feature some way along the west side of the fort where the precipice is less pronounced.

Duchary Rock

82 BEN FREICEADAIN, CAITHNESS

1st millennium BC.

ND 059558. About 13 km SW of Reay. B870 and minor road to Dorrery. Stop opposite hill (not ridge with wireless mast, but hill north of it) and walk over moorland. (40 mins. to fort)

An extensive fort known as Buaile Oscar occupies the plateau-like summit of the hill. The steep slopes on the north and east sides had no artificial defences, but a substantial rampart, now overgrown, encloses the rest of the hill. Most unusually, this rampart is set partway down the hill, taking advantage of a slight natural terrace. In

Ben Freiceadain, aerial view

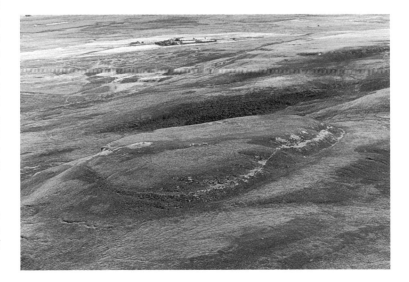

places, cliff-like exposures of flagstone immediately behind the rampart seem to have been quarried for building material, while elsewhere quarry pits have been dug to the rear. The only visible entrance is to the north-east, where one stone slab still lines the back of the rampart.

Within the fort is a grass-grown mound, the remains of a neolithic chambered cairn. On the low ground between the fort and the road there are a number of other structures, ranging from abandoned crofthouses to neolithic and bronze-age cairns; several are indicated on the OS map.

83 DUN TELVE, BROCH, GLENELG, WEST INVERNESS -SHIRE

Late 1st millennium BC/Early 1st millennium AD. (Photograph p.132)

NG 829172. Minor road from Shiel Bridge through Glenelg; about 500 m S of Glenelg turn E into Glen Beag. Broch beside road in Glen Beag.

Historic Scotland.

This spectacular broch stands on the valley floor near the river, a position offering no apparent defensive advantages. About one third of the wall still stands to a height of some 10.10 m, and only the broch of Mousa in Shetland is better preserved.

Dun Telve broch, the entrance

The outer wall of the broch tapers inwards as it goes up in the characteristic 'cooling-tower' profile. The base of the wall is largely solid, but above this there are still four galleries and part of a fifth. The double wall construction, bonded together by slabs forming the ceiling of one gallery and the floor of the next, can be seen in the broken ends of the wall. The entrance has one door check and a good bar-hole. A cell opens off the entrance passage to the right. Inside to the left is a doorway leading to a cell with corbelled roof on the left, and a stairway on the right, with seventeen steps remaining. The rest of the stair is lost for it runs into the fallen part of the wall, but it may well have led to a passage or landing, as at Dun Troddan (no. 84) with a door onto the upper floor, before continuing up to the wallhead.

This broch has two scarcement ledges, and the upper one some 8.90 m above the floor is a unique survival, not found anywhere else. It possibly supported a conical thatched roof completely covering the interior.

The first gallery, level with the floor carried on the first scarcement ledge, has carefully finished walls and was obviously used, if only for storage, but the walls of the other, narrower galleries are extremely rough with sharp stones sticking out. Above the entrance door a series of apertures or voids in the inner wall are carried up to the present top of the wall. This was, at least in part, a design to lessen the weight on the lintel over the door. Another set of voids starts high in the wall and there was originally a third set above the stair door. These puzzling voids did not give access to the galleries, for they are crossed by many lintels with only narrow gaps between, but they would have admitted air and may have helped to ventilate the galleries and stop them getting damp and smelly. Among the objects found in the broch when it was cleared out in 1914 were three stone lamps, used with oil and a floating wick, several rotary quernstones and some spindle whorls.

Outside the door to the broch are further structures built of very large blocks, including an outer entrance with passages leading off right and left round the broch. This may be part of an outer wall which once surrounded the whole broch, forming an enclosure with houses in it. However the rectangular structure with very thick walls to the left of the entrance could be considerably later than the broch and not necessarily of the same date as the outer entrance.

---

84 DUN TRODDAN, BROCH, GLENELG, WEST INVERNESS-SHIRE

Late 1st millennium BC/early 1st millennium AD.

NG 833172. Dun Troddan is 500 m along the road E of Dun Telve (no. 83).

Historic Scotland.

Dun Troddan is set on a terrace on the side of a hill, looking down on its neighbour Dun Telve from a little further up the glen. About one-third of its wall still stands to a height of some 7.6 m, making it the third best preserved broch after Mousa and Dun Telve, and in its structural details it is very like Dun Telve.

From the entrance with its door checks a long cell, now only partly roofed, leads off to the left. Inside the broch a doorway opens to a cell on the left, with its corbelled roof intact, and to a stair on the

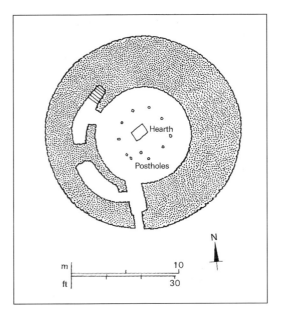

Dun Troddan broch plan

right. Nine steps lead up to a level passage running round inside the wall for some 5.50 m; after this the stair rose again, though only one step of the second flight has survived. It is probable that here, as at Totaig (no. 85), a doorway gave access from the passage onto the floor supported on the scarcement, but at Dun Troddan this part of the wall has fallen and no trace of such a door remains. Like Dun Telve, Dun Troddan has a series of voids over the door to the stairs and another set high up in the wall. Three galleries survive in the wall of which only the lowest, at first-floor level, would have been used by the inhabitants. The hollow walls and the slabs forming the galleries can be seen clearly in the broken ends of the walls. A good idea of the blank and impregnable appearance of an intact broch can be got by looking at the highest part of the wall from outside.

Dun Troddan was cleared out by the then Office of Works over a number of years, and its floor excavated, though not to modern standards, in 1920. A ring of postholes were found which would have held wooden posts to support the upper floor, and a central stone hearth, which had been rebuilt several times. Later hearths were built above a layer of rubble and seem to show continued use of the structure as a dwelling after the upper part of the tower had fallen. Part of a rotary quern can still be seen in the paving of the lowest hearth. Among the few objects found in the broch were stone spindle whorls and a tiny yellow glass bead.

Dun Troddan broch, mural galleries (Left)

It is unusual to find brochs so close together as Dun Troddan and Dun Telve, but a few other instances are known such as Keiss (see no. 44).

Dun Troddan broch

85 CAISTEAL GRUGAIG, BROCH, TOTAIG, WEST INVERNESS-SHIRE

Late 1st millennium BC/early 1st millennium AD.

NG 866250. Minor road from Shiel Bridge along shore of Loch Duich to Totaig; then on foot by track and path through forestry plantation to broch.

Forestry Commission.

The broch stands on the hillside overlooking the junction of Loch Alsh, Loch Duich and Loch Long, a view now partially obscured by forestry plantations. It is built of substantial stones giving a particularly solid appearance, and much of the outside wall stands clear of debris.

Caisteal Grugaig broch
(Below and Right)

The interior was cleared out in 1899, so many structural features are visible despite its ruined state. The floor inside is the natural surface of a rocky knoll and is very irregular, dropping some 1.50 m from southwest to northeast. The entrance is at the lowest point, and has a fine triangular lintel, one set of door checks, a bar-hole to the right and a guard chamber, now blocked, on the left. Further round the wall on the inside a small doorway opens into a round cell with high corbelled roof. Next to this, a larger doorway leads to a short flight of stairs, rising to a level passage, now partly blocked by tumble. From this passage a doorway opens onto the scarcement ledge, while beyond it the stairs once continued upwards. The high doorway is an interesting feature, probably once common in many brochs, but not often preserved, though there is another at Rhiroy (no. 86). It led out onto a wooden floor supported by the scarcement ledge, here less than a metre above the ground. On the opposite side of the broch yet another door opened into two long cells running right and left within the wall, both now blocked by tumble, but partly visible amid the rubble of the walls. Such long cells may have been used, like souterrains, as cool stores.

On the way back, look for bait holes in the rocks. These are east of the Totaig slipway, at the first corner in the road, on rocks under a tree above the shore. They were used for crag fishing, when shellfish such as limpets were pounded up in the

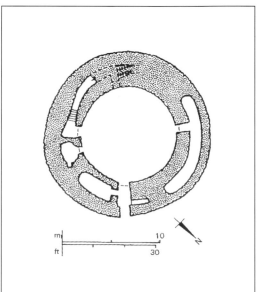

holes and thrown into the water to attract fish into frame nets.

features in the wall have been blocked up to preserve them. A scarcement ledge can be seen in the highest part of the wall. It is only 1.20 m above ground level on the uphill side, though as the floor sloped down it would have been some 2.50 m above the floor on the other side. Inside the broch, some 4 m left of the entrance is a blocked doorway leading to a chamber in the wall on the left, and a stairway going up on the right (the low 'lintel' to this door is only part of the modern blocking). From a landing on the stair a door led out onto a wooden floor above the central court, supported on the scarcement ledge. Beyond this is the stairs went up again. In the highest part of the wall are the remains of a narrow gallery with a few lintel slabs still in position.

Excavation inside the broch showed there had been a central hearth and a ring of posts to support the upper floor. A flat rotary quern was found in one posthole (this, and the few other finds are in the Hunterian Museum, University of Glasgow). Two other postholes by the entrance may have held an inner door. Various phases of reuse after the broch had been partly dismantled were identified.

Caisteal Grugaig, the entrance (Left)

The excavator has suggested that this broch did not have a hollow wall all round, but had a straight stretch of much thinner, solid wall above the precipice and should therefore be called a 'semi-broch'. Since this part of the wall is missing one cannot be too sure of its structure, but there would have been room to build a wide wall all round if about 1.50 m of cliff has fallen away since the iron age.

86 RHIROY, BROCH, ROSS AND CROMARTY

Late 1st millennium BC/early 1st millennium AD.

NH 149900. On SW side of Loch Broom. Leave A835 12 km S of Ullapool by side road leading N beside Loch Broom through Rhiroy to village sign 'Loggie'; the broch is then uphill on the left.

The broch stands on an open hillside on the edge of a small precipice. On the uphill side it is still some 3.50 m high; on the lower side it has collapsed to its foundations. The approach is from the south, where the rectangular walls of a modern sheep pen and dip are built against the broch. Here the fallen stone has been cleared from the broch walls, though piles of rubble remain elsewhere (the large stone piles beside the sheep dip are excavation dumps).

The entrance, now infilled, was through the low part of the wall on the southeast. The inside of the broch has been cleared of stone, but most of the

87 CLACHTOLL, BROCH, SUTHERLAND

Late 1st millennium BC/early 1st millennium AD.

NC 036278. B869 from Lochinver to Clachtoll. Stop near cemetery just N of Clachtoll, walk to beach, then 400 m SW along shore to broch.

The broch is built on a rocky knoll right on the edge of the sea and still looks impressive, though part of the wall has now fallen over the low cliff. The broch has not been cleared out and the interior is full of stones which hide most of the inner wall-face, but much of the outer wall can be seen.

On the east side there is an outwork, a stone wall running obliquely some 5 m-18 m from the broch, with an entrance passage through it. This outer wall goes round the south side of the broch and runs out to the cliff at each end. Between the outer wall and the broch there is now a confused mass of rubble, but originally there would have been stone huts with a path between them leading to the broch entrance. The inner end of this path seems to have been a lined and roofed passage, as at Carn Liath (no. 90), but modern walls have been built in this area which confuse the ancient features.

Dun na Maigh broch (Right)

Clachtoll broch

The broch entrance has a massive triangular lintel diverting the weight of the wall above. The entrance passage is partly filled with rubble, but it is possible to crawl in and see first the door checks with a bar-hole beyond on the right, and then openings to small chambers on either side. Opposite the entrance, on the other side of the broch, the remains of a gallery can be traced in the wall.

Dun na Maigh broch, the stairs (Right)

88 DUN NA MAIGH, BROCH, SUTHERLAND

Late 1st millennium BC/early 1st millennium AD.

NC 552530. On hill at S end of the Kyle of Tongue. Park on hard standing below rock face, and follow path uphill to broch.

Dun na Maigh is built on a rocky knoll at the north end of a ridge overlooking the Kyle of Tongue, with a fine view over the estuary and the hills either side.

On the west side the ridge is precipitous, but to the north and south the slopes are less steep and the remains of an outer defensive wall can be seen.

The broch has collapsed, but much of the remaining wall stands clear of the surrounding tumble, and several characteristic features can be seen. The entrance is on the east, with some lintels still in place. There are two sets of door checks for two wooden doors, and the door to a blocked cell between them on the right, but the fallen stone in the entrance passage has not been cleared down to floor level. Inside, again on the right, is a door leading to the remains of a cell in the wall on the left, and a stair on the right. One lintel remains in place at the top of the stair. Opposite the stair there seems to be a doorway to some other feature, now blocked. A short stretch of modern wall has been built near the stair.

89 DUN DORNAIGIL, BROCH, SUTHERLAND

Late 1st millennium BC/early 1st millennium AD.

NC 457450. On minor road about 6 km S of Loch Hope.

Historic Scotland.

This broch, often known as Dun Dornadilla, stands beside the road on a low terrace above the valley of the Strathmore river. From the outside it is very impressive, as a section of the wall over the entrance still stands some 6.7 m high, and all the fallen stone has been cleared away. Only the outer skin of this piece of wall survives, for the inner wall has fallen away and has been replaced by a modern buttress. Three galleries were seen within the wall in the 18th century. Apart from the high section, the wall has collapsed almost to floor level. Over the blocked entrance is a fine triangular lintel like those at Clachtoll (no. 87) and Totaig (no. 85); the door seems very low, but this is because it is partly blocked up. There is no access to the rubble filled interior, but one can appreciate the fine masonry and the curious way in which the broch is sited on the edge of the terrace, so that the foundations have had to be built up considerably on the downstream side.

90 CARN LIATH, BROCH, SUTHERLAND

Late 1st millennium BC/1st millennium AD.

NC 870013. Beside the A9, 4 km N of Golspie. Carpark and signpost.

Historic Scotland.

The broch is built on the edge of a terrace looking out over a flat coastal strip to the sea. The knoll on which the broch stands may have been artificially steepened in places and is defended by a stone wall round its edge. Within this, and sometimes into this, a series of houses have been built and rebuilt, some perhaps contemporary with the broch, others certainly later. (The site was excavated in the late 19th century and the records are inadequate.)

Carn Liath broch

The broch entrance is on the east and is approached by a stone-walled passage leading from the outer wall. This passage was once lintelled over and has checks for a wooden door. The broch entrance has its own set of door checks, here vertical slabs set at right angles to the passage wall, and a bar-hole, and beyond these a door to a chamber on the right. Inside the broch a doorway opposite the entrance opens onto the stairs, which can be climbed to the present top of the wall. This has been grassed over for its protection. A thick secondary facing, now of irregular height, hides much of the inner wall-face; it is the wall of a house constructed out of the broch remains after the highest part of the wall had fallen. In the top of the original wall-face there are traces of a scarcement ledge. Little can be seen of the galleries but there are some traces high up near the entrance.

Sunk in the floor of the broch were three curious round 'chambers', apparently not water cisterns, perhaps storeholes, now filled in. Evidence for the manufacture of beads, rings and bangles from the local shale was found, also iron slag from iron-working. There are finds from the broch in Dunrobin Castle Museum.

91 DUNBEATH, BROCH, CAITHNESS

Late 1st millennium BC/late 1st millennium AD.

ND 155304. Start in Dunbeath at carpark/picnic place by mill below bridges, and follow path beside Dunbeath water for 800 m (15 minutes).

Dunbeath broch

Just before the broch is reached, the path crosses a minor burn on a small suspension bridge with iron columns cast at the Ness Iron Works, Inverness. Leave the path and climb a grassy slope to find the broch on a knoll overlooking the Dunbeath Water, set in a grove of trees surrounded by a modern wall. The broch was excavated in 1866 but then decayed until in 1990 it was cleared out and consolidated.

The wall is only a metre or so high at the entrance, but rises to some 4 m at the far side. A small chamber opens from the entrance passage between two sets of door checks, and a wooden draw-bar for one door may have been operated from here. On the far side of the broch there is an entrance to a larger chamber opening out either side of the door. The way such chambers were roofed can be well seen, the sides being gradually corbelled in until the remaining space could be bridged with slabs (which often formed the floor of the gallery above). There is also a scarcement ledge to support a wooden floor some 2 m up. These are the only features to survive, and the staircase to the wallhead must have been reached by an opening in the wall above ground level, as at Rhiroy (no. 86) and Yarrows (no. 105). Steps would have led up to

the opening. Much of the stone from this broch and any outworks has been robbed for later walls and buildings in the strath.

Beyond the broch the path continues up a most attractive wooded strath. A leaflet from Dunbeath Heritage Centre (off the A 9, on the old road southeast of the new bridge; exhibition and audio-visual programme) describes a trail along the strath through hazel, birch, rowan and bird-cherry woodland, passing various archaeological sites. Out and back, this trail is some 13 km (8 miles) long and would take most of a day; at the end the trail leaves the path and involves a scramble up a hill. At the far end, there are two round chambered cairns and a long horned cairn at Loedebest, and a standing stone and a stone quarry where such slabs may have been obtained on Cnoc na Maranaich, all of which can be reached more easily by a back road from Dunbeath.

A siege of Dunbeath in AD 680 is recorded in the Annals of Ulster. The broch would then have been a collapsed mound of stones. The most likely place for an important 7th-century settlement is the headland occupied by Dunbeath Castle (which can just be glimpsed from the A 9); its situation may be compared with dark-age sites at Burghead (Moray) and Castle Rock, Dunottar (Kincardine).

92* NYBSTER, BROCH, CAITHNESS

Late 1st millennium BC/early 1st millennium AD.

ND 370361. On the A9 at Auckengill, just S of the Northlands Viking Centre, take turning signed to Harbour Broch. From carpark follow fenced path to broch.

The broch here is only a low circular wall, but the interest lies in the associated structures found in the excavations by Sir Francis Tress Barry of Keiss Castle at the end of the last century. Unfortunately these structures have since decayed and are overgrown with long grass in summer. Nevertheless, some of the plan can be made out. The broch is built on a high rocky headland between two inlets, defended by a stout rampart faced with stone walls and a large curved ditch, only partly excavated. The entrance through the rampart has checks for two wooden doors, and there are the remains of stairs inside leading from ground level to the wall top. (Stone slabs bridging some of the holes on the site are modern, put there to assist visitors.) The entrance to the broch is round the far side. This was a solid-based broch, the entrance to the stair and any galleries being higher in the wall and now lost. There are a few partition slabs and a stone tank set in the broch floor.

All the rest of the headland is covered with the remains of buildings which seem mostly to be a contemporary settlement, in contrast to Forse Wag (no. 94) and Yarrows (no. 105) where the outbuildings are clearly later. These are now rather a jumble of ruins, with a large mound among them which is the excavator's spoil dump.

On the cliff near the broch is a strange monument known as Mervyn's Tower, built of rough stones and adorned with a number of grotesque heads. This was erected to Tress Barry by John Nicolson, the local farmer and sculptor who helped with his excavations. There are more sculptures in the garden of Nicolson's house, between the carpark and the museum. Back at the carpark is a picnic place, and a path down to the tiny harbour. More information about the broch and other local sites, with an excellent video 'Caves, Cairns and Castles', can be found in the Northlands Viking Centre in Auckengill.

Nybster broch

---

93 KILPHEDIR, BROCH, HUT CIRCLES AND SOUTERRAIN, SUTHERLAND

Later 1st millennium BC/early 1st millennium AD.

NC 994189 (broch). In Strath of Kildonan. A897 to bridge over Kilphedir burn, 6.5 km from Helmsdale; park in quarry, then sheep track up hill.

The broch is on the hill east of the burn but cannot be seen from the road by the bridge. A sheep track just east of the bridge leads up the hill, bearing slightly right, and passes through a deserted crofting settlement under the line of the electricity poles; there are the foundations of a longhouse, and some smaller buildings and a kiln barn. From the first skyline the broch is visible on the hillside above, some 15 or 20 minutes walk from the road.

Nybster broch, monument (Left)

The broch is set on a prominent knoll with good views up and down the valley. It is ruinous, and appears as a great mass of rubble spilling down the hill, but it has a particularly impressive set of outer defences, now all covered with heather so that the stone walls look like banks. There are terraces east and west of the broch defended by an inner rampart, a deep ditch and a stout outer rampart. At the west end, the entrance is protected by an extra short stretch of rampart.

Just below the broch is a good path along the side of the hill; follow it west to find three hut circles on the edge of the ravine above the burn (NC 991190). One hut circle has much thicker walls than the other two, and this one has a souterrain leading out of it beneath its wall. The far end has been broken into, so light comes in, but it may be full of water and gumboots are needed. A muddy hole, originally provided with steps, drops down into the narrow souterrain passage; the latter has drystone walls and a lintelled roof and is about 9.50 m long.

There are more hut circles up the burn and on the west bank. Some of the latter were excavated in the 1960s, and shown to have interior posts that supported their thatched roofs, while radiocarbon dates from two huts suggest they were occupied in the last few centuries BC. A number of clearance cairns round these and other hut circles are probably of the same date and show that some patches of ground were cultivated. Many other hut circles can be seen on the hill slopes along the north

Forse Wag, broch entrance from within (Right)

Kilphedir broch

side of the Strath of Kildonan, some indicated on the OS map, and at least six other souterrains have been found, three still attached to hut circles. Part of one at Suisgill (NC 897250) is close to the east side of the road; only the far end survives, with lintelled roof and a curved end-wall, in which is a small built-in recess or cupboard.

94 FORSE WAG, BROCH AND SETTLEMENT

Later 1st millennium BC/early 1st millennium AD.

ND 204352. Take A 895 N from Latheron, after 2 km park in first marked layby; walk E along gated track to gate in stone wall on right, through gate and down hill to site.

Forse Wag now appears as a great spread of stones with structures emerging out of the tumble. It was partially and rather clumsily excavated between 1939 and 1948. The settlement began as a group of stone huts that were replaced by a broch, which was in turn robbed to build a series of pillared houses. 'Wag' is the local name for these houses and may derive from a Gaelic word meaning 'little cave'.

On the north is the circular wall of the broch, with its entrance flanked by a stair and a gallery in the wall. Most of the interior of the broch and its south wall were destroyed when a long rectangular house was built over it. Another long house stands west of the broch. This is 12 m long and has the remains of two rows of upright, pillar-like stones inside which

supported the roof. Stone lintels crossed from wall to pillar, and between pillars, so that the areas between could easily be roofed with flagstones, perhaps then covered with turf. One lintel is still in position. There is a long entrance passage with door checks, and two side entrances lead off to other rooms or houses, one of which is round and has one stone pillar still standing. Beyond is a complex series of buildings, some early, only partly excavated. The L-shaped structure west of the site is the excavator's stone dump.

In the fields round Forse Wag a number of other structures can be found, including hut circles to the west. Looking south, a noticeable green hump by an old stream bed is the grassed-over remains of three burnt mounds, while over to the northeast a large grassy mound in the distance is an unexcavated broch. Most of the stone field walls round the broch belong to a more recent, though pre-improvement, farming settlement. Traces of cultivation strips can be seen within the walls.

95 THE ORD, HUT CIRCLES AND CHAMBERED CAIRNS, LAIRG, SUTHERLAND

Hut circles, 1st millennium BC; chambered cairns, 4th-3rd millennia BC.

NC 5705. From Lairg take A839 across river, turn right and follow signs to Ferrycroft Countryside Centre, carpark and start of marked Archaeological Trail. Leaflets from centre.

The Ord is a low hill at the south end of Loch Shin. Prehistoric settlers here had ready access to both cultivable and grazing land, and salmon in the river for nine months of the year. There are remains of occupation from many different periods here: two neolithic chambered cairns, several bronze-age burial cairns, a large number of bronze-age or iron-age hut circles, and post-medieval enclosures and ploughed fields.

The trail joins a track which leads uphill towards the television mast where a large cairn of bare stones stands near the top of the hill. This chambered cairn was excavated in 1967, and the chamber, antechamber and passage have been refilled, but some of the passage and its lintels are visible. The cairn is about 27 m in diameter with a shallow forecourt. Cremation burials, sherds of pottery and flint flakes were found in the chamber, while bones from earlier burials may have decayed. When the tomb was blocked a stone platform with a boulder kerb, now grassgrown, was built round it. Above the collapsed corbels of the chamber a later cremation burial was found. On the highest part of the hill are the remains of another chambered cairn, of which only the large slabs in the chamber and passage remain, with mere vestiges of cairn material.

The Ord, chambered cairns

The Ord, Lairg, plan

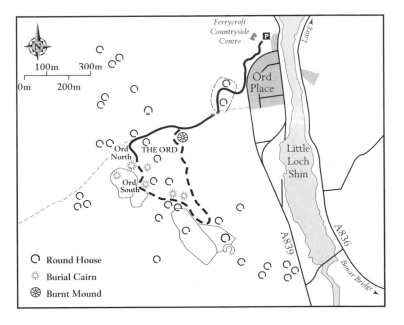

Scattered across the hill are a number of hut circles. Some 23 or so have been recorded, and it should be possible to locate at least 15 with the aid of the sketch plan given here. They may be of various dates and built and rebuilt over many centuries. There are also a large number of clearance cairns of unknown date dotted around this area, and a few traces of what may be prehistoric field walls. The cairns are particularly noticeable each side of the track before the path diverges from it. The hut circles are overgrown, but most make a noticeable circle in the heather. Occasionally the facing stones in the wall, or the entrance gap, usually on the southern side, can be seen. Just south of the chambered cairn on the very top of the hill is a bronze-age round cairn with much of its kerb traceable. Immediately east of this is a hut circle in grass and so easier to see.

Other features on The Ord include the overgrown stone walls of more recent enclosures, within which and also outwith which the ridge and furrow of plough cultivation has been seen on air photographs and can be seen on the ground when the sun is low. Towards the south end of the area, with an enclosure wall crossing it and a recent fence intruding on its ditch is an enigmatic structure marked by two circles on the plan. This has been considered to be an unusual form of ditched ring cairn, but it consists of something very like a hut circle within a ditch and an outer bank, and it could be a fortified hut. There are a few similar sites in the Highlands, but none has yet been excavated.

There are more hut circles and clearance cairns between Lairg and Invershin on the slopes east of the A 836 as shown on the OS map; excavation has shown that these hut circles range in date from the 2nd millennium to the mid-1st millennium BC.

An audio-visual programme in the Ferrycroft Countryside Centre shows human impact on the landscape and archaeological sites.

96 LAID SOUTERRAIN, SUTHERLAND

1st millennium BC.

NC 428612. Beside A838 W of Loch Eriboll, about 600 m N of turning to Portnancon and 100 m N of turning to Port Camul. Torch and gumboots needed.

The entrance to the souterrain is marked by two small stone cairns on the east verge, but these are hidden by bracken in summer. Opposite, west of the road, is a prominent rock, and hard ground on which to park north of the burn. The souterrain once led out of a hut circle, but this has been destroyed in road works. It is quite typical of the small souterrains found in the northern Highlands: a flight of twelve stone steps leads steeply downwards into the souterrain proper, which is a curved passage some 8.5 m long and up to 1.65 m high and 1.5 m wide. The drystone walls are built roughly into courses with larger boulders at the bottom and the far end rounded off, the roof is lintelled over the large slabs and the floor is of earth. Unfortunately altered drainage patterns, perhaps to do with road works, mean the souterrain is now usually flooded with water too deep for gumboots, but it is still possible to go down the steps and look along with a torch. Originally this would have been a perfectly dry storage cellar for the house above.

Laid Souterrain

CAIRNS AND STANDING STONES

**Clava cairns,
Inverness-shire**

Surviving traces of bronze-age and neolithic man in the Highlands are mostly their burial places, ceremonial sites or enigmatic standing stones.

Standing Stones

There are few examples of free-standing stone circles and they are not particularly impressive. One large stone circle at Guidebest, Caithness (ND 180351) is much obscured by vegetation. Related to stone circles is the most unusual and impressive U-shaped stone setting at Achavanich, Caithness (no. 97). Some fine stone circles can also be seen round Clava tombs (nos 99, 100).

Multiple rows of small stones, set parallel or in slightly spreading fan shapes, are unique to Caithness and eastern Sutherland: eg Mid Clyth (no. 98), Yarrows (no. 105), Garrywhin (no. 103). Being so small, they are easily damaged and others may have been completely destroyed by agriculture. Some settings seem to focus on early bronze-age cairns on top of low hills. Professor Thom has argued that the fan-shaped settings, together with observations of the moon, were used to calculate the moon's movements, which are complex and involve an 18.6 year cycle as well as the four week one. While these movements would have been important to early man, the calculations suggested are very complicated and there is no proof that this is what the rows were intended for, nor is it clear that they were ever set out with the precise accuracy needed. Some stone settings or cairns may incorporate alignments on sun- or moon-settings or risings or the like, but it is unlikely that these were worked out from the monuments in the first place.

Standing stones, on their own or in pairs, are found in the Highlands as elsewhere in Scotland. We do not know why they were erected. Among many examples are those beside the A 9 north of Ospisdale, Sutherland (NH 716894), at Yarrows (no. 105) and near the road at Rangag (ND 176448), both in Caithness. There is another at Edderton, Easter Ross (no. 72), reused by the Picts.

Camster long cairn, inside a chamber

Round Cairns

The typical bronze-age burial monument was a round mound, in the Highlands almost always a cairn of stones. The cairn, normally retained by a kerb of boulders, covered one or more cist graves, a small boxlike structure of stone slabs covered with a large capstone which held a 'crouched' burial, that is a body bent up to fit in the grave. A good example of such a cist can be seen at Embo (no. 102). Without excavation, bronze-age cairns cannot always be distinguished from earlier neolithic round cairns, but the latter, which covered burial chambers, were generally larger. Of many bronze-age cairns there are some at The Ord, (no. 95), and one on top of Warth Hill near Duncansby, Caithness (ND 371698), known to have covered two cists. Towards the end of the 2nd millennium BC, the practice of burying under cairns seems to have died out.

Cup-marks and cup-and-ring marks

Cup-marks and cup-and-ring marks are found on bronze-age and neolithic monuments such as the cairns at Clava (no. 99) and Corrimony (no. 100), and also on exposed rock surfaces or natural boulders, such as the group on a large boulder south of Lochan Hakel (NC 569526), at the end of the Kyle of Tongue. Why such hollows and grooves were carefully pecked into the stones is unknown.

Chambered Cairns

Most impressive of the early prehistoric monuments in this area are the chambered cairns, great mounds of pale grey stones standing out against the dark heather-covered hills and moors, within which were chambers built with large slabs of stone. The capstones sometimes weigh several tonnes, and, like standing stones, were manouvered into position by prehistoric Stronachs and Telfords using, not machinery, but ropes, wooden levers and muscle power. These cairns were used many times for burials, with earlier remains pushed to one side or even taken out. Objects such as pots, stone arrowheads, and bird and animal bones which may have been food offerings were put in the tombs too. Unfortunately many were excavated in the last century and the records were inadequate.

Clava, cup-and-rings on kerb-stone of cairn

So that the tomb could be reused, an entrance led out to the edge of the mound. Most cairns in the Highlands are passage graves, where the burial chamber is distinct from a narrow access passage. The chambers vary in shape, some divided into two or more compartments by vertical slabs. There is usually a curved recess or forecourt in the face of the cairn at the entrance, where ceremonies may have been performed at the time of burial or later. The shape of the mounds varies too; many are simply round, but some are long, and there are also short rectangular cairns. The long and short cairns often have forecourts at both ends with elongated corners, and they are known as horned cairns.

It has only recently been realised that these cairns often have a long history of use and development, rather like medieval parish churches; and they may equally reflect changing rites and changing beliefs over the centuries. The earliest monuments were probably simple chambers inside small round cairns. Some small cairns were later enlarged and long cairns added to them, sometimes with extra chambers. Outstanding examples are Camster Long and Camster Round (no. 101). Chambered cairns were probably used by neolithic people through most of the 4th and 3rd millennia BC, and sometimes early bronze-age pottery is found in the final blocking of their entrances or even with the last burials inside.

Clava Cairns

An unusual group of chambered cairns found in northern Inverness and Nairn Districts with a very few outliers have been called after the fine group of three cairns at Clava (no. 99). One feature of these cairns, unique in Scotland, is the circle of standing stones which invariably surrounds them. This, together with the fact that usually only one or two bodies seem to have been buried in the cairns, has led to them being attributed to the very late neolithic, though no secure dating evidence has been recovered. There are two kinds of cairn, passage graves with a central chamber that was once roofed, and ring cairns, with a closed chamber. The ring cairns are generally larger, and the chambers probably too wide for corbelled roofs, so they may have been filled up with earth and stones. Beside Clava and Corrimony (nos 99, 100), there is ready access to another more ruined example of a ring cairn in a housing estate on the north of Aviemore (NH 896134), near the fire station.

The passages of most chambered tombs in Scotland face roughly east or southeast, but the passages of Clava tombs face southwest. They seem to focus intentionally on the setting of the sun or moon at a particular time of year, in contrast to earlier interest in their risings. The two passages at Clava face midwinter sunset, while the passages at Corrimony faces the minor southern moonset. It has been suggested that these may have been symbolic alignments, intended for the dead as much as the living.

97 ACHAVANICH, STONE SETTING, CAITHNESS

2nd millennium BC.

ND 187417. South of Loch Stemster, close to the E side of a minor road from Lybster which joins the A895 at Achavanich.

A remarkable setting of large stones, arranged in an unusual way as a long U-shape with one open end. Some 36 slabs or stumps survive, but some stones are missing, and there may originally have been around 54. The average size of the stones is about 1.2 m to 1.5 m, and the tallest is nearly 2 m high. Many of the stones have been taller, but their tops have weathered and split off. The broad faces of the stones are set at right angles to the perimeter of the setting, in contrast to the practice at stone circles. Only one comparable monument is known, a ruinous U-shaped setting at Broubster, Caithness (ND 047608). The purpose of these settings is unknown, but their date is thought to be bronze age from their general similarity to stone circles.

Just outside the stones, close to their northeast corner and also along the east side, are some small slabs set on edge, which may be the remains of cist graves, perhaps added to the monument long after its initial purpose was forgotten. A short distance southeast of the stones, on a low hillock, are the remains of an earlier neolithic round cairn with traces of a central chamber.

Mid Clyth stone rows

98 MID CLYTH, STONE ROWS, CAITHNESS

2nd millennium BC.

ND 295384. Beside minor road at Mid Clyth, 14 km S of Wick; signposted off A9.

Historic Scotland.

The best preserved example of these settings of small stones, which are unique to Caithness and Sutherland, is appropriately known as the 'Hill o' Many Stanes'. The stone rows run down the

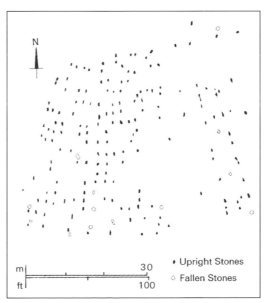

Achavanich stone setting (Left)

Mid Clyth stone rows plan

southern slope of a low hill. Around 200 stones are arranged in at least 22 rows running north and south, and fanning out slightly towards the south end. The small flat slabs are less than 1 m high, and wedged carefully upright with their broad faces in line with the rows. In 1871 around 250 stones were visible, and if the pattern was once complete there may have been over 600 stones originally. There seems to be a main fan pattern in the centre, with a separate fan on the west that is bent towards the north end, and a few stray slabs on the east. The rows are generally regarded as of bronze-age date, but this is more or less guesswork, as no stone rows have yet been excavated in Scotland.

Clava cairns

---

99 CLAVA CAIRNS, CHAMBERED CAIRNS, EAST INVERNESS-SHIRE

Later 3rd millennium BC.

NH 757444. About 8 km E of Inverness. Leave B9006 just E of Culloden Visitor Centre on minor road S, cross B891, and follow signposts to cairns.

Historic Scotland.

Three impressive round cairns, each surrounded by a ring of standing stones, are now fenced off within a wooded enclosure. They have given their name to a whole group of similar burial cairns found only in Inverness and Nairn Districts and in the Black Isle. The three cairns at Clava are set in a line, the central cairn being a ring cairn while the other two, known as the NE and SW cairns, are passage graves. All have been dug out at different times without proper record. The ring cairn at Clava was dug by modern methods in 1953, but owing to previous disturbances little was found except some scraps of cremated human bone. As seen today, the cairns are open in the centre, but they would not have been like this originally. The chamber walls of the passage-graves would have been corbelled inwards until the gap could be covered with one large capstone, the passages roofed with flat slabs and then the whole structure covered with more stones, so the cairns would have been 3.10 m high or more, while the ring cairn, which has no passage, and has a larger central space, is thought to have been filled, after burial, with earth and stones up to the top of the surrounding walls.

All the cairns have a graduated kerb with larger boulders near the entrance on the southwest side. The passages and chambers are lined with slabs, graduated in the chambers, and carrying upper courses of drystone walling. Round the cairns are set circles of standing stones, varying in number, but having taller or more impressive stones on the south or southwestern side. The modern road cuts between the SW cairn and part of its circle of stones.

Unique features of the three cairns at Clava are the low stone platforms surrounding the cairns, and the cobbled 'causeways' linking the platform round the ring cairn to three of the standing stones. Excavation in 1994 showed the causeways to be contemporary with the ring cairn and its stone circle. Several stones in the cairns have cup-marks made before the stones were set in place; the clearest are those in the NE cairn (nearest to the carpark) which has cup-marks on the innermost lefthand slab in the passage, while a fine cup-marked boulder with a ring round one cup is set in the kerb on the north of the same cairn.

Just west of the central cairn, against the fence, is a small ring of stones 3.7 m in diameter. This may be the surviving kerb of a late type of bronze-age cairn known as a kerb cairn, where a low cairn generally covered a cremation burial within the kerb.

100 CORRIMONY, CHAMBERED CAIRN, WEST INVERNESS-SHIRE

Later 3rd millennium BC.

NH 383303. In Glen Urquhart; minor road signposted to cairn off A831 from Drumnadrochit.

Historic Scotland.

This cairn is a well-preserved passage grave of Clava type. As usual, the cairn is retained by a ring of large boulders. A long passage leads through the cairn material into the small central chamber, and part of this passage is still roofed with the original stone slabs, whereas at Clava these are missing. The passage is only about one metre high, and so can only be entered crouched or crawling. The walls of the chamber have a basal ring of boulders, above which is drystone walling that oversails in its higher courses but is now open in the centre. The roof was originally corbelled inwards until the top could be closed with one large slab, and then covered with the stones of the cairn. The massive cup-marked slab now lying on top of the cairn was probably the capstone. The passage and chamber had a cobbled floor. In the 19th century the chamber had been dug out down to this floor and refilled. New excavations in 1953 discovered the stain of a single crouched body buried below the cobbled floor.

A ring of eleven standing stones surrounds the cairn, and though there seems to be space for a twelfth it may never have been erected. The four circle stones closest to the passage entrance have been re-erected at some time, and the two west of the entrance are not original, but made out of two lintels from the passage roof.

101 CAMSTER, CHAMBERED CAIRNS, CAITHNESS

4th and 3rd millennium BC.

ND 260440 (round) and 260442 (long). 8 km N of West Clyth, beside minor road to Watten; signposted from A9.

Historic Scotland.

Corrimony cairn
(Left)

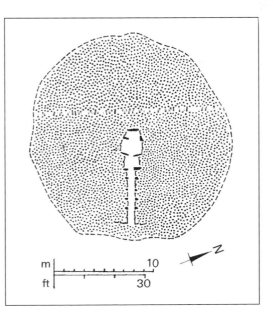

Camster round cairn

The Grey Cairns of Camster are two of the best-preserved neolithic chambered cairns in Britain. These huge mounds of grey stone, one round and one long, stand in open moorland close to the modern road. Careful restoration has made their chambers accessible to visitors, and rooflights make torches unneccessary. The passages are low, so be prepared to get your knees muddy.

Camster long cairn

Camster Round is almost intact and stands some 3.7 m high and 18 m in diameter, though some collapse round the sides has buried its original drystone kerb. A passage leads to the central chamber which still has its original corbelled roof, a rare survival. The walls are of drystone masonry and large vertical slabs divide the chamber into three parts. The cairn was excavated in the 19th century when burnt bones, pottery and flint tools were found in the chamber and the remains of several skeletons in the chamber and passage.

Camster long cairn, plan

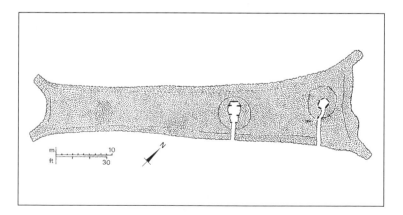

Camster Long is an enormous elongated mound of stones, 69.5 m long, with short horns at each end

defining forecourts. There are two burial chambers in the cairn, both at the north end with their entrance passages to the east. One is a simple, polygonal chamber formed of vertical slabs, the other is more elaborate and divided into three compartments by slabs. The original roofs had collapsed, so both are now roofed with fibreglass domes. Any burials in the chamber were destroyed in 19th-century excavations.

New excavations over a period of years were completed in 1980 and the cairn has since been restored. It is a complex structure of several phases. The northern chamber and probably the southern one also were originally contained in small freestanding round cairns. Later on the great long cairn with its horned forecourts was built over them, and may itself have been built in several stages. The long cairn was retained by drystone walls which have been repaired as far as possible with the original materials. The passages of the chambers had to be extended by the ancient builders to reach the edge of the new long cairn. The south end of the cairn had been robbed to build a modern sheep stell, the round structure east of the cairn, and the facade at this end has been restored with new stone of a deliberately different colour to distinguish it from ancient work. The north forecourt has an unusual stone platform, now grassed over for its protection.

102 EMBO, CHAMBERED CAIRN, SUTHERLAND

4th to 2nd millennium BC.

NH 817926. In Embo, 3 km N of Dornoch. Cairn in carpark at S end of Embo, by the petrol pumps.

A low mound excavated in 1956 and 1960 was found to be the remains of a stone cairn containing two neolithic burial chambers and also bronze-age graves. Only the base of the structures is preserved, but the excavated chambers can be viewed with the covering mound removed and give an excellent view of the overall plan and of features not visible in other cairns.

The main chamber is entered from the south, where a short passage with drystone walls leads first into an antechamber and then into the chamber proper, an oval area constructed of six upright slabs with drystone walling between. Most of the original corbelled roof had been destroyed before excavation. At least six adults and nine children had been buried in this chamber before it was blocked up. At the other end of the cairn a short passage opens into a second ruined chamber formed of five upright slabs originally linked by drystone walling. Most of this chamber had been disturbed before excavation. Bones of animals and birds, including dog, pig, otter, great auk, duck, guillemot and gannet were found both in the filling of the main chamber and in the body of the cairn.

Part of the original cairn material remains on the west side and beside the passage on the south. The original mound would have been higher, but something the shape of the fenced area. The neolithic cairn was again used as a burial place in the early bronze age, when two stone cists were inserted into the mound. In one, which has been removed, a woman was buried with a food vessel pot and a necklace of black jet beads. The other cist can be seen in the centre of the cairn between the two chambers. It is formed of four stones set on edge and was covered by a flagstone. It contained the bones of two babies, a food vessel pot and a corded beaker. Later in the bronze age cremation burials were inserted into the cairn, one with a bronze razor.

103 CAIRN OF GET, CHAMBERED CAIRN, CAITHNESS

4th or 3rd millennium BC.

ND 313411. About 11 km S of Wick. From A9 by telephone box in Ulbster take minor road N, in about 400 m park at notice. Path to cairn.

Historic Scotland.

There is a remarkable series of prehistoric and later monuments in the area, including several chambered cairns and an iron-age fort. The path to the Cairn of Get is marked by black and white poles; from the cairn one can walk to other monuments.

The Cairn of Get lies just over the first low ridge. It is a short horned chambered cairn excavated in 1866, when the bones of seven or more people were found in the antechamber, and a deposit of wood ash, burnt and unburnt human and animal bone, flint arrowheads and fragments of pottery in the main chamber. The chamber, which is divided by upright stones, has lost its roof and lies open to view. The two leaning slabs at the back of the chamber were set that way deliberately; above them heavy corbel stones project over the chamber as the start of the roof. The walls facing the sides of the horns can be seen in places.

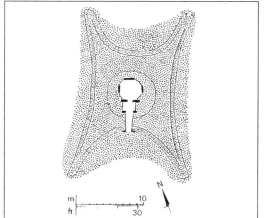

Cairn of Get

Cairn of Get plan

Some 30 m back from the Cairn of Get, in the heather on the inside of a bend in the path approaching it, is a small cairn some 10 m in diameter with a cist grave exposed in it. It is uncertain if this is a bronze-age cairn, or more unusually a Pictish grave of the 1st millennium AD. Beyond the Cairn of Get is a fine stone dam, retaining a now silted loch. This was probably built in the 19th century as part of the works to provide a head of water for Whaligoe Mill (see no. 14). The dam points conveniently to the Fort of Garrywhin (ND 312413) immediately to the north and occupying the top of a broad flat hill some 150 m long, with steep sides. A single stone rampart, now much tumbled, runs right round the hill with an entrance at each end. At the north end the rampart was doubled in width and faced with very large upright slabs, of which three survive and give an idea of the original height of the rampart. The interior is now covered with peat and heather, but near the south end are the remains of a stone structure, possibly a later hut circle, while further north is the remains of a small stone cairn, perhaps bronze age.

On the slopes south of the fort, between it and the loch, are a line of three rather dilapidated hut circles, best distinguished by the bracken growing on them. About 150 m east from the south end of the fort, and across a fence, is a denuded early bronze-age cairn on a small knoll; it was excavated in 1865, and a burial with beaker pottery found in a central cist. Radiating down the slope from it to the south are 7 or 8 lines of small grey stones, with at least 11 stones in the most complete row. Only 30 stones remain today, but originally there must have been around 80. Some other very ruinous stone rows exist nearby, one group 220 m ESE of the Cairn of Get, and another 200 m SSW, the latter also aligned on a cairn, but both hard to see now. On a ridge some 400 m east of the Cairn of Get, looking down on Loch Watenan, are the grassgrown remains of a broch within an outer defensive work (ND 317411) and there is another broch further north on the same ridge (ND

318414). Cairn Hanach, or Kenny's Cairn (ND 310408) is built on the edge of higher moorland and shows up on the skyline from Cairn of Get, from which it lies some 450 m southwest. Traces of crofting settlements can be found on the low ground between Cairn Hanach and Groat's Loch.

104 CNOC FREICEADAIN, CHAMBERED CAIRNS, CAITHNESS

4th or 3rd millennium BC.

ND 012653. On Cnoc Freiceadain, 5.5 km E of Reay. Signposted path off minor road leading N from Shebster to Achreamie.

Historic Scotland.

Two impressively long cairns of stone, now both grass-grown, are set at right angles to each other on top of the hill. For much of their length the mounds are low, but the south cairn has higher mounds at both ends, and the north cairn has a round mound at the south end. These three prominent humps clearly provided the name Na Tri Shean (the three fairy mounds) now applied only to the south cairn. It is probable that three separate round chambered cairns were incorporated into two later long structures, the north cairn being given an unusual northeast-southwest alignment to fit it onto the crest of the hill. Low horns can be seen at both ends of the south cairn, and at the north end of the north cairn, defining rectangular forecourts. Neither cairn has been excavated.

The south cairn seems to be virtually intact, and at 71 m long is one of the longest of its type. There is probably a chamber under the round mounds at either end, and two tilted slabs at the east end may be collapsed capstones from the roof of one chamber. The north cairn at 67 m is nearly as long, but the body of this cairn has been extensively disturbed down the centre. As well as a presumed chamber at the south end, some projecting slabs suggest another at the northern end. A few isolated slabs near the centre of this cairn may belong to later cist burials inserted into the existing mound. From the top of Cnoc Freiceadain, the site of two of the oldest monuments in Caithness, one looks down on one of the newest, Dounreay Atomic Power Station, and there are extensive views from this hill across much of Caithness and Orkney.

Cnoc Freiceadain long cairn

105 YARROWS ARCHAEOLOGY TRAIL, CHAMBERED CAIRNS, STANDING STONE, BROCH, CAITHNESS

4th or 3rd millennium BC (chambered cairns) to early 1st millennium AD (broch and outbuildings).

ND 305435 for start of trail; trail leaflets from Tourist Information Centres at Thurso or Wick. Minor road from A9 at Thrumster to Loch of Yarrows, and down west side of loch to South Yarrows farm and carpark. Trail on private land: NO DOGS please.

The whole trail from South Yarrows farm to the top of Warehouse Hill and back again takes some two hours or more, and involves steep climbs and some boggy areas, but the first two long cairns are quick and easy to reach. The trail is a mown path through heather, but the further cairns are off the path. Take this map or the trail leaflet with you to identify the cairns.

From the carpark go down to the loch (two stiles over fences) to see a broch with outer defences and outbuildings, 1. These were cleared out in 1866-7 but have since become somewhat ruinous and also partly flooded since the level of the loch was raised. There is a long chamber in the wall of the broch leading off the side of one entrance, and the stairs once rose opposite this. A later wall has been built round the inner side of the broch to make it into a house, and the second entrance may be connected with this. The outbuildings belong to this secondary phase and include long curved structures which had rows of upright slabs inside to support the roof, as at Forse Wag (no. 94). The whole site was cut off by a ditch and bank running out to the loch at each end.

Return to the start, and take the mown grassy path uphill through the heather to a series of cairns. Nearest to the carpark are two very long horned cairns which lie east-west across the flat top of the hill, some 30 m apart. Both were excavated in 1865. The north cairn, 2, is somewhat overgrown with grass and heather and has a chamber at the higher east end where horns, not now visible, defined a semi-circular area in front of the entrance. This part of the cairn is divided by a narrow gap, possibly original, from a long rectangular

extension with short horns at the west end. The south cairn, 3, a little higher up the hill, is 78 m long and its horns are visible at both ends, as are traces of the wall-face that ran all round it. The chamber in the higher east end was divided into three compartments, the inner one still covered by a capstone, but there is confusing modern walling and dumps in the outer chamber and forecourt.

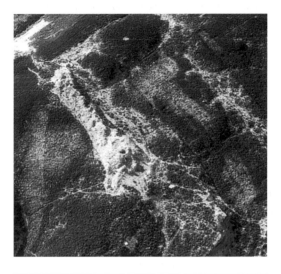

South Yarrows, aerial view of long cairn

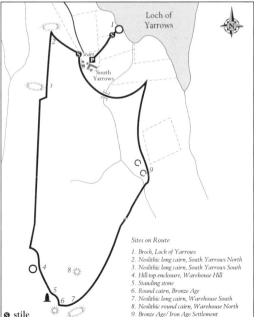

Sites on Route

1. Broch, Loch of Yarrows
2. Neolithic long cairn, South Yarrows North
3. Neolithic long cairn, South Yarrows South
4. Hill-top enclosure, Warehouse Hill
5. Standing stone
6. Round cairn, Bronze Age
7. Neolithic long cairn, Warehouse South
8. Neolithic round cairn, Warehouse North
9. Bronze Age/ Iron Age Settlement

S stile

The trail then continues up to Warehouse Hill. The next site reached is a flat-topped hill with steep sides that seems to have been a fort, 4, though the defences are hard to see. There are slight traces of rampart footings on the west side, and a heather-covered bank and ditch on the south; the location is very similar to Garrywhin (see no. 95). Next comes a standing stone, 5, with a larger slab lying by it which may have split off its face. Erected in the 2nd millennium BC, it has more recently been used as a parish boundary marker. The prominent stone cairn highest up the hill is also bronze age (though until recently confused with a different neolithic cairn). A cist or stone-lined grave some 2.5 m long, with human bones and a bronze spearhead, was found in it in the last century, perhaps a warrior buried with his spear. Little can be seen now but a hole in the middle, and disfiguring modern marker cairns (please do not add to these).

Nearby is another neolithic chambered cairn, 7, apparently just a large round mound, but when the heather was burnt off in 1982 it was found to extend southwest as a long, low rectangle with horned ends. Part of the chamber can be seen. The last chambered cairn, 8, is now turf-covered. Many of the cairn stones have been removed and the whole passage and chamber with the dividing slabs lie open to view.

Skelpick long cairn

From Warehouse Hill the path descends back north towards the loch. Just before a square fenced enclosure are two hut circles, 9, one east and one west of the path, part of a scattered settlement; these are quite hard to see in the heather. The trail returns to the carpark passing west of the farmhouse.

From the carpark a pair of standing stones can be seen on the ridge east of the loch, where there is another chambered cairn. Also east of the loch at ND 312440 is a group of stone rows some 43 m long, originally at least eight rows set roughly parallel to one another, but now reduced to the remains of six, at a place called Battle Moss. These are only some of the early sites in the neighbourhood, and one wonders where the people who built all these monuments lived? Their tombs have been found but not their dwellings.

106 COILLE NA BORGIE, CHAMBERED CAIRNS, SUTHERLAND

4th or 3rd millennium BC.

NC 715590. In Strathnaver about 3 km S of Bettyhill. Leave A836 at bridge on minor road to Skelpick. Cairns close to road.

A huge elongated mass of grey stones protrudes through the heather above the road. On closer inspection, there are substantial remains of at least two and probably three long chambered cairns set in line. Best preserved is the south cairn, some 72 m long, with traces of somewhat rectilinear forecourts, defined by short horns, at either end. The cairn is widest and highest where the chamber is, and the north forecourt is marked by a series of tall upright slabs, once linked by drystone walling. The chamber and passage are set at an angle to the axis of the cairn, and may have been covered by a small round cairn before the long cairn was built. The chamber is divided into compartments by the usual pairs of upright slabs. Its roof has collapsed, and much of the structure is visible.

The status of the northern structure is uncertain. Sometimes regarded as one cairn, it may in fact be two cairns set in line. There are traces of a forecourt at either end, and a chamber at the north end now hidden by a horrid modern rubbish dump. All these cairns were cleared out around 1867 when 'only a few bones were found' and 'no account was taken of them'. The use of upright stones in the facades of these cairns is unique in the north of Scotland, though quite usual in the south and west. The use of these cairns may have continued through most of the 3rd millennium BC.

There are several other chambered cairns at Skelpick; particularly impressive is another long horned cairn at NC 722567, some 2.5 km south of Coille na Borgie, and east of the Skelpick Burn.

MUSEUMS AND VISITOR CENTRES

CAITHNESS

Northlands Viking Centre, Auckengill, has displays and an excellent video on local archaeology.

Castletown Flagstone Centre, Castletown; displays in the centre supplement the trail round the flagstone works and harbour (no. 15).

Dunbeath Heritage Centre, Old School, Dunbeath; local displays, information and audio-visual programme.

Clan Gunn Centre, Latheron, Caithness; a local display in the 18th-century church.

Last House Museum, John O'Groats, a tiny museum of evocative old photographs in a cottage.

Thurso Museum, High Street, Thurso, has two Pictish cross-slabs and a Norse gravestone, also exhibits on such subjects as the flagstone industry, coastal transport and fishing.

Wick Heritage Museum, West Argyle Street, Wick, in an old curing house, has displays on the herring industry and coopering, a kipper kiln and other maritime exhibits (see no. 7).

SUTHERLAND

Strathnaver Museum, Bettyhill, in the old church of Farr, has exhibits on crofting, clearances, a Clan Mackay centre, and a Pictish cross-slab outside (no. 59).

Dunrobin Castle Museum, Golspie, houses an important collection of Pictish stones (no. 74) and local archaeological material, also hunting trophies from all over the world, in a Victorian setting. (See also no. 33).

Timespan, Helmsdale; displays on local history and Highland life, including panning for gold in the Strath of Kildonan, with audio-visual programme.

Ferrycroft Countryside Centre, Lairg; a Tourist Information Centre and Visitor Centre in one, with displays for adults and children, video and audio-visual programmes on the landscape and man's impact on it; also the start of a Forest Trail and the Ord Archaeological Trail (no. 95).

ROSS AND CROMARTY

Avoch Heritage Exhibition, Avoch; displays of old photographs and some artefacts, summer only.

Cromarty Court House, Church Street, Cromarty; imaginative displays with 'talking heads'. Tape tours of Cromarty available (see no. 3).

Dingwall Museum, Town House, Dingwall; a small museum with local exhibits in the old Tolbooth.

Gairloch Heritage Museum, Gairloch, has local displays on a variety of subjects from archaeology (with a Pictish symbol stone) to crofting; reconstructions include a crofthouse interior.

Groam House Museum, Rosemarkie; a fine Pictish cross-slab (no.70) and other Pictish stones found locally, with information and video on Picts.

Highland Museum of Childhood, The Old Railway Station, Strathpeffer; small, nostalgic collection with dressing-up box for children in a Victorian railway station with roses growing by the rails.

Tain Museum, Visitor Centre and St Duthac's Church (no. 59; signposted 'Tain Through Time'). The museum has local exhibits and is the Clan Ross centre. Tape tours of Tain available (see no. 4).

Ullapool Museum, West Argyle Street, Ullapool; local displays in a Telford church with most of the original fittings.

Loch Broom Museum, Ullapool; a small collection of local geological and natural history specimens and a few antiquities.

INVERNESS-SHIRE

Fort Augustus Abbey, Fort Augustus. In the Victorian Abbey building, much of which can also be seen, is an extensive exhibition with electronic surprises. Themes include General Wade's fort, its destruction in 1746 (sound and light), origins and history of monasticism and the Scottish Highlander.

The Regimental Museum, Fort George (see no. 41), is the museum of the Queen's Own Highlanders (Seaforth and Cameron).

Inverness Museum and Art Gallery, Castle Wynd, Inverness; the displays portray many aspects of the Highlands including archaeology and natural history, and there is a collection of Pictish stones.

Drum Tower Exhibition, The Castle, Inverness; changing exhibitions of local interest.

Culloden Battlefield and Visitor Centre, near Inverness (NTS); audio-visual programme, and entry to Culloden Cottage (no. 27).

Landmark, Carrbridge; Highlander multi-screen audio-visual progranme, Sawmill, Nature Trail and other features.

Grantown Museum, The Square, Grantown-on-Spey; local history exhibition.

Highland Folk Museum, Duke Street, Kingussie, has open-air reconstructions of a island blackhouse and a horizontal mill, and extensive indoor exhibits on farming and Highland life.

Highland Folk Park, Newtonmore; a new venture including a working 19th-century croft, an open-air museum of buildings (starting with a corrugated-iron church), and ambitious plans for the future.

Clan Macpherson Centre, Newtonmore; clan and local history.

NAIRN

Nairn Fishertown Museum, Laing Hall, King Street, Nairn; display on the old fishertown of Nairn and maritime exhibits.

Nairn Literary Institute Museum, Viewfield House, Nairn, has a small collection of local objects.

Highland Railway Museum, British Rail Station, Nairn; a railway museum in the 1885 station building.

Also of interest are centres related to Highland wildlife and geology: these include:

Flow Country Visitor Centre, Forsinard, Caithness; information on the geology and natural history of the area, and Tourist Information Centre.

Knockan Cliff Geology and Nature Trail, near Elphin, Ross and Cromarty (Nature Conservancy Council).

Torridon Deer Museum, The Mains, Torridon, Ross and Cromarty.

The Highland Wildlife Park, Kincraig, East Inverness-shire; animals and birds once indigenous to the Highlands.

The Cairngorm Reindeer Centre, Glenmore, Aviemore, East Inverness-shire.

Osprey Hide, Loch Garten, East Inverness-shire, RSPB.

EDINBURGH

The National Museums of Scotland hold important collections from the Highlands, including objects from brochs, Viking finds from Caithness, and Pictish stones including the magnificent carved slab from Hilton of Cadboll, Ross and Cromarty. Part or all of the museum, now in Queen Street, may be shut from 1995 onwards, in preparation for the move to a new building in Chambers Street, Edinburgh, opening in 1998.

BIBLIOGRAPHY

Baldwin, JR (ed) *Caithness: a Cultural Crossroads*, Edinburgh, 1982.

Baldwin, JR (ed) *Firthlands of Ross and Sutherland*, Edinburgh, 1986.

Baldwin, JR (ed) *Peoples & Settlement in North-West Ross-shire*, Edinburgh, 1994.

Beaton, E *The Doocots of Caithness*, Dundee, 1980.

Beaton, E *Ross & Cromarty: an illustrated Architectural Guide*, Edinburgh, 1992.

Beaton, E *Sutherland: an illustrated Architectural Guide*, Edinburgh, 1995.

Burl, A *Prehistoric Astronomy and Ritual*, Haverfordwest, 1983.

Burt's *Letters from a Gentleman in the North of Scotland*, (1st ed 1754), Edinburgh, 1974.

Cameron, AD *The Caledonian Canal*, Lavenham, 1972.

Chapman, RW (ed) *Journey to the Western Islands of Scotland (Johnson) and Journal of a Tour to the Hebrides (Boswell)*, London, 1970.

Close-Brooks, J *Pictish Stones in Dunrobin Castle Museum*, Derby, 1989.

Cruden, S *The Scottish Castle*, Edinburgh, 1981.

Davidson, J and Henshall, AS *The Chambered Cairns of Caithness*, Edinburgh, 1991.

Dunbar, JG *The Historic Architecture of Scotland*, London 1966; revised edition, 1978.

Dunlop, J *The British Fisheries Society 1786-1893*, Edinburgh, 1978.

Fawcett, R *Scottish Medieval Churches*, Edinburgh, 1985.

Fawcett, R *Scottish Abbeys and Priories*, London, 1994.

Feachem, RW *A Guide to Prehistoric Scotland*, London, second edition, 1977.

Gifford, J *The Buildings of Scotland: Highlands and Islands*, London, 1992.

Hackett, S and Livingston, N 'Scottish parliamentary churches and their manses,' in Breeze, DJ (ed) *Studies in Scottish Antiquity*, Edinburgh, 1984.

Haldane, ARB *The Drove Roads of Scotland*, London, 1952.

Haldane, ARB *New Ways through the Glens*, London, 1962.

Hay, G *The Architecture of Scottish Post-Reformation Churches*, London, 1957.

Henshall, AS *The Chambered Tombs of Scotland*, 2 vols, Edinburgh, 1963 and 1972.

Henshall, AS and Ritchie, JNG *The Chambered Cairns of Sutherland*, Edinburgh, 1995.

Hume, JR *The Industrial Archaeology of Scotland, vol 2, The Highlands and Islands*, London, 1977.

Kermack, WR *The Scottish Highlands, A Short History*, Edinburgh, 1957.

MacKie, EW *Scotland: an Archaeological Guide*, London, 1975.

MacLean, A *Telford's Highland Churches*, Inverness, 1989.

MacLean, L (ed) *The Middle Ages in the Highlands*, Inverness, 1981.

Mair, C *A Star for Seamen*, Frome, 1978.

McNeill, P and Nicholson, R (eds) *An Historical Atlas of Scotland, c 400—c 1600*, St Andrews, 1975.

Meldrum, E (ed) *The Dark Ages in the Highlands*, Inverness, 1971.

Omand, D (ed) *The Caithness Book*, Inverness, 1972.

Omand, D (ed) *The Moray Book*, Edinburgh, 1976.

Omand, D (ed) *The Sutherland Book*, Golspie, 1982.

Omand, D (ed) *The Ross and Cromarty Book*, Golspie, 1984.

Price, R J *Highland Landforms*, Inverness, 1976.

Richards, E *A History of the Highland Clearances*, London, 1982.

Ritchie, A *Scotland BC*, Edinburgh, 1988.

Ritchie, A *Picts*, Edinburgh, 1989.

Ritchie, A and Breeze DJ, *Invaders of Scotland*, Edinburgh, 1991.

Ritchie, JNG *Brochs of Scotland*, Princes Risborough, 1988.

Ritchie, G and Ritchie, A *Scotland; Archaeology and Early History*, Edinburgh, 1991.

Royal Commission on the Ancient and Historical Monuments of Scotland, *An Inventory of Monuments and Constructions in the County of Caithness*, Edinburgh, 1911.

Royal Commission on the Ancient and Historical Monuments of Scotland, *An Inventory of Monuments and Constructions in the County of Sutherland*, Edinburgh, 1911.

Salter, M *Discovering Scottish Castles*, 1985.

Scott, Sir W *Northern Lights: or a Voyage in the Lighthouse Yacht in 1814*, ed Laughlan, WF, Hawick, 1982.

Smout, TC *A History of the Scottish People, 1560-1830*, London, 1969.

Southey, R *Journal of a Tour in Scotland in 1819*, London, 1929.

Tabraham, C *Scottish Castles and Fortifications*, Edinburgh, 1986.

Taylor, W *The Military Roads in Scotland*, Newton Abbot, 1976.

There are also guide booklets or leaflets to individual sites in the care of Historic Buildings and Monuments, published by HMSO, Edinburgh. Leaflets describing individual hydro-electric schemes and a booklet, Power from the Glens, can be obtained from the North of Scotland Hydro-Electric Board, 16 Rothesay Terrace, Edinburgh.

INDEX OF PLACES

Printed in Scotland for HMSO by (3808)
Dd 293089   C50 8/95